CONTENTS

1   PROFESSIONAL FRAMEWORK

2   SERVICE LOCATIONS

3   CLIENT GROUPS AND SERVICE PROVISION

FOREWORD

In 1990, the first edition of "Communicating Quality" was described by Council as "a journey through speech and language therapy", a guide to good practice and a source of information for those responsible for providing and commissioning services.

In 1996, the second edition of "Communicating Quality" remains an essentially practical document with the same specific purpose. Its strength lies not so much in the actual text, as in the application and the influence of the text upon the lives of speech and language therapists, their clients and purchasers. Through the annual Registration procedures, speech and language therapists agree to adhere to the Code of Ethics and Professional Practice contained within these pages as the professional, clinical and organisational principles guiding all speech and language therapy activities

The standards and guidelines in the book have been drawn on evidence which relies heavily upon practitioners' clinical experience and knowledge. This concurs with national directives on the establishment of clinical guidelines, which should be based upon evidence from "expert committees, reports or opinions and/or clinical experience of respected authorities" (AHCPR, 1994).

These standards and guidelines represent the benchmarks of speech and language therapy practice, and, as such, they should provide measurable criteria against which compliance can be judged. Using such statements and guidelines will assist the profession in its quest to demonstrate evidence based practice.

Charles Handy, in his reflections on the future of work, wrote; "change comes from small initiatives which work, initiatives which, imitated, become the fashion. We cannot wait for great visions from great people. We must light our own small fires in the darkness."

"Communicating Quality" is one such initiative which, if well used, can become a source of light and inspiration.

EDITOR'S ACKNOWLEDGEMENTS

This book is the outcome of countless hours of dedication. It has been revised, revisited, reworded, restructured and reviewed by speech and language therapists and others working individually and collectively to produce a new edition of a hugely successful text.

Particular thanks must go to:

Caroline Fraser, chair of the Communicating Quality Working Party, who has worked relentlessly on the revisions with her colleagues Julia Appleton, Maria Farry, Christine MacCarthy and Sue Stevens,

Tessa Duffy, whose vision, skill and tenacity were the driving force behind the first edition. Her contribution as an advisor to the Working Party on the second edition has been greatly valued,

Members of Specific Interest Groups, Local Groups, TASLTM and many individual members throughout the country, who have committed themselves to revising sections of the text on behalf of their colleagues,

Sue Nosworthy, Bridget Ramsay and Sandy Bennett at College and Jenny Dowson for secretarial and administrative support,

Tom Montgomery of M and M Press, Gary Burnett and John Young at Opticol, whose dedication to detail has been so consistent,

Members of Council, in particular Pam Enderby, Sandra Walker, Aileen Patterson, Liz Jepson, Sue Roulstone, Pam Evans and Christine Skinner who have guided this edition through various stages,

Colleagues at the department of Speech and Language Therapy, University of Strathclyde, whose advice, support and forbearance has been greatly appreciated.

Particular thanks must also go to Shirley Davis, Carol Miller, Colm O'Keefe, Jois Stansfield, Ketron Morrison, Marcia Beer, Margaret Gordon, Myra Lockhart, Sally Millar, Jennifer Reid, Roger Lanyon, Alex Giles, Chris Mowles, Simon Halliday, Maureen Ainley, Dot Reid, Hope Docherty, Davie Robertson and all College members.

Anna van der Gaag
Editor

Richmond House

79 Whitehall

London SW1A 2NS

Telephone 0171 210 5150-3

Fax 0171 210 5407

From the Chief Medical Officer

Sir Kenneth Calman KCB MD FRCS FRSE

I am very pleased to welcome the revised professional guidelines produced by the Royal College of Speech and Language Therapists. Speech and Language Therapy is an important element of the National Health Service and has a key role to play in helping people of all ages with communication difficulties. The heavy demands on the service make it particularly important that standards are set and regularly reviewed so that a high level of quality can be maintained. I congratulate speech and language therapists on being among the leaders in the development of exacting clinical standards designed to achieve this aim.

SIR KENNETH CALMAN

Chief Medical Officer

April 1996

Introduction
The User's Guide

This is the second edition of "Communicating Quality", a text which, in its first edition, was widely acknowledged as a seminal work on professional standards for speech and language therapists. Its publication in 1991 marked a new era in the history of the profession, and its subsequent practical application across the range of client groups with which speech and language therapists work, was unprecedented. Since that time, the profession has progressed into new areas of service, absorbed new legislative requirements, and changed its practice to incorporate technological advances and demographic shifts.

This edition of "Communicating Quality" has been produced in the light of these changes, and in recognition of the profession's commitment to ongoing growth and development. Much of the text remains the same. Some sections have undergone considerable updating, and some chapters now present alphabetically for ease of access. An index and bibliography have been included.

"Communicating Quality; Professional Standards for Speech and Language Therapists" has been written with three groups in mind;

1   Members of the speech and language therapy team, including clinicians, educators, managers, students, co-workers and assistants.

2   Commissioners and purchasers of speech and language therapy services

3   Consumers of speech and language therapy services, including individual consumers, consumer representatives and colleagues in other professions

The aim of the text is to provide information which contributes to decision making and delivery of services. Specifically, the text sets out to;

- inform the decisions taken by commissioners and purchasers on supply and demand issues, service agreements, and the ongoing delivery of quality services.

- inform consumers of the range of service and the model of care which they can expect to receive.

- inform members of the profession and their colleagues of the consensus on appropriate models of care available to consumers, ethical and legal issues, professional development issues, management issues, skill mix issues and resource requirements.

Certain sections of the text include 'standards' and 'guidelines' for good practice. These summarise current consensus on the parameters of a quality service, and demonstrate a commitment to ongoing improvement in service delivery. The 'standards', highlighted in bold type, are statements against which existing services can be measured. Further information on how these might be applied is given in "Audit: a manual for Speech and Language Therapists", published by the College.

Chapter one outlines 'core' professional issues, including the core professional standards and guidelines which apply across the whole range of services, the code of ethics and professional conduct, and information on clinical accountability and research.

Chapters two, three and four contain guidelines and professional standards relevant to specific service locations, specific clients groups and specific communication disorders. This may seem a somewhat artificial distinction to make, as there is an obvious overlap between these three aspects of service delivery. However, this distinction does allow the reader ease of access to information for different purposes.

For example, a purchaser may wish to obtain information on the service specification for a rehabilitation centre. This information is outlined in Chapter Two. Alternatively, the purchaser may be placing a contract for a population of clients who have suffered a stroke. This information is provided on Chapter Three.

Speech and language therapists are more likely to refer to information across these three chapters, rather than requiring information from one chapter alone. For example, a speech and language therapist may receive a request from a general practitioner to assess a dysphasic client who has suffered a stroke and who needs to be seen at home. The speech and language therapist would refer to three sections of the text;

Chapter Two - Domiciliary services
Chapter Three - Cerebro vascular accident
Chapter Four - Adult aphasia

Service location , client group and communication disorder can occur in a variety of combinations. It is therefore necessary to outline each aspect in some detail, so that effective cross referencing can occur. Each chapter contains the identical headings;

Description/Definition of the Service
Aims/Principles of Service Delivery
Protocols for;
Referral
Assessment
Intervention
Discharge
Interface/Liaison with Other Professionals
Skill mix
Resource Requirements

The disadvantage of this approach is that some descriptions are repeated in different but related sections. The advantage is that the reader can use each section separately where this is required.

The remaining chapters focus on particular aspects of professional practice. Chapter Five outlines guidelines for good practice in record keeping and report writing. This is an essential part of good professional practice.

Chapter Six gives details on relevant legislation and its implications for practice. It provides information on contributing to legal statements, appearing in court as a witness and observing confidentiality. New sections on the NHS and Community Care Act, the Disabled Persons Act and the

Code of Practice, are included.

Chapter Seven describes professional development from the pre-entry to postgraduate stage and beyond. It discusses pre-qualification training, and outlines the role of the speech and language therapist in clinical training. It describes the transition to clinical autonomy and the importance of continuing professional development initiatives throughout the working life of a speech and language therapist. It also highlights the need for research and ongoing evaluation of clinical effectiveness.

Effective clinical management is as essential to quality professional practice as ongoing professional development. Chapter Eight contains information on the management process in speech and language therapy services. It outlines the role of speech and language therapy managers, the requirements of service planning and development, service specification and business plans. The importance of audit as an integral part of service delivery is discussed. The chapter also considers manpower and recruitment and retention issues as they relate to speech and language therapy services. Equal opportunities, terms and conditions of employment, health and safety at work, personal safety issues and guidelines on accommodation and equipment are also addressed.

Chapter Nine considers the "skill mix" of speech and language therapists and support personnel. It provides a description of the recent changes in the terminology of skill mix. The terms "specialist", "specialised" and "generalist" speech and language therapist have been superseded by "speech and language therapist with specific

responsibilities" and "speech and language therapist with specific duties". Readers are advised to familiarise themselves with this terminology before referring to the sections on Skill Mix in Chapters 2,3, and 4.
The chapter also describes the role of speech and language therapists' assistants, bilingual co-workers and volunteer helpers.

Chapter Ten outlines the major professional networks within the speech and language therapy profession on a national and international level. These include management organisations, educational and regional advisory committees, international committees and associations, and voluntary organisations concerned with clients with communication disorders.

Chapter Eleven address key issues relating to independent practice. It includes information on the relationship between the independent practitioner and colleagues employed by the health service.

Chapter Twelve provides guidance on health promotion principles and practice as they apply to speech and language therapy services. It examines child surveillance issues for speech and language therapists.

Editor's Note
Terminology

Each section of this text has been crafted by speech and language therapists with particular expertise. Differences in style and terminology are inevitable, as speech and language therapists work in health, education or social services settings, all of which have their own character and emphasis.

The following editorial changes have been introduced in order to maintain some continuity of style, whilst respecting the diversity within the profession and its practice.

The term *client* has been used throughout the text to describe the *patient, child,* or *adult* who may be receiving speech and language therapy. The term *carer* has been used throughout the text to refer to *partner, spouse, parent, sibling, relative, friend* and *professional carer.* This reflects current trends in the public domain, as well as providing a more manageable, if less personal, description of those individuals with whom the speech and language therapist may work. The terms *therapy* or *intervention* have been used in preference to *treatment,* as these terms reflect the broader nature of speech and language therapy work with clients and carers.

1

PROFESSIONAL FRAMEWORK

The Role and Function of the Royal College of
Speech and Language Therapists
Mission Statement
Code of Ethics and Professional Conduct
Core Guidelines and Professional Standards
Clinical Accountability

THE ROLE AND FUNCTION OF THE ROYAL COLLEGE OF SPEECH AND LANGUAGE THERAPISTS

*T*he Royal College of Speech and Language Therapists is the professional body governing speech and language therapy in the United Kingdom. It is the licensing body with power invested by the Secretary of State. The certificate to practise, issued by the College on behalf of the Secretary of State, and registered membership of the College, provide recognition of professional status.
Registration applies to speech and language therapists who are 'practising', i.e. directly engaged in professional activities in the following categories:

■ clinical practice;

■ research;

■ management;

■ higher education.

The College accredits all qualifying courses in the United Kingdom through a process of peer review conducted by the Academic Board. The College holds a register of speech and language therapists. In addition to registration, speech and language therapists may become members of the College. This provides them with membership services including professional indemnity insurance, monthly bulletins and a quarterly journal.

The College has procedures for dealing with professional conduct and complaints both from consumers and clinicians.

The College does not enter into national or local pay negotiations on behalf of its members. This role is undertaken by the unions representing speech and language therapists employed by statutory and other bodies. The majority of speech and language therapists belong to the Manufacturing, Science and Finance Union.

The College is served by an elected council. Each councillor fulfils a particular role as well as holding a corporate responsibility for council decisions.

The College supports purchasers and providers of speech and language therapy services as well as individuals. The College offers professional advice to commissioning authorities on service delivery and organisation. On an individual basis, members of the College are able to access support and advice on issues such as professional practice, career development and working in the independent sector. The College is considering expanding its existing role to cover accreditation and service reviews.

The College provides members and clients with a comprehensive information service on request.

The College informs the Secretary of State and the Ombudsman of appropriate advisors for professional advice on complaints within the NHS.

MISSION STATEMENT OF ROYAL COLLEGE OF SPEECH AND LANGUAGE THERAPISTS

The Royal College of Speech and Language Therapists (College), through its members, develops policies governing the work of the profession.

The College accredits pre-qualifying education of speech and language therapists, and grants certificates to practise.

The College ensures the advancement of the profession of speech and language therapy by requiring members to continue their professional development through training and research.

The College sets professional and ethical standards for practitioners, and through a system of registration, encourages its members to provide and maintain the highest quality of client care.

The Organisational Structure of RCSLT

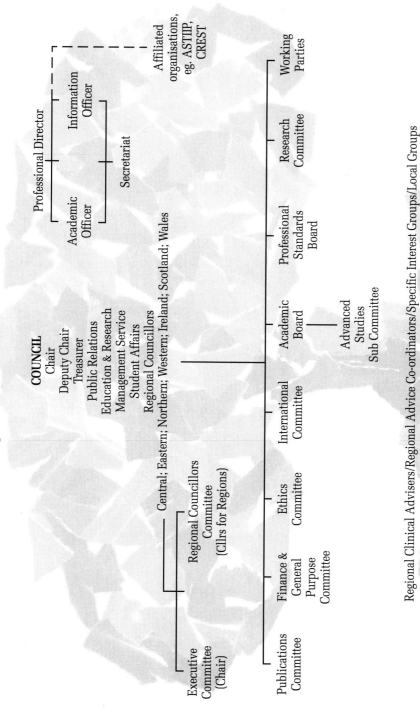

COUNCIL
Chair
Deputy Chair
Treasurer
Public Relations
Education & Research
Management Service
Student Affairs
Regional Councillors

Professional Director

Academic Officer

Information Officer

Secretariat

Affiliated organisations, eg. ASTIIP; CREST

Central; Eastern; Northern; Western; Ireland; Scotland; Wales

Executive Committee (Chair)

Regional Councillors Committee (Cllrs for Regions)

Publications Committee

Finance & General Purpose Committee

Ethics Committee

International Committee

Academic Board

Advanced Studies Sub Committee

Professional Standards Board

Research Committee

Working Parties

Regional Clinical Advisers/Regional Advice Co-ordinators/Specific Interest Groups/Local Groups

MEMBERS

Map showing RCSLT Regions

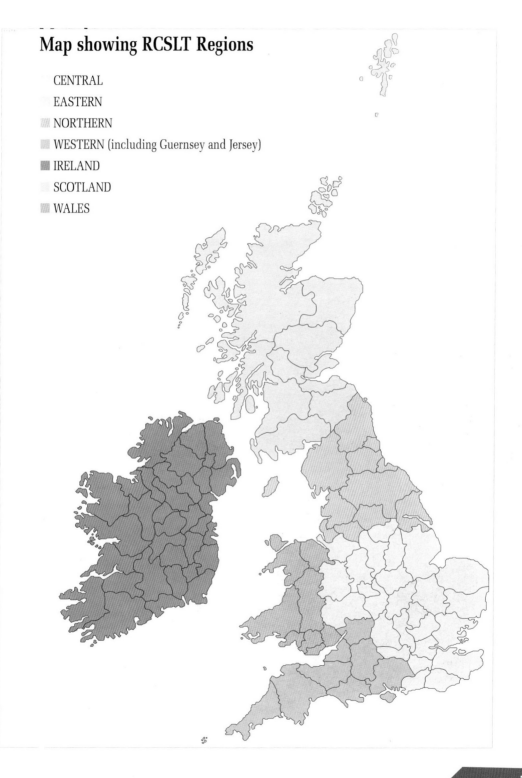

CENTRAL
EASTERN
NORTHERN
WESTERN (including Guernsey and Jersey)
IRELAND
SCOTLAND
WALES

CODE OF ETHICS AND PROFESSIONAL CONDUCT

The paramount concern of speech and language therapists is the well-being of their clients. The College, therefore, requires its members to be professionally competent and to maintain the highest professional and personal standards in the performance of their duties. Speech and language therapists should strive to maintain objectivity in all their judgements and must be personally accountable for their conduct.

Personal conduct:

Speech and language therapists should:

- respect the legal, social and moral norms of the society and the communities in which they work;

- refrain from activities which might bring themselves or the profession into disrepute.

Professional Competence:

Speech and language therapists should:

- hold an appropriate professional qualification and be registered with the College;

- maintain and continually update professional knowledge and skills, reflecting technical and clinical progress;

- operate only within the parameters of their own competence and cease to practise if that competence becomes impaired for any reason. Onward referrals of clients should be made as appropriate;

- be competent in the spoken and written language of the client group receiving therapy. In specific circumstances where this is not possible, appropriate measures should be taken to ensure that therapy will be effective with the client.

Professional conduct:

Speech and language therapists have the following duties:

- to refrain from discrimination on the basis of race, religion, gender or any other consideration. Selection for therapy should only be made on the basis of relevant client information and accepted standards of best practice:

- to avoid activities which may give rise to a conflict of interest, and to make explicit to all concerned any necessary and relevant conflicts of interest;

- to disregard prospects of professional advancement or personal gain when making professional decisions;

- to decline gifts or hospitality from clients which could be construed as inducements to gain preferential therapy;

- to abstain from undertaking unnecessary therapy, or prolonging therapy unnecessarily, by continually monitoring therapy effectiveness;

- to refrain from guaranteeing the results of therapy and from making false or exaggerated claims when advertising. All advertising should conform to the College guidelines;

- to agree fees in advance in accordance with the College recommended norms;

- to obtain approval for research projects, including studies where only medical records are used, from the appropriate Ethics Committees;

- in association with the College, to educate and inform the public regarding communication disability and to ensure the accuracy of such information.

Responsibility towards clients:

Speech and language therapists have the following duties:

- to respect the needs and opinions of the clients to whom a duty of care is owed;

- to ensure that the well-being of clients is not compromised by any action or omission on the part of the speech and language therapist;

- not to enter into inappropriate or disruptive personal relationships with clients;

- to inform clients of the nature and likely course of proposed intervention and of the status of those involved in their care. Consent must be gained from the client or his/her carer and consent can be withdrawn at any time. Consent must not be assumed, and should be in writing for research purposes, or when videotaping;

- to retain the strictest confidentiality of information including that acquired in the course of non-clinical duties, except in the following cases:

  - where there is valid written consent by the client or the client's authorised representative;

  - where necessarily imparted to a close carer in the client's best interests when, due to the nature of the client's impairment, it is not possible for consent to be gained;

  - where required by the order of a court or if there is a wider ethical duty to disclose information.

When releasing confidential information, there is a responsibility to help protect the client from the consequences of the disclosure.;

- to ensure familiarity with national guidelines and relevant legislation on data protection and to ensure that these are observed by all staff for whom the therapist has responsibility;

- to ensure that the presentation and reporting of research results protects the anonymity of subjects.

Responsibility towards professional colleagues, students and support staff:

Speech and language therapists have the following duties:

- to ensure adequate supervision of students and support staff, delegating to them only such duties as fall within their competence and to accept full responsibility for their actions;

- to share information, knowledge and skills with fellow professionals and, to an appropriate level, with students and support staff;

- to refrain from collaboration in therapy with practitioners who are not appropriately qualified;

- to maintain liaison with professional colleagues in cases of concurrent therapy;

- to refrain from disparaging the competence or character of colleagues;

- to make concerns regarding professional competence of colleagues known to the appropriate professional and/or employing body.

Responsibility towards employer:

Speech and language therapists have the following duties:

- to work to the highest level of their ability within an agreed job description;

- to endeavour to satisfy the requirements of the employer except when:

  - this conflicts with the best interests of the client;

  - the employer gives false information or issues misleading statements;

  - the directions of the employer conflict with agreed professional standards.

It is in their clients' best interest that speech and language therapists exercise independent professional judgement at all times.

CORE GUIDELINES AND PROFESSIONAL STANDARDS

The following guidelines and professional standards are described as 'core', and form the basis of good practice. There are specific standards and guidelines in each chapter of the document, but reference should always be made to the 'core' standards and guidelines outlined below. Standards have been highlighted.

ACCESS

1 **An open referral system will operate.**

2 **Speech and language therapists will uphold non-discriminatory practices at all times.**

3 **Admission to and discharge from speech and language therapy will be at the discretion of a qualified speech and language therapist.**

4 **All referrals will be acknowledged and the acknowledgement will indicate when the client can expect to be seen for an assessment.**

5 Prior to the initial appointment, the client will receive details of the service being offered.

6 **If the referral relates to an in-patient, that in-patient will be seen within two working days.**

For community or out-patient referral the initial appointment will be offered within eight weeks of the receipt of referral.

These recommended response times pertain unless specific location, client or disorder guidelines recommend otherwise.

7 An initial appointment will be offered at the nearest appropriate speech and language therapy location.

8 All appointments should take into account:

- the clinical needs of the client;

- the most mutually convenient location and time for the client.

9 Access to the service will include the appropriate involvement of carers.

10 Re-referrals after discharge for failure to attend should be discussed with the referring agent and will not necessarily receive priority.

ADMISSION TO SERVICE

1 The client will be offered a timed appointment of a specific duration. Under normal circumstances, this will be offered with no less that two weeks notice.

2 All clients will be seen punctually. If there is unavoidable delay, an explanation will be given.

3 The speech and language therapist will be adequately prepared to receive the client with all relevant information available.

4 The client will be informed that the purpose of the assessment is to establish a diagnosis and to form an opinion as to intervention and outcome. This may include an appropriate range of formal and informal assessments and observations, as well as a complete and relevant case history, which will be recorded in the notes.

5 Therapists will have access to a range of assessment tools.

6 The initial assessment will be repeatable, to allow for measurement of change at a later date.

7 On completion of the assessment procedure, which may take more than one appointment, the findings and implications for future management will be discussed with the client and carer. This will include an explanation of the diagnosis and prognosis, where appropriate. These findings will be recorded in the notes.

8 The outcome of assessment will be recorded and made known to the client, carer and relevant professionals. The outcome may be one of the following:

- no communication difficulty detected;

- client/carer declines therapy;

- therapy not appropriate;

- referral to other agency/service for further opinion or action, prior to speech and language therapy intervention;

- referral to multi-disciplinary team;

- advice with access to re-assessment within a given time-scale;

- therapy programme recommended with a given time-scale.

9 Following the assessment, the speech and language therapist will advise the referrer in writing of the findings of the assessment.

10 The assessment findings will include an opinion as to the appropriate timing of intervention. Therapy will commence within a specified time following assessment. The period of time will not be of a duration that renders the assessment 'out of date' by the time the therapy programme has commenced.

11 Information on relevant voluntary organisations will be given to clients and carers by the speech and language therapist.

CRITERIA FOR ACCEPTANCE FOR THERAPY

Acceptance for a programme of therapy will depend upon the following:

- the clinical judgement of the individual speech and language therapist based upon the assessment findings and upon discussion with the client and carer;

- the competencies of the speech and language therapist;

- the client's agreement to participate in a programme of therapy;

- the expected outcome of therapy.

PROGRAMMES OF THERAPY

1 All episodes of therapy will be negotiated and agreed between client and carer and the speech and language therapist.

2 The responsibility of the client and carer for active participation in therapy will be explained. The nature of their participation will be agreed.

3 Achievable goals will have been identified and agreed between the speech and language therapist and client and carer. These will include expected outcomes and time-scales.

4 The psychological adjustment of client and carer to the communicative disability must be an integral part of every programme of therapy and should be identified within the overall programme.

5 There will be ongoing evaluation of the effectiveness of the programme by both speech and language therapist and client and carer, with modifications as necessary.

6 The repeatable assessment used at the initial contact will serve as the baseline to determine change over time.

7 In the event of any concern regarding the effectiveness of the programme or its application, the client and carer or the speech and language therapist may ask for a second opinion.

8 Where a programme requires contact of client and carer with a speech and language therapy assistant or volunteer, this will be explained to client and carer. In all cases, overall responsibility for the speech and language therapy management of the client remains with the speech and language therapist.

9 Throughout the period of contact, the speech and language therapist will ensure that any other professionals or agencies involved with the client and carer will be kept informed of progress, as appropriate. Specific advice and training by the speech and language therapist of other professionals/carers in regular contact with the client may be required.

10 The speech and language therapy programme may form part of a multi-disciplinary programme of care and may include joints aims and intervention.

11 **Any significant change in client and carer status will be communicated, with clients' and carers' consent, to the appropriate agency.**

12 **Any change in therapist will be communicated in advance to the client and carer concerned and appropriate agencies.**

13 The client and carer will be adequately prepared for the cessation of therapy.

OUTCOMES/REASONS FOR DISCHARGE

1 Speech and language therapists have a responsibility to be aware of the effectiveness of their therapy. The outcomes of a programme of therapy should be related to the goals of that therapy programme. These may be associated with the specific speech, language or swallowing problem, the functional consequences, or the impact on the client and carer. Methods for determining, collecting and analysing outcomes of clients receiving speech and language therapy should be specified within the contract between client, carer and speech and language therapist.

2 The reason for discharge of a client from speech and language therapy will be one of the following:

- achieved communication potential;
- achieved goals for current episode;
- therapy no longer appropriate;
- therapy deferred;
- transfer to other agency;
- transfer out of district;
- transfer out of health service;
- client/carer self discharged;
- failure to attend, inadequate compliance;
- health deterioration or death of client.

This should be recorded in the notes.

3 Procedures dealing with clients failing to attend appointments or comply with therapy will be available.

4 **The outcomes of therapy and reason for discharge along with future management will be recorded and reported to the referring agent and other relevant professionals/agencies.**

5 Clients who are between episodes of therapy may be given clear, written guidance to encourage consolidation and/or continuation of progress.

6 The reason for discharge and outcome of therapy should be clearly explained to the client and appropriate carers. On final discharge clients and carers may be given guidelines for maximising their communicative ability. This may include

referral to other statutory or voluntary agencies (as appropriate for specific care groups).

7 Routinely, information will be given by the therapist to the client and carer of a process of re-referral or re-accessing the service.

ADMINISTRATION AND LIAISON

1 Reports will normally be provided following assessment and on completion of therapy.

2 Clients' contact records will be kept up to date and will be concise and factual. All client and carer contacts, direct and indirect, will be recorded.

3 The speech and language therapist will endeavour to attend any relevant case conferences, review meetings etc. called by another agency to discuss the client's progress. A report should be provided when attendance is not possible.

4 There will be adequate written guidelines and advice available for individual clients and carers and all relevant client groups.

5 Written consent will be obtained from all clients and carers for any recording, film or sound, which may be used for teaching or publicity purposes.

6 The speech and language therapist will ensure that advice and/or training is available and provided for any individuals, other professionals and voluntary agencies relevant to a specific client group.

7 Time and resources must be allocated for speech and language therapists to maintain and develop appropriate clinical standards for each client group.

CLINICAL ACCOUNTABILITY

INTRODUCTION

1 As professionals, speech and language therapists accept clinical accountability for their clients. The principle of clinical accountability applies to:

- assessment and diagnosis;

- decision whether to provide therapy or not to provide therapy;

- determination of therapy plan;

- therapy itself;

- evaluation of the effectiveness of therapy;

- decision to terminate therapy;

- organisation of caseload;

- relationship with assistants, co-workers and carers.

2 Speech and language therapists establish competence in their profession from their initial education, qualification, ensuing clinical experience and continuation of in-service training. Clinical advances, professional development and training allow speech and language therapists to expand their professional competence throughout their working lives.

3 The College advises on professional responsibilities and is the registering body

for the profession in the United Kingdom. However, each district/area health authority (or equivalent employing authority) is a separate body authorised to determine its own rules, with responsibility for whatever service is provided by that authority and with a duty for the safety and well-being of clients committed to its care. Speech and language therapists should be aware of their own authority's policy, of their own department's clinical policy and of the details outlined in their own job descriptions. The authority to which a speech and language therapist is accountable is the district/area health authority (or other equivalent employing authority), through their professional head of service. Independent practitioners assume their own professional accountability through the College.

4 The profession of speech and language therapy within the National Health Service is covered by National Health Service Acts. The unified profession stems from the National Health Services Reorganisation Act (1973) (effective 1st April 1974). The employment of speech and language therapists is governed by the National Health Service (Speech Therapists) Regulations (1974) as amended by Statutory Instruments No.47/85 National Health Service England and Wales and No.208 (S20/85) National Health Service (Scotland).

LEGAL RESPONSIBILITY

1 The employing authority is vicariously liable for torts committed by its employees within the scope of their duties. Where speech and language therapists are working within the scope of their employment, the employing authority should in all normal circumstances (i.e. provided the charge is not a criminal one) support them should there be litigation. However, the authority's support could depend upon whether the speech and language therapist was deemed to be performing duties outlined in the job description. It should also be noted that an authority could proceed against an employee after that employee had been found negligent or otherwise blameworthy in a legal action, either seeking an indemnity for damage and costs incurred or through the authority's own disciplinary machinery.

2 Accountability

Speech and language therapists are accountable to the employing authority for any action or process they are authorised to carry out or, being so authorised, fail to carry out. They have a duty of care towards the client and would be negligent if there was a breach of that duty which resulted in harm or damage to the client. The 'duty of care' is that expected of a reasonable therapist in the situation concerned. Therapists remain at all times responsible for their own acts and omissions. The definition of what is reasonable is that which a 'respectable body of opinion within the profession' would confirm.

3 Negligence

Negligence is any act or omission from which follows harm or damage which could or should have been foreseen by a reasonable therapist. The standard by which therapists are judged is that expected from their position, standing and declared competence. The higher the standard claimed, the higher the expectation of competence. However, speech and language therapists must recognise and observe the limits of their own professional expertise and competence.

Negligence could be proved where:

- intervention should only have been undertaken by someone more highly experienced or with special responsibilities in that field; or

- where onward referral should have been made and such referral was not made.

4 Autonomy

The speech and language therapist must recognise and observe the limits of clinical autonomy. In accepting the duty to take reasonable care of their clients in all circumstances, therapists have a duty to take into account the known medical condition of the client and to ascertain (when it would be reasonable to do so) what that medical condition is, if it is not clear. The therapist is, however, personally responsible for the assessment and the diagnosis of the communication disorder, consequent therapy, for decisions on the continuance of therapy, and for the safety and well-being of the client when undergoing diagnosis or therapy.

The therapist must therefore take appropriate precautions to ensure reasonable care of the client in all circumstances.

5 Delegation

Speech and language therapists are responsible for another's actions or failure to act, if they have delegated the care of the client to someone whom they employ or whom they can be seen to direct.

The therapist has to be satisfied that the other person is appropriately trained and competent. In leaving someone else to carry out some action for a client, the decision has to be reasonable, and the instructions or advice have to be such that they could reasonably be carried out by the person to whom given in that particular situation.

The reasonableness of the speech and language therapist's decision to delegate is therefore the primary concern in this context.

Summary:

The standards expected of each speech and language therapist are those of a reasonable person in such a position. Each is responsible for any decision or omissions and for precautions taken or not taken, particularly where there is an element of risk which was known or could reasonably have been foreseen. Each is responsible for harm or damage which occurs directly or as a result of any act or omission. To the extent outlined above, speech and language therapists are therefore accountable to their employing authority for the safety and well-being of clients committed to their care.

EXTENSION OF ROLE-RELATED SKILLS

1 A speech and language therapist's initial education provides the foundation for later specialisation. The competence to take on increased responsibilities and to apply new techniques or therapy methods is then initially assessed by a senior or more skilled colleague. The growth in competence thereafter is likely to come either from a programme of continuous development involving attendance on specialist courses followed by practice or from a period of supervised experience.

2 The duties which speech therapists in the health service or independent sector are required to carry out are set out in general terms in their conditions of service. Many techniques which have been adopted over the years by the profession in its service to the client are a normal and understood part of the therapist's duties. On the other hand,

as new therapies or techniques are evolved, some speech and language therapists will be required to undertake them or will themselves be developing these new techniques and their job descriptions should be amended accordingly.

3   Research
Those undertaking research should follow the College ethical guidelines for research.

4   Employing Authority
Where a speech and language therapist wishes to introduce new techniques or methods of therapy beyond those covered by her/his job description, the employing authority should be informed of this and assured of the therapist's competency. Supervising speech and language therapists should be aware of the different specialised techniques being carried out by those for whom they are responsible.

5   Working in a Multi-disciplinary Team
Speech and language therapists should exchange necessary information with other members of the team and agree on the allocation of responsibility. Speech and language therapists should be alert to their own professional responsibilities in these circumstances.

LIFE-THREATENING SITUATIONS

1   From time to time, speech and language therapists may be required to come to a decision to enter into a situation involving risk to a client. Other speech and language therapists will be entering such situations on a regular/daily basis. Their actions must be those which could be reasonably expected in such situations. The competent speech and language therapist is aware of the risks involved but takes all reasonable precautions to safeguard the client. In the event of difficulties occurring, a positive duty to act arises and the speech and language therapist is required to do whatever would reasonably be expected.

2   The prime responsibility for taking a decision, which could bring about a new life-threatening situation, must remain with the medical practitioner concerned and the speech and language therapist should, if necessary, insist that a potentially dangerous situation is authorised in writing. A distinction is drawn between entering a medically dangerous situation with therapy, and undertaking therapy which carries risks.

In the former case, the medical practitioner should be requested to agree in writing to therapy for his/her client, while in the latter case, the speech and language therapist alone is fully responsible for the client and for the therapy. Where the possibility of a threat to life exists, the responsibility of therapists is to act with forethought and in good faith at their level of competence.

3   In a situation where there is the possibility of danger to the client, speech and language therapists should be trained in recovery techniques. They must know what equipment or personal help might be required, the time limit for its arrival and how to call for help in an emergency. Speech and language therapists should have adequate up-to-date competence in first aid. The level of competence and support that is required relates to the perceived degree of risk, the client's condition and the environment in which the client is receiving therapy.

CLIENT'S CONSENT

1   Speech and language therapists should obtain the consent of the client or of his/her representatives to the course of therapy being adopted. In the case of children, consent will normally be obtained from parents or guardians. Providing the therapist is of the opinion that the child (under 16) is able to understand the rationale, course and likely outcome of therapy, the child is able to consent on his/her own behalf. In the case of services that are delivered in an educational setting, the head teacher cannot legally take responsibility. Where consent is sought, the therapist need only have consent from one parent for the course of action; the other parent does not have a veto.

2   Parents cannot dictate courses of action to therapists. In deciding on a course of therapy, professional judgement should be paramount. The duty of care includes follow-up and continues until the client is discharged. Parents/carers must be informed of the arrangements throughout.

INSURANCE

1   Provided speech and language therapists are working within the scope of their employment, they should be supported by the employing authority should they become involved in litigation. In the past, it has been held that insurance should not be needed. However, the College has become aware that attitudes are changing and that in the event of a claim, legal support from an employing authority could depend upon prior knowledge or agreement to the course of therapy. In such cases, the terms of the job description could be crucial.

Since therefore:

■   speech and language therapists are legally accountable for their professional actions and for any negligence - whether by act or omission or injury; and

■   speech and language therapists, having started therapy, have a duty of care towards the client which must be properly discharged,

The College recommends that all speech and language therapists should obtain professional indemnity cover. The policy offered by the College is to cover claims against members of the College (whether practising or non-practising) arising from alleged professional negligence or breach of professional conduct. Claims are to be covered during the policy period regardless of when the actual incident giving rise to the claim occurred. Territorial limits are to be world-wide but excluding the USA and Canada.

2   Independent Practice
The policy outlined above will also cover the College members in independent practice.

3   Speech and language therapists covered by the insurance are required to follow the guidelines outlined in Chapter 8.

2

SERVICE LOCATIONS

*T*his chapter describes the model of care offered by speech and language therapists in a range of locations.

The content serves to provide 'guidelines' to good practice in any one location. A number of points have been highlighted and form 'standards' of good practice. These standards may be taken as indicators of good practice on a wider basis. They may be of particular interest to purchasing authorities and speech and language therapists engaged in drawing up quality indicators for service specifications.

ACUTE HOSPITALS

Description/Definition of the Location:

A service provided in a hospital setting to both in-patients and as part of an out-patient speech and language therapy department. The service may take place at the bedside or in the speech and language therapy department. The service may include combined clinics with medical and other colleagues.

Aims/Principles of Service Delivery:

1 To assess, diagnose and treat clients referred both as in-patients and out-patients.

2 To work within a multi-disciplinary framework.

3 To provide an appropriate service, in terms of timing and in terms of the skills of the speech and language therapist, to clients referred to the hospital department.

4 To offer a range of therapy models including individual, group and intensive options.

5 To contribute to the education of medical, nursing and paramedical staff regarding communication and swallowing, thereby raising awareness pertaining to referral and recovery.

Referral:

1 **The hospital department will provide a service to all referrals received within the context of their operational policy. This should include self-referrals.**

2 **Referrals will be acknowledged in the following ways:**

In-patients - the results of the initial assessment will be detailed in the client's medical notes to act as acknowledgement.

Out-patients - the referring agent will receive an acknowledgement letter.

3 The client referred will receive an acknowledgement letter.

4 **All in-patients will be seen within two working days of referral.**

5 **Out-patient swallowing referrals will be seen within five days of referral.**

6 **All other out-patients will be seen within eight weeks of referral.**

Assessment:

1 **All referrals will receive an initial assessment.** This will generally take the form of an informal interview. Once completed, four possible courses of action will be forthcoming:

- additional in-depth assessment;

- advice to client and carers regarding appropriate management of the communication and/or swallowing problem;

- referral on to other agencies;

- discharge.

More than one course of action may be taken for any one client.

2 Assessment procedures may include:

- interviewing the client;

- informal assessment;

- use of formal standardised assessment protocols;

- observation of the client's communication abilities;

- interviewing the carers;

- obtaining information from the multi-disciplinary team and other agencies.

3 Assessment will usually cover:

- specific speech and language abilities;

- oral/facial musculature;

- swallowing abilities;

- cognitive abilities;

- emotional/psychological factors;

- social factors;

- medical factors.

4 **A speech and language therapy record sheet will be completed for every client referred.**

5 **Speech and language therapists will take a thorough case history** to facilitate a holistic approach to client care.

6 Notification of initial appointment will be given by letter to the client, at least one week in advance.

7 Notification of any review appointment will be given by letter to the client, at least one week in advance.

8 Where possible, the client will be offered preferred appointment times.

9 Where necessary initial assessment may be offered on a domiciliary basis for those clients unable to travel to the hospital.

Intervention:

1 Speech and language therapists will work within the multi-disciplinary framework to facilitate a team approach to client rehabilitation.

2 **A care plan for each client will be compiled prior to the commencement of therapy.** This care plan will be made available confidentially to the speech and language therapists, assistants and volunteers and other appropriate professionals who are working with the client. The care plan will

be updated regularly.

3 Therapists will liaise with all relevant agencies and carers of the client to ensure continuity of approach.

4 **The amount of therapy to be offered, review times and aims of therapy will be discussed with the client** and shared with:

- the carers (subject to the client's permission);

- the multi-disciplinary team;

- the referring agent;

- other relevant agencies.

5 Therapy may take the form of individual and/or group therapy. The amount of therapy offered will vary depending on the client's needs and the stage of the therapy programme. It may vary from three times a day in the acute stages of the intervention period, to review appointments at the end of the intervention period.

6 **Detailed notes will be kept regarding all intervention with clients.**

7 Speech and language therapists will regularly update:

- client's medical notes;

- nursing care plans;

- speech and language therapy care plans;

- speech and language therapy notes;

- group files.

8 Reports will be written following the assessment and circulated as appropriate.

Discharge:

1 Discharge may take place at any stage during involvement with the client:

- after initial assessment;

- if the client has no speech/language and/or swallowing problem;

- if the client declines therapy;

- if the client is too ill to receive therapy;

- if the client is to be transferred to a more local speech and language therapy service;

- if the client is not considered appropriate for therapy after a period of therapy or review;

- if maximum potential has been reached;

- if further therapy is no longer considered appropriate by the client and/or therapist.

2 The reasons for discharge will be discussed fully with the client, the carer and relevant others.

3 The client and carer will be put in contact with social networks available after discharge from active therapy, e.g. stroke clubs, self-help groups, etc.

4 All clients and their carers will be notified of direct access to speech and language therapy for advice and support after discharge.

5 The referring agent will be notified of the reasons for the discharge via reports or details in medical notes.

6 Clients being transferred out of the area

will have all reports and copies of their therapy notes sent on to the relevant service (subject to the client's permission).

Interface/Liaison with Other Professionals:

1   The speech and language therapist working within a hospital setting will work in close conjunction with the multi-disciplinary team which may include hospital-based staff, e.g.:

- medical staff;
- therapists;
- social workers;
- nursing staff;
- dieticians;
- psychologists.

2   The speech and language therapist based in a hospital is charged with the responsibility of representing the needs of clients with communication problems in terms of facilitating early referral, securing co-operation with therapy programmes and of influencing the communication environment of clients living in ward-based accommodation. Furthermore, speech and language therapists recognise the need to be aware of and make full use of community-based services and primary health care teams as required by individual clients.

3   Speech and language therapists will attend team meetings and case conferences as appropriate.

Skill Mix:

Hospital-based departments traditionally treat clients suffering from a wide range of acquired and occasionally developmental disorders.

It is therefore important to create an appropriate management structure which includes a distribution of speech and language therapists with specific responsibilities and specific duties. In order to gain the necessary experience to progress to such posts, speech and language therapists need to have the opportunity to work with the range of client groups and presenting disorders that occur in a hospital setting. Where speech and language therapists are engaged in service delivery, they should be able to refer to colleagues with specific responsibilities for a particular disorder.

Assistants and volunteers may be used in carrying out therapy programmes as appropriate to the specific needs of the client, and under the direct supervision of a speech and language therapist.

See specific guidelines under Client Groups (Chapter 3).
See guidelines on skill mix (Chapter 9).

Resource Requirements:

See general guidelines for accommodation and equipment (Chapter 8).

CHILD DEVELOPMENT CENTRES

Description/Definition of the Location:

A centre for children and their carers working towards a detailed assessment of abilities. These assessments are carried out by a multi-disciplinary team.

This assessment results in the evolution of a client centred plan of care to meet the child's identified needs. The centre may provide an assessment or assessment and intervention service.

Aims/Principles of Service Delivery:

1 To provide a specialist assessment and diagnostic service for children with difficulties in a variety of areas including communication.

2 To provide a service within a multi-disciplinary model of care.

3 To act as a resource to speech and language therapists undertaking the therapy of the child referred.

4 To provide education and training to other members of the multi-disciplinary team in order to contribute to the most effective management of a child with communication and swallowing difficulties.

Referral:

1 Referrals are usually made to the centre co-ordinator or consultant in accordance with the centre's published referral procedure.

2 Referrals will usually be discussed at the team meeting and the appropriate agencies will be identified for involvement in the child's assessment.

Assessment:

1 Assessment may take place with other team members.

2 The assessment procedure will be specific to the child's case history.

3 The speech and language therapist will liaise with other team members and carers when making recommendations.

4 The speech and language therapist will ensure that the carers have an opportunity to discuss the assessment results and follow-up recommendations.

5 **A written report will be compiled detailing the assessment findings.**
This will form part of the overall team report.

Intervention:

1 The actual model of intervention will depend upon the child development centre concerned. Some centres offer an assessment service only with intervention being carried out by the child's local service.

2 Where intervention is offered, the programme will be drawn up in conjunction with the other team members and have clearly defined aims and objectives for therapy.

3 Intervention may be provided individually and in groups. These groups are likely to involve other members of the multi-disciplinary team. The contribution of the

team members should be clearly defined.

4   The speech and language therapist working in a child development centre will promote and facilitate access to augmentative and alternative communication as appropriate for individual children.

5   **Progress will be monitored on a regular basis and goals updated accordingly.**

Discharge:

1   Discharge will normally be a team decision taken after an assessment or a period of intervention.

2   **If the discharge is to another speech and language therapist, for example, in the case of a child attending a special educational facility, the discharge will be accompanied by a full report detailing the child's strengths and needs. The report will include information relating to intervention.**

3   The carers will be involved in the decision to discharge.

Interface/Liaison with Other Professionals:

1   Due to the multi-disciplinary nature of child development centres the speech and language therapist works in close conjunction with all team members by attending team meetings and case conferences. The speech and language therapist may act as a key worker for particular children with whom she/he is centrally involved.

2   Speech and language therapists must have clearly defined links to others in the team and other colleagues within speech and language therapy.

Skill Mix:

The speech and language therapist with specific responsibilities in a child development centre must have had a period of experience working with a general paediatric caseload and with children with special needs. This would normally be for a period of not less that three years.

The speech and language therapist with specific responsibilities will have undertaken post graduate training in relevant subjects and will be a member of the appropriate College Specific Interest Group.

Speech and language therapists with specific duties working in a child development centre will do so with the support of a colleague with specific responsibilities relevant to this client group.

Resource Requirements:

See general guidelines for accommodation and equipment (Chapter 8).

COMMUNITY CLINICS

Description/Definition of the Location:

A service delivered from a community clinic/health centre to the local population, where the speech and language needs of the client can be met most efficiently by services provided in local settings.

Aims/Principles of Service Delivery:

1   To acknowledge that every client referred to speech and language therapy has a right to access local services.

2 To provide a speech and language therapy service to every client whose speech and language need can be most appropriately met by attendance at a local clinic.

3 To assess and provide intervention and advice where indicated to the client.

4 To work with other professionals in the primary health care team ensuring that the client's needs are met from a locally-based setting.

5 To work in close conjunction with colleagues e.g. in education and social services, establishing and maintaining a holistic approach to client care.

Referral:

1 **The referral procedure must ensure that all clients have equal access to the service, irrespective of age, sex, race and presenting speech and language difficulty.**

2 Referrals will be accepted directly from the client or carer, or from any professional involved with the client providing they have gained the client's/carer's consent.

3 Guidance information should be available to all interested parties as follows:

- referral agents will be given information regarding the referral procedure;

- referring agents will be informed of the need to give appropriate information upon referral e.g. biographical details, results of audiological assessments and any known relevant information from the client's social, developmental or medical histories;

- referring agents will be informed of the need to describe the presenting speech and language problem as far as possible;

- referring agents will be given information on possible outcomes following referral.

4 **The referral will be acknowledged to the referring agent and client/carer.**

5 Policy on re-referral will be agreed and implemented as appropriate.

Assessment:

1 **Following the receipt of a referral, an initial appointment will be offered to the client within eight weeks of the date of referral or within local guidelines.**

2 The initial appointment may be used for discussion with the client/carer, for case history taking, or initiating formal/informal assessment.

3 A case history will be taken including relevant details of medical, social, psychological, educational and communication status.

4 Assessment may involve a range of formal or informal assessments and may take place or be continued outside the clinic e.g. in the home or school, in order that a full profile of the client's communication skill may be completed.

5 As part of the assessment process the client may be referred on to another agency in order that a full and detailed assessment may be completed.

6 During the assessment process a second opinion may be sought as required by the

assessing therapist or if requested by the client/carer.

7 Following assessment a management decision will be made and discussed with the client/carer and all other parties will be informed.

8 An initial report will be written, and circulated as appropriate.

Intervention:

1 Following assessment, the techniques, timing and length of the period of intervention will be discussed and agreed with the client/carer.

2 Intervention may take the form of:

- advice;

- direct/indirect/facilitated therapy;

- individual/paired/group therapy;

- regular/intensive/block/review appointments;

- a programme for service delivery outside the clinic location, for example, in a nursery or school.

3 Intervention may be:

- contracted for a specified period of time;

- offered regularly on site;

- offered off site e.g. facilitated intervention by the carer in the home.

4 All intervention will be planned and recorded in the case notes.

5 Following intervention, a case management decision will be made, and consequently:

- reassessment may take place;

- discharge may take place;

- the client may be placed on review if it is anticipated that a further episode of care is likely to be needed.

6 At all stages during the intervention, the client/carer should be fully involved in the decision-making process.

Discharge:

1 The client may be discharged at any point following referral, after a case management decision to do so.

Normally, the decision to discharge will be taken by the therapist(s) responsible for the client's care in the light of progress and/or change in performance and should always be discussed with the client/carer. **The criteria for discharge will be locally agreed and clearly defined.**

2 For clients who are discharged for failure to attend, the client/carer will be informed that discharge procedures are to be initiated and will be given a date of discharge.

3 A discharge report will be written and circulated as appropriate.

4 All relevant personnel will be informed of the conclusion of the episode of care and the reasons for the decision to discharge.

5 Procedures of re-referral will be made clear as appropriate to the client/carer.

Interface/Liaison with Other Professionals:

As attendance at a community clinic/health centre is a routine part of the well-person's lifestyle, it is essential that the speech and language therapist working in such a location actively seeks out the other professionals who are relevant to the client at the time of the speech and language therapy referral. The establishment and maintenance of these relationships are paramount to the holistic multi-disciplinary approach to the client's needs. By definition, the client attending clinic is part of the community "at large" and therefore there is no finite list of professionals with whom the speech and language therapist will liaise. It is incumbent upon the therapist, as part of the assessment procedure, to identify other professionals with whom formal/informal contact must be made. Contact may be made in writing, by phone or by face-to-face contact and is facilitated by attendance at primary health care team meetings, liaison committees etc.

Skill Mix:

It is important that speech and language therapy managers acknowledge that the skills required for the potential client groups in clinic require the full staffing skill mix. There should be an identified manager of the service and clinicians with specific responsibilities available in addition to clinicians with specific duties.

Speech and language therapy assistants also have a role within community clinics, as do speech and language therapy students.

Levels of staffing for a clinic service will vary significantly according to the structure and resources of the district/areas that are available to the client. However, waiting times should be within agreed standards.

There should be easy access to therapists with specific responsibilities in regionally- and nationally-based specialist centres and therapists available locally to provide second opinions.

Resource Requirements:

Community clinics/health centres require a range of equipment and test materials that can be used with all clients, regardless of age, sex, race and speech and language diagnosis. Equipment should be safe, complete and regularly updated.

The accommodation provided must be appropriate for the client/carer and the model of care. It should be safe, accessible to the client and physically comfortable, with a designated waiting area and access to lavatory and changing areas.

See general guidelines for accommodation and equipment (Chapter 8).

DAY CENTRES
[including Social Education Centres, Adult Training Centres and Resource Centres]

Definition/Description of the Location:

Day facilities within the community provide services on either a full- or part-time basis for specified client groups. These client groups may include elderly people, clients with a physical and psychological/psychiatric disability and clients with a learning disability. The centres may offer a social, educational, recreational or work-based activity schedule.

Adult training centres, social education centres and resource centres in particular aim to make maximum use of the local community facilities and where appropriate aim to facilitate an 'outreach' service. Centres aim to maximise the independence of the clients attending by providing a full range of learning experiences.

Aims/Principles of Service Delivery:

Speech and language therapy services are provided to day centres with the following aims and principles:

1 To maximise the communicative potential of each client attending the centre.

2 To facilitate an understanding of the needs of clients attending.

3 To assist the centre staff in building a communication environment that is conducive to the development of communication skills.

4 To assist the centre staff in building an environment which encourages communicative participation and the development of self-advocacy.

5 To provide an appropriate service that meets the needs of the client group in their daily environment. This will necessitate the provision of services within the client's daily activities group.

6 To contribute to the knowledge and skills of the centre staff, thereby enabling them to take into account the client's communicative strengths and needs.

7 To work as a member of the total staff team.

Referral:

1 **Referrals will be accepted from any source provided that the client's consent has been obtained.**

2 The speech and language therapist will discuss the referral with the client and carer prior to actioning the assessment.

3 Clients referred should have access to an audiological assessment prior to commencing speech and language therapy.

4 On receipt of the referral, the speech and language therapist will ascertain the reason for the referral, the keyworker involved and the expected outcome of intervention.

5 A pre-assessment questionnaire may be completed by centre staff, giving details of the client's perceived communication strengths and needs.

Assessment:

1 An assessment of the communication environment of the centre as it pertains to the individual client will be carried out and the results communicated to the staff group as part of the total assessment findings.

This assessment may include assessment of environmental factors such as:

- noise levels;

- seating;

- opportunities to exercise communicative ability;

- choice through communication;

■ the nature of the communication used by significant others in the day centre towards the client.

2   The client will be fully involved at all stages of the assessment process and the subsequent decision-making.

3   **At least one other person who knows the client well will be actively involved in the assessment.**

4   It is necessary to assess the staff's expectations of and aspirations for the client's communication performance as their perceptions will be instrumental in planning intervention and deciding the appropriate level of staff training.

5   Assessment may take place in a range of settings, including the client's natural centre group setting, during community participation opportunities and at home. It is vital to gain an overview of the client's strengths and needs in the fullest range of settings in order to gain an accurate and comprehensive assessment result.

6   Assessment procedures appropriate to the specific client group will be carried out.

7   **A profile of the client's specific communication strengths and needs and his/her personal communication environment will be drawn up and circulated for discussion to all staff concerned.**

Intervention:

1   All goals for intervention should be drawn up with the active participation of the centre staff.

The centre staff will be required to work closely with the speech and language therapist in implementing the communication programme. It is, therefore, important that they are involved in deciding which goals are appropriate for the client.

The client will be involved in this process wherever possible.

2   Due to the nature of communication it is imperative that the 'programme' of intervention is integrated into the client's regular centre activities. Speech and language therapy should not be seen as separate from the rest of the client's activities.

3   If a decision is made, based upon the assessment results and the client/staff views, to implement a programme, the speech and language therapist should enlist the support of a 'keyworker' to implement the therapy goals. This person should be a member of the centre staff who is in frequent contact with the client.

4   Intervention may take place on a one-to-one basis with the client, implementing through direct therapy a goal plan which states short- and long-term goals of intervention.

5   In addition to the above, intervention will integrate the goal plan into the client's everyday programme through the involvement of centre staff and other centre users.

6   Intervention may involve the setting up of specific therapy groups to develop and practise certain skills. At least one member of the centre staff will be required to participate in these groups.

7   Whichever intervention programme is selected (it may be a combination) it is incumbent upon the speech and language therapist to make full use of the centre environment in assisting the client to develop and use skills.

8   Goals will be functionally-based in order to be meaningful for the client and staff.

9   The speech and language therapist working with clients who are making full use of community facilities or who are engaged in work opportunities must be prepared to take the assessment results and goal plans into these environments.

10 **The goals of therapy will be rigorously monitored and updated accordingly.** It is important to gain the commitment of centre staff to a period of therapy, at the end of which goals may be re-evaluated and further goals reset.

11 If the agreed goal plan has not been implemented consistently, it is unlikely to be successful and the efficacy of intervention may be called into question.

12 Intervention will usually require staff training by the speech and language therapist in either general communication concepts or more specific skills targeted at the actual goal plans in operation.

13 The speech and language therapist recognises the social function of the centre and must respect the rights of the client to

enjoy social and recreational activities without an undue emphasis on 'learning'. Appropriate intervention programmes should also allow for time and space for the client.

Discharge:

1   The speech and language therapist should seek to negotiate the termination of therapy with the client and keyworker.

The speech and language therapist must retain the right to discharge on the basis of clinical judgement.

2   **A full report will be completed and circulated prior to discharge detailing:**

- a summary of the client's initial assessment;

- a summary of the initial aims and objectives;

- progress since assessment;

- reasons for discharge.

3   The process for re-referral should be made clear to the client and keyworker.

Interface/Liaison with Other Professionals:

1   Speech and language therapists aim to provide intervention in a fully integrated manner, contributing as part of the wider team. Therefore, speech and language therapists working in a day centre should consider themselves part of the total centre staff team whilst remaining aware of their unique contribution.

2   It is advisable for the speech and language therapist to attend staff meetings and participate in discussions regarding the

centre's organisation and role.

3 The speech and language therapist has a clear educative role with other professionals within the inter-disciplinary team in representing the needs of clients with communication and swallowing difficulties.

The speech and language therapist is responsible for facilitating an understanding of the nature of communication difficulties in carers and other staff and for involving others in the therapeutic process.

4 Speech and language therapists will participate in client reviews and planning meetings as appropriate.

Skill Mix:

The skill mix of the speech and language therapist required to deliver a service to a day centre will depend upon the actual client group attending the centre. The clients may, for example, constitute an elderly persons group, clients with a physical disability or clients with learning disabilities. See Chapter 3 for information on specific client groups.

It should be recognised that in most instances, therapists working in adult day facilities take on a 'visiting' role and will need to have the necessary skills to provide an integrated seamless service for the clients in their care.

Resource Requirements:

Speech and language therapists will require access to a range of on-site assessment and therapy materials. Due to the functional nature of the integrated intervention, the speech and language therapist will require

access to existing resources in the centres.

The speech and language therapist will require access to office space for administration purposes and individual assessment/intervention where appropriate.

See general guidelines for accommodation and equipment (Chapter 8).

DOMICILIARY

Definition/Description of the Location:

Domiciliary services are those offered to clients in their own homes either as part of an agreed service initiative, or as part of a total care plan involving concurrent delivery in other locations.

Aims/Principles of Service Delivery:

1 To optimise the client's communication within the care unit.

2 To observe clients' communicative functioning in their day-to-day environment and to observe their interaction with others.

3 To provide assessment/intervention for clients who for practical, medical and/or emotional reasons, may be unable to access or benefit from intervention outside of their own home environment.

4 To enhance liaison with community-based primary care or specialist teams e.g. district nurses/health visitors, and to encourage a co-ordinated approach to client care.

5 To facilitate the delivery of services in the most appropriate environment for the client.

6 To enable close contact between the

speech and language therapist and the client's family and friends in order to develop a clear understanding of the client's communication needs within a natural context.

Referral:

1 **Referrals will be accepted from any source provided that the client's consent has been obtained. Clearly defined and published referral procedures will be available to all potential referring agents.**

2 A nominated base for receipt of referrals will be agreed and noted in the guidance to referring agencies.

3 On receipt of referral, the appropriateness of domiciliary service provision will be evaluated and appropriate action taken.

Assessment:

1 Prior to undertaking an assessment, the speech and language therapist will contact the relevant member of the multi-disciplinary team with the details of the planned visit.

2 Speech and language therapists should give careful consideration to the environment in which the client is assessed and managed. Speech and language therapists must be aware of any procedure that is likely to involve risk to the client e.g. a dysphagia assessment, and must ensure appropriate support before proceeding with the assessment.

3 At the initial assessment the speech and language therapist should assess whether home visits are the best location if further intervention is required.

4 **Speech and language therapists must be aware of safety procedures relevant to home visits** including how to deal with challenging behaviour and medical emergencies e.g. if a client suffers an epileptic fit.

5 Speech and language therapists should take the minimal amount of case note information to a home visit. The main case notes should remain at the working location base.

6 When case notes are written they should always stipulate "Home Visit" if a client has been treated in their own home.

7 Speech and language therapists involved in a home visit must carry an identification badge.

8 **Following assessment, the members of the multi-disciplinary team will be informed of the outcome of assessment results and the proposed therapy plan.**

Intervention:

1 Appropriateness of home visits should be reassessed after the agreed period of intervention.

2 The client/carer should be informed at the outset of any likely change to the domiciliary service in the event of a client's altered circumstances e.g. improvement in health allowing for out-patient therapy; commencing school with on-site speech and language therapy.

Discharge:

1 The client/carer will be informed how to contact the speech and language therapy department should they need to be re-referred.

2 If a client is discharged from the domiciliary service and referred on to another aspect of the service e.g. a pre-school special needs child passed on to a therapist within education, the domiciliary therapist will normally pass on all case notes and relevant information.

Interface/Liaison with Other Professionals:

1 Where there is involvement of a community team the members of this team should be informed of the speech and language therapist's involvement.

2 Joint visiting may be appropriate as in the case of a physiotherapist and speech and language therapist visiting a client at home.

3 Attendance at individual case conferences is to be encouraged where possible.

4 The general practitioner is to be kept informed of the plan for intervention.

Skill Mix:

Speech and language therapists involved in domiciliary visiting should have the necessary specialist and non-specialist skills appropriate to the client group they are serving.

Speech and language therapists engaged in domiciliary care need to have undertaken training in:

- first aid and the primary management of emergencies e.g. epilepsy;

- management of challenging behaviour and personal safety.

Resource Requirements:

1 A budget for travelling expenses.

2 A range of equipment to be used during home visiting appropriate to the needs of the client group.

See general guidelines for accommodation and equipment (Chapter 8).

LONG STAY INSTITUTIONS

Description/Definition of the Location:

A service which is delivered to clients living in an institutional setting. The clients will have lived or are expected to live in this setting for some considerable time.

The location is characterised by high staffing ratios, and ward-based accommodation. The institution will normally provide day and recreational activities for its clients. Some institutions may be in the process of closing and transferring residents into smaller, locally-based provision within a community setting.

Aims/Principles of Service Delivery:

1 To maximise the communication potential of the client living in a long-stay institution by identifying, modifying and enriching the communication environment in which the client resides.

2 To enable the staff caring for the client to have an understanding of their client's communication strengths and needs.

3   To contribute to the staff's skills and knowledge in interacting with clients who have a communication impairment.

4   To facilitate the client's access to services such as audiology and dentistry which will contribute to their communication skills.

5   To represent clients with communication needs as a particular group within the long-stay institution.

6   To assist in decisions pertaining to the grouping of clients and skill development, prior to moving to a home of their own in the community.

7   To work as part of the total care team which may include medical staff, nursing staff, paramedical staff, instructors and care staff.

Referral:

1   **The speech and language therapist working in a long-stay institution will be required to develop a referral procedure which allows straightforward, equal access to the service provided by the department. Referrals will be accepted from any source provided that the client's consent has been obtained.**

2   The speech and language therapist will communicate this referral procedure to the institution, including the wards, day facilities, recreational departments and other paramedical departments.

3   The referral procedure will ensure that clients themselves may request an appointment with the speech and language therapist.

4   With clients' changing needs and circumstances it may be appropriate for clients who have previously been discharged from the service to be re-referred. Procedures for re-referral should be straightforward. Staff may need to be given advice and feedback as to the appropriateness of making a re-referral.

Assessment:

1   **Clients referred to the service will receive a full assessment of their strengths and needs as appropriate to speech and language therapy.**

2   This will involve assessing clients in all their natural environments, as appropriate, e.g.:

- ward base;

- day centre;

- recreational activity.

3   Assessment may include a range of formal and informal procedures specific to the particular client group or suspected communication difficulty.

4   **Assessment will be undertaken with the help of the significant people in the client's life;** i.e. those who are in regular contact with the client and who know him/her well.

5   Joint assessment with other paramedical staff may be appropriate.

6   An assessment of the client's communication environment is of particular importance in a long-stay institution where environmental deprivation may be a significant factor affecting the client's communication performance.

7   Assessment will include an evaluation of the following;

- client's motivation to communicate;

- client's need to communicate;

- client's opportunities to communicate.

8   **A written assessment report will be compiled, discussed where possible with the client, and communicated to the relevant staff.**

9   **The referring agent will be given information as to the outcome of the assessment.**

Intervention:

1   A multi-disciplinary care plan should be completed where possible, which includes the communication strengths and needs of the client and aims and objectives of therapy.

2   Intervention may take the form of a programme of facilitated intervention delivered by the ward-based or day service staff. This may include a programme for changing factors within the environment which have been identified at the assessment stage as affecting the client's communicative performance.

3   As part of the intervention programme, the speech and language therapist may need to deliver specific staff training relevant to the therapy programme for the client concerned.

4   In the case of clients who may be leaving the institution to live in community-based accommodation, the speech and language therapist has an important role to play in preparing the client for the new demands that may be placed upon his/her communication skills in his/her new environment. Intervention may include advising the wider team of the implications of the client's communication for group selection planning.

5   Residents in a long-stay institution may not have had access to ENT and audiology services. It is particularly important to pay close attention to these factors and arrange for the necessary referrals to be made. The speech and language therapist may actively need to support the client in attending appointments with other agencies and at times assist in the testing procedure or examination the client may be asked to undergo, particularly if appointments are offered in community settings.

6   Speech and language therapists may need to develop intervention programmes with non-speaking clients who may have an associated physical disability. These clients may benefit from augmentative and alternative communication systems.

7   Staff turnover in long-stay institutions is often high. The speech and language therapy department may therefore need to initiate a continuous programme of staff training on general and specific communication skills issues.

8   It should be recognised that securing staff motivation and commitment in an institution that is subject to closure is often a difficult task. The speech and language therapist is able to contribute to the morale of staff by involving them in communication assessments and therapy and valuing their contribution to the care plan.

9   It is likely that intervention will prove

unsuccessful if the significant others in the client's life are not actively involved in the therapeutic process. They must therefore be adequately supported by the speech and language therapist.

10 **Goals of intervention will need to be integrated into the general communication environment of the client, written down and communicated in a style that ensures an understanding of the goals by the staff involved with the client on a day-to-day basis.**

11 Speech and language therapists are advised to select only one or two areas for intervention with a client at any one time in order that the staff and the clients themselves are able to co-operate with the programme.

Discharge:

1 Discharge may take place at any stage during the intervention, after full consultation has taken place with the client/team.

2 **A decision to discharge will be accompanied by a discharge report.**

3 The relevant staff should be informed of the process for re-referral.

4 If the discharge involves a referral to another speech and language therapist, e.g. in the case of a client moving on to another residence, a full report detailing background information, assessment results and intervention plans should be passed on to the agency receiving the referral.

Interface/Liaison with Other Professionals:

The speech and language therapist has an educational role with other staff within the inter-disciplinary team. The working arrangements of the speech and language therapist must allow for her/him to participate fully in the life of the residency in order to be acknowledged as a team member. It is only in this way that the speech and language therapist can ensure that clients with communication needs will be recognised and referred to the speech and language therapy department. The speech and language therapist will therefore participate in case conferences and individual programme plans as appropriate.

Skill Mix:

The skill mix of the speech and language therapy service to a long-stay institution will depend upon the actual client group attending the institution. The clients may, for example, constitute an elderly persons group, clients with a physical or psychiatric disability or clients with a learning disability. See Chapter 3 for information on specific client groups.

The speech and language therapist working unsupported by senior staff will have had experience of working within an inter-disciplinary environment and delivering the service through carers and others involved in clients' everyday lives.

Resource Requirements:

Speech and language therapists will require access to a range of on-site assessment and therapy materials. Due to the functional nature of the intervention programme, the speech and language therapist will require access to existing resources in the long-stay institutions.

The speech and language therapist will require access to office space for administration purposes and for the individual assessment of clients, as appropriate.

See general guidelines for accommodation and equipment (Chapter 8).

PRE-SCHOOL FACILITIES

Description/Definition of the Location:

A day provision that is exclusively for pre-school children. Facilities may include social service/health service day nurseries, educational day nurseries, opportunity playgroups and state and independent day nurseries.

Aims/Principles of Service Delivery:

1 To ensure the early detection of pre-school children with speech and language difficulties.

2 To offer advice and support to other professionals/staff in pre-school facilities to enable them to work effectively with pre-school children with speech and language difficulties.

3 To recommend and implement the appropriate intervention to meet the needs of a child in liaison with other staff and carers.

4 To provide in-service training for other professionals and carers.

Referral:

1 **Carer consent for referral will always be obtained prior to an assessment.**

2 Written service agreements should be made when there is an agreed level of input into a pre-school facility - this should be agreed with the manager or teacher of the nursery and take the form of a joint operational policy.

Assessment:

1 Carer involvement in initial assessment is desirable to enable a full case history to be taken.

2 Assessment may be formal and/or informal according to a child's individual needs and may therefore take place in a range of locations.

3 Following assessment, the speech and language therapist and the pre-school facility staff and carers will work together in planning the intervention programme.

4 **Reports detailing the findings of the assessment will be completed and shared with carers and staff.** Further onward referrals may be made with the carers' permission.

Intervention:

1 Intervention may be carried out directly by the speech and language therapist or indirectly via programmes devised by the speech and language therapist and carried out by staff/assistants/carers.

2 Carers will be informed of the plans for intervention.

3 Whether intervention is direct or indirect, the speech and language therapist remains responsible for the child's care, for renewing goals and revising programmes.

4 Liaison with other professionals should be maintained. Close contact must be maintained if another profession and/or carer is carrying out a programme of therapy with the child.

5 The speech and language therapist may initiate a referral for an educational psychology/audiology/ENT assessment if this is thought to be appropriate. This would always be done with carer permission and discussed with appropriate staff.

6 The location for intervention may change if it becomes more appropriate for intervention to occur e.g. within a community clinic.

Discharge:

1 Any proposed discharge will be fully discussed with carers and staff at the pre-school facility.

2 Carers will be informed when a child is to be discharged, and made aware of the method of re-referral.

3 When the child moves into full-time education the speech and language therapist will liaise closely with colleagues in education.

Interface/Liaison with Other Professionals:

1 Efforts will be made to work closely with the child's carers.

2 A wide range of professionals may be involved with the child. The speech and language therapist will actively seek out the 'team' concerned with the child and involve them as appropriate.

3 Close liaison will be maintained with pre-school facility staff.

4 Referrals on to other appropriate professionals should occur as necessary.

5 The speech and language therapist may be asked to contribute to the child's statement/record of special educational need.

Skill Mix:

The appropriate skill mix for a child attending a pre-school facility will depend upon the disorders with which the child presents. See Chapters 3 and 4 on client groups/presenting disorders.

Resource Requirements:

Speech and language therapists working in these facilities will require access to a quiet room in order to undertake formal assessments of the child's communication skills and to offer individual therapy where appropriate. Accommodation suitable for group work should also be made available when required.

See guidelines for accommodation and equipment (Chapter 8).

REHABILITATION CENTRES

Definition/Description of the Location:

A centre which exists to provide intensive therapeutic rehabilitation to a designated client group or groups.

The services are offered in order to enable clients to reach their potential and therefore maximise their long term functioning. The therapeutic services are provided within an inter-disciplinary framework.

In most instances, the clients are medically stable and may be at any stage in their recovery.

Aims/Principles of Service Delivery:

1 To provide an intensive therapeutic service to the client who may not benefit as fully from less intensive models of care.

2 To provide therapeutic management within a fully inter-disciplinary framework.

3 To provide a specialist assessment, diagnostic and therapy service to the client presenting with communication difficulties.

4 To provide information and clinical management support to others involved in the rehabilitation of the client.

5 To represent the communication needs of the client in the overall rehabilitation process.

6 To contribute to the education of professionals and carers in relation to the client presenting with communication and swallowing disorders.

Referral:

1 Referrals to the rehabilitation centre will normally be received via a medical source. The referral to speech and language therapy may be from a local therapist or team member. **Referrals will be accepted from any source provided that the client's consent has been obtained.**

2 **The referral will be acknowledged and full liaison with the previous speech and language therapist will take place prior to undertaking the assessment of the client.**

Assessment:

1 On receipt of the referral to the rehabilitation centre, the client will be invited to attend for an assessment interview. This will normally extend over a period of one to two days and consist of a screening assessment by all services, in order to establish the requirements for intensive rehabilitation.

2 The speech and language therapist will participate in this screening assessment, offering a verbal and written report as necessary.

3 Following admission to the rehabilitation centre a period of assessment/intervention will be offered usually extending over a period of two to six weeks. During this time a full speech and language assessment will be carried out. This may include an assessment of swallowing and/or eating skills.

4 **The assessment procedure will be specific**

to the apparent disorder and case history information.

5   The assessment procedure will be inter-disciplinary and the speech and language therapist will work closely with the other team members. For example, the physiotherapist and the speech and language therapist may jointly assess posture, breathing and voice presentation; the occupational therapist, the clinical psychologist and the speech and language therapist may jointly assess cognition, reasoning and memory skills.

6   **The assessment will be carried out in conjunction with the carers, therapists and nursing staff,** and may include observation and assessment in a range of settings including:

- assignment-based assessment of the client in the local neighbourhood;

- ward-based assessment;

- one-to-one therapy situations.

7   The speech and language therapist will need to consider whether speech and language therapy within the rehabilitation centre offers a model of care which will benefit the client to an extent above that which can be offered in other settings. It is only if a client is considered to be able to make greater progress within a rehabilitation centre setting that therapy should be offered within that location.

8   Following the assessment a joint report and care plan will be drawn up by the team. A priority skill or skills will be identified in the plan, and communicated to all those involved with the client. Wherever possible this decision is to be made in conjunction with the client and his/her carers.

9   The care plan will be 'client-centred' and will be written in such a way as to facilitate common understanding within the team. The speech and language therapist will be required to work within a holistic model of care and to integrate communication needs into the overall care plan.

Intervention:

1   The inter-disciplinary care plan compiled at the end of the assessment period will identify the communication needs of the client. The speech and language therapist will translate these needs into aims and objectives of therapy.

2   The aims of therapy will change over time.

The initial aims of therapy will be to restore lost functions, to rehabilitate the client towards pre-traumatic level of performance.

Once the anticipated level of ability has been reached, the aims will be directed towards a functional approach to therapy. This will involve assisting the client in adjusting to persisting disabilities and capitalising upon existing skills.

3   Most rehabilitation centres employ an eclectic approach to therapy. There is a recognition that each client requires an individual management plan; the intervention approach will therefore be based upon the presenting needs of the client.

4   Intervention will take place within individual and group situations in a range

of locations. Full use will be made of 'natural' settings including local community facilities. The intensity of interventions will vary from between several short sessions per day to twice weekly speech and language therapy sessions, depending upon the needs of the particular client.

5 **The identified priority areas for therapy will be addressed and integrated into each specific therapy plan regardless of discipline.** This pattern of intervention will at times identify an inter-disciplinary approach as the most appropriate model of care.

6 In this way the aims of the speech and language therapist's programme will be reinforced throughout the client's daily schedule.

7 The speech and language therapist will need to be sensitive to the client's physical and psychological state in delivering a therapy programme.

8 Speech and language therapists are required to be flexible and resourceful in the timetabling and delivery of their services.

9 **The client's progress and response to therapy will be fully recorded, discussed with the client/carer and reported to the team at regular team briefings.**

Discharge:

1 **The decision to discharge will be a team decision taken after full consultation with all team members, the client and carers.**

2 The discharge may be to:

■ a local speech and language therapist;

■ another rehabilitation unit;

■ the care of another professional group.

In the event of the above, a full report detailing assessment, intervention and response to therapy will be compiled either individually or as part of the team report and passed on to the relevant agency.

3 Therapy should be terminated if there is no evidence that the client and carer are benefiting. In the case of a discharge which does not involve a 'referral on' the client should be adequately prepared for the cessation of intervention and offered further support and advice as appropriate.

Interface/Liaison with Other Professionals:

1 The speech and language therapist has a clear educative role with other professionals within the inter-disciplinary team in representing the needs of the client with communication difficulties.

2 The speech and language therapist is responsible for facilitating an understanding of the nature of communication difficulties in carers and other staff and for involving others in the therapeutic process. In order to participate in the delivery of therapy plans, all speech and language therapy personnel require appropriate training and support.

3 The speech and language therapist working in the rehabilitation centre is required to work within an inter-disciplinary model of care at times developing into a trans-disciplinary model.

Rehabilitation centres are characterised by such joint professional working practice and the speech and language therapist has a responsibility to actively participate within this framework.

4 Consequently, the speech and language therapist will participate in team meetings and case conferences as required.

Skill Mix:

Speech and language therapists delivering services to clients attending rehabilitation centres will have specialist skills relevant to the particular client group.

For a rehabilitation centre serving neurologically impaired clients, the speech and language therapist with specific responsibilities will have had experience of usually not less than three years duration in working with clients presenting with dysphasia, dysarthria, dysphonia and dysphagia, within an acute and/or educational setting as part of a multi-disciplinary team.

For a rehabilitation centre serving clients with traumatic brain injury, the speech and language therapist with specific responsibilities will have experience gained through post-graduate education or clinical practice of the associated difficulties of cognitive impairments, physical disability and behavioural challenges, including an understanding of theoretical models relating to personality and behaviour and basic learning strategies.

These skills may be acquired through a programme of supervised continuous development and/or post-graduate education experiences.

The speech and language therapist working in a rehabilitation centre will have a clear understanding of the role of other members of the team including physiotherapists, occupational therapists, clinical and educational psychologists and nursing staff/teaching staff.

Speech and language therapists working in rehabilitation centres who do not fulfil the above criteria will be fully supervised by a senior colleague. This supervision should be available on site in order that management decisions can be taken after discussion with a senior colleague.

The expectations and required justifications from within the team will also necessitate the full support of a specialist colleague who has a knowledge of all clients attending the centre.

Speech and language therapists working within rehabilitation centres are advised to belong to relevant College Specific Interest Groups and national societies and associations.

Rehabilitation centres are recognised as being ideal locations for undertaking research into clinical activity. This is to be encouraged wherever possible.

Assistants:

Due to the fully inter-disciplinary model of care delivered within the rehabilitation centres the role of assistants is likely to be confined to the preparation of rooms and equipment for therapy, administrative tasks and assisting in group therapy interventions.

See specific client group/speech and language disorder guidelines (Chapters 3 and 4) for the use of assistants.

Resource Requirements:

1 The speech and language therapist providing services within a rehabilitation centre requires access to therapy rooms suitable for group and individual therapy.

2 The therapist requires transport facilities and/or expenses budget to facilitate community participation.

See general guidelines for accommodation and equipment (Chapter 8).

SERVICES TO EDUCATION

Mainstream Schools

Description/Definition of the Location:

A service delivered within the mainstream school to children who need support for and development of their communication skills. This will include children with statements/records of special educational need.

Aims/Principles of Service Delivery:

1 To provide a service which involves a high degree of shared knowledge, skills expertise and information among all those involved with the child.

2 To provide speech and language therapy assessment and intervention for children with speech and language difficulties as an integral part of their school life, ensuring that speech and language therapy input is part of a total programme for the child.

3 To recognise and implement highly flexible working practices with the focus on the everyday social and learning context of the child.

4 To acknowledge that a speech and language therapy service in a mainstream school is a specialist service and not simply a speech and language therapy 'clinic' located in a school.

5 To deliver the service in such a way as to enable education staff to incorporate the aims of the speech and language therapy programme in the planning of the language programme in the context of the broad curriculum.

Referral:

1 The referral procedure will ensure that all children identified in accordance with the local service description have equal access to the service, irrespective of age, sex, race, presenting communication difficulty or named mainstream school.

2 Referral will be accepted directly from the carer or any professional involved with the child, providing the guidelines pertaining to 'consent to treat' have been followed.

3 Referral to the service will operate in accordance with the referral policy for the employing authority, which must be available to any interested party and should be updated as appropriate.

4 Guidance information should be available to all interested parties (see referral procedures for Community Clinics above).

5 It is probable that a high percentage of children receiving speech and language therapy within a mainstream school will previously have attended speech and language therapy at a local clinic/health centre. The model of care for these children will differ when they are referred to the mainstream service and are identified as part of the mainstream population receiving speech and language therapy input in school.

6 **The referral will be acknowledged to the referring agent and client/carer.**

7 Further referrals will be initiated when appropriate in accordance with the model of care for assessment/intervention/discharge.

8 Policy on re-referral will be agreed and implemented as appropriate.

Assessment:

1 Following receipt of referral an initial appointment will be agreed with carers and education staff as appropriate.

2 The format for the appointment will depend upon the information already known by the therapist, e.g. the appointment may be used for case-history taking, discussion, classroom observation, assessment, reassessment, review, intervention, and will be described to carers and education staff, who will be requested to contribute.

3 Assessment may take place over a number of appointments, may involve a range of formal or informal assessments, may take place in different locations within the mainstream school and may be continued outside the school. It will include other professionals' assessment of the child's communication skills and other areas of functioning, particularly noting the findings of the educational psychologist, where appropriate.

4 As part of the assessment process the client may be referred on to another agency in order that a full and detailed assessment can be completed.

5 Liaison with other agencies will be initiated as appropriate.

6 During the assessment process a second opinion may be sought as required by the assessing therapist or if requested by carers or education staff.

7 Following assessment, a management decision will be made in conjunction with and following full discussion with carers and education staff. This decision will take into account the perceptions of all those involved, and will be made in the social/learning context. All other parties will be informed.

Intervention:

1 **Following the management decision, the method, timing and length of intervention will be discussed and agreed by all parties.**

2 Intervention may take the form of:

- direct/indirect/facilitated therapy;

- individual/paired/group therapy;

- regular/intensive/block/review intervention.

3 Intervention may be:

- initiated immediately;

- planned for a future date.

4   The length of the period of intervention will be confirmed.

5   **All intervention will be planned and written up, so that the outcome of the intervention may be audited.**

6   Following intervention, a management decision will be made, as a result of which one of the following will happen:

- reassessment;

- discharge;

- review recommended if it is anticipated that a further episode of care is likely to be required.

7   As service delivery is within the school setting, intervention should include provision of a written programme outlining assessed areas of difficulty and details of intervention. This should be planned with members of the school's staff to fit in with the child's overall education programme and address issues currently significant in the child's educational life.

8   Intervention will include facilitating access to the National Curriculum/ 5-14 Curriculum.

9   Intervention will normally include the provision of in-service training to all staff involved with the child, on both a formal and informal basis.

Discharge:

1   **Criteria for discharge will, where appropriate, be agreed locally and be clearly defined.**

2   Although the service is delivered within the school setting, the therapist responsible for the child's care must recognise the rights of the carers to withdraw the child from therapy. In these instances the speech and language therapist must consider the implications of The Children Act upon 'consent to treat'.

3   **A discharge report will be written and circulated as appropriate.**

4   Procedures for re-referral must be made clear to carers and education staff.

Interface/Liaison with Other Professionals:

1   It is essential that the speech and language therapist working in a mainstream school acknowledges her/his role as a member of the multi-disciplinary team. Intrinsic to service delivery in a mainstream school is the acknowledgement of the primacy of the child's educational needs.

2   A mainstream service where the speech and language therapist and education staff work together will improve communication and increase opportunities for sharing expertise. This service aims to develop understanding of the nature and implications of speech and language difficulties and develop confidence, knowledge, skills and expertise in dealing with children with speech and language difficulties. Therapists and education staff must recognise that sharing knowledge and skills will enhance their respective professional roles. This requires formal agreement on time allocated for such discussion.

In addition, the therapist working in such a location must seek out other professionals who may provide a service to the child, and establish and maintain those professional relationships that are paramount to the holistic, multi-disciplinary, multi-agency approach to the child.

Skill Mix:

The nature of the appropriate skill mix required to deliver the service will depend upon the identified caseload within the mainstream school. Employing authorities will need to identify the range of skills which will allow the service to be maximally effective. Levels of staffing for a mainstream service will vary significantly according to the demands of the identified caseload, but caseloads should be deemed manageable and waiting times within agreed standards.

There must be an identified manager of the service and speech and language therapists with specific responsibilities available. There may be a role for speech and language therapy assistants and speech and language therapy students.

See guidelines on skill mix (Chapter 9).

Resource Requirements:

A service delivered within a mainstream school requires a full complement of equipment and test materials that can be used appropriately with all clients, regardless of age, sex, race and speech and language disorder. Equipment should be safe, complete and regularly updated.

Speech and language therapists working in mainstream schools require access to education in the curriculum and in classroom practices.

Accommodation:

Therapists working within mainstream schools will normally be accommodated for periods of intervention rather than on a regular basis and therefore need to acknowledge the demands that are made by those using the accommodation regularly as well as other visiting professionals. If accommodation outside the mainstream classroom is identified as essential, e.g. for formal testing, then the provision of such accommodation must be agreed upon before the service is introduced.

The therapist is responsible for ensuring that any accommodation provided by the local education authority is safe and accessible.

Special Schools
[including Classes and Units]

Description/Definition of the Location:

A speech and language therapy service provided to a special educational establishment for children with statements/records of special educational need. The service is based within the school and is provided in close collaboration with the school staff.

Aims/Principles of Service Delivery:

1   To provide assessment and intervention for children with communication and/or eating and drinking difficulties as an integral part of their educational life.

2   To deliver the service in such a way as to enable the education staff to incorporate the aims of the speech and language therapy

programme into the language curriculum for each child with a speech and language difficulty.

3   To work with the school staff, carers and other professionals to facilitate the child's development, to carry out specific therapy where appropriate, to serve as a resource for the school staff in preparing any school policies and to be available as a resource for relevant areas of the curriculum.

4   To contribute to workshops for staff and carers on topics relating to communication and/or eating and drinking.

Referral:

1   **The referral procedure will ensure that all children who are identified as requiring a referral to speech and language therapy have equal access to the service irrespective of age, sex, race, or presenting difficulty.**

2   Referrals will be accepted directly from the school staff providing the guidelines pertaining to 'consent to treat' have been followed.

Assessment:

1   On receipt of the referral the speech and language therapist will attempt to gain the relevant information pertaining to the child. This would normally include: medical information, personal/social and educational background of the child and information relating to previous speech and language therapy.

2   **The carers will be invited to take part in the assessment process.**

3   An audiological assessment should be available to the speech and language therapist prior to the commencement of the assessment.

4   The speech and language therapist will liaise closely with the school staff throughout the assessment process taking their perceptions into account in formulating both the assessment protocol and subsequent interpretation of the assessment findings.

5   Assessment may take place in a range of locations including, for example, the classroom, in a separate room with the speech and language therapist, in the dining room during mealtimes or in the child's home.

6   The assessment should be designed in such a way as to allow the child to be seen within the educational context.

7   The assessment will take into account the assessment results of other professionals involved with the child.

8   The assessment will include an evaluation of the child's communication environment and its effect upon the child's communication performance.

9   During the assessment a second opinion may be sought.

10 **Following the assessment, the findings and the implications for intervention will be circulated to and discussed with carers and other staff involved with the child.**

Intervention:

1   **Following the assessment, long- and short-term goals will be formulated in conjunction with the school staff.** These goals

will be discussed with carers and then documented. There will be an ongoing evaluation of the effectiveness of the intervention with modifications as appropriate.

2 All episodes of care will be negotiated and agreed between the carers and the speech and language therapist. The responsibilities of the carers and school staff for active participation in therapy will be agreed.

3 Where intervention requires the involvement of speech and language therapy assistants, students or volunteers, this will be explained to the carers.

4 Intervention may take various forms, depending on the individual needs of the child. It may require direct face-to-face therapy in a group or on an individual basis, indirect intervention via programme planning in the classroom setting or at home. The type of intervention should be agreed with carers and appropriate staff and should be reviewed regularly.

5 In order for the speech and language therapy to be successful, arrangements should be made to integrate the work done by the speech and language therapist with the child's daily life in school and at home. If therapy is to be generalised it must be seen to be important to all aspects of the child's educational and social life. Therefore the contribution of the teaching staff, assistants, nursery and child care staff and carers is essential.

6 In order to plan realistic strategies for helping language development within the classroom setting the speech and language therapist should understand the environment and its influence upon the child's communication behaviour.

7 Where appropriate, the speech and language therapist should work within the classroom setting, in order that the most natural communication environment may be accessed.

8 The intervention programme may be offered in a variety of ways.

9 Intervention should include the speech and language therapist participating in workshops and staff training.

10 **Clear, precise and up to date records will be kept at all times, and reports written as necessary.**

11 The speech and language therapist will contribute to the child's statement/record of educational need and annual reviews.

12 Where regular therapy is no longer indicated the child may be placed on review.

13 The purpose and length of the review period should be discussed with the carers and appropriate staff.

14 Following the review period the child should be reassessed to determine future intervention requirements.

Discharge:

1 Therapy should be discontinued if there is no evidence that the child/carers are benefiting.

2 Although the service is delivered in the school setting, the speech and language therapist must recognise the rights of the carers to withdraw the child from therapy.

In these circumstances, the speech and language therapist must carefully consider the content of 'The Children Act' (1989) (where appropriate), and its reference to 'consent to treat'.

3 A discharge report will be written and circulated as appropriate.

4 Procedures for re-referral will be made clear to carers and school staff.

Interface/Liaison with Other Professionals:

1 It is essential that the speech and language therapist working in a special school acknowledges her/his role as a member of the multi-disciplinary team involved in the child's education. Intrinsic to the service delivery is the acknowledgement of the primacy of the child's education and the place of communication in that educational process.

2 The service aims to develop confidence, knowledge, skills and expertise in dealing with children with speech and language difficulties. It is important that the therapists and educational staff work in close collaboration, sharing skills and roles in order that the most effective service may be delivered. This requires formal agreement on time allocated for such discussion.

3 Opportunities for discussion between the staff and therapist are essential. Arrangements should be made to incorporate this into the child's programme. Plans should be organised to include all staff who work with the child or children.

4 Where possible the speech and language therapist should be involved in parent evenings and meetings.

5 The therapist will contribute to the annual review and the statement/record of educational need.

6 In the case of home visits the therapist may accompany staff or visit unaccompanied. Care should be taken to inform the headteacher of any proposed visits.

Skill Mix:

The nature of the skill mix will depend upon the identified case load of the children in any particular school. See Chapter 9 for guidelines on skill mix.

It should be recognised that the nature of the inter-agency service requires that services to special education be delivered under the direction of an identified manager.

Where possible therapists may work in close collaboration with other colleagues in order to provide the most effective service.

Resource Requirements:

Speech and language therapists working in special schools/units/classes require access to education on the curriculum and on classroom practices. This type of training is often more effective if therapists can attend training with their teaching counterparts.

The resources as outlined in accommodation and equipment guidelines in Chapter 8 should be available to therapists working in special schools.

Other resources to be provided by local agreement.

A range of assessment and therapy materials will be available as appropriate to the client group.

Language Units
[including Schools and Classes]

Description/Definition of the Location:

A service delivered within a designated unit/class/school to an identified population of speech- and language-impaired children, where the criteria for admission to the unit/class/school have been based upon educational principles. The primary educational needs will have been recognised as resulting from the presenting speech and language disorder. It should be noted that this population will normally be identified as statemented/recorded and as having educational needs that can be met by placement in the language unit.

Aims/Principles of Service Delivery:

1 To provide a service which involves a high degree of shared knowledge, skills expertise and information among those involved with the child.

2 To provide speech and language support, assessment and intervention for the child attending the unit as an integral part of school life. This would ensure that speech and language therapy input is implicit in the child's educational programme, acknowledging that ownership of that programme is with the education authority.

3 To recognise that primacy of care is with the education authority for the holistic management of the child's speech and language difficulties.

4 To implement working practices that accommodate all the needs of the child, in addition to those needs specifically identified by the speech and language therapist's assessment.

5 To acknowledge that educational placement in a language unit recognises that the child's speech and language difficulties have implications for his/her education, and that a positive statement is being made about the child's overall needs being intrinsic to his/her speech and language needs.

6 To deliver the service in such a way as to work with education staff, incorporating the aims of the speech and language therapy programme in the planning of the language programme.

Referral:

1 The referral to the speech and language therapist working in the language unit will normally be made by the therapist who has initiated or been involved in the decision that the child requires language unit placement. Whilst the decision to place the child in the language unit will normally be an educational decision and made by personnel in education, it is imperative that a speech and language therapist is involved in the decision-making process, either by submission of a report, or by forming part of the panel/board that ratifies placement.

2 Once the child is attending the unit, he/she must have equal access to speech and language therapy, irrespective of age, sex, race or presenting speech and language difficulty.

3 The guidelines pertaining to 'consent to treat' must be followed.

4 Referral to the service will operate in accordance with the referral policy for the education/health authority, which will be available to any interested party and will be updated as appropriate.

5 It must be noted by all parties that the model of care provided by the speech and language therapy service within a language unit is likely to be different from that offered in other locations which the child may have attended previously for therapy. Language unit placement is a unique acknowledgement by all parties of the child's speech and language needs as part of his/her education, and the model of care provided will reflect the difference between this educational placement and all others.

6 The referral will be acknowledged to the appropriate parties.

7 Further referrals will be initiated when appropriate in accordance with the model of care for assessment/intervention/discharge.

Assessment:

1 As the child attending a language unit must have been assessed by a number of professionals including the speech and language therapist (in order for the placement decision to have been made), an assessment will precede the child's admission to the unit and be available to the speech and language therapist.

2 It is incumbent upon the speech and language therapist to decide how much further assessment is required when the child is admitted to the unit. Further assessment

may include all/any of the assessment procedures described in the section on Developmental Speech and Language Disorders in Chapter 4.

3 It is essential that the education staff and the speech and language therapist working in the language unit share assessment findings so that a complete profile of the child's speech and language skills and other skills can be identified and common aims and objectives agreed.

4 The re-assessment process may require that the child be referred on to another agency in order that a full and detailed assessment can be completed.

5 Liaison with other agencies will be initiated as appropriate.

6 During any re-assessment process, a second opinion may be sought as required by the assessing therapist or if requested by carers or education staff.

7 Following assessment, a management decision will be made in conjunction with education staff. It will be based upon the whole needs of the child and will be made in conjunction with the overall educational management of the child. Carers will be involved in the decision making. All other parties will be informed of the outcome.

Intervention:

1 Intervention is likely to be as described in the section on Developmental Speech and Language Disorders, although it is likely that direct/indirect facilitated intervention will co-exist during the child's placement in the language unit, as may individual/paired/group intervention.

2 The speech and language therapist working in a language unit must ensure that education staff in the unit are kept fully informed about the nature of intervention and the therapist is kept fully informed about the child's speech and language performance in the classroom, in the playground, during community-based activities, etc.

3 The speech and language therapist must also ensure regular contact with the carers of the child attending the unit, so that all parties are kept fully informed of the child's speech and language functioning.

4 The speech and language therapist should seek to include in-service training of education staff as part of intervention.

Discharge:

1 Discharge will occur according to agreed guidelines.

Interface/Liaison with Other Professionals:

1 It is essential that the speech and language therapist working in a language unit acknowledges her/his role as a member of the multi-disciplinary team involved in the child's education. The speech and language therapist in other paediatric locations may assume exclusive ownership of the management of the child's speech and language difficulties. In the language unit setting this ownership must co-exist with the education authority's ownership of the educational management of the child presenting with speech and language difficulties, which will assume primacy of care.

2 A language unit service where the speech and language therapist and education staff work together will improve communications and increase opportunities for sharing knowledge and developing understanding of the nature and implications of speech and language difficulties. The therapist and education staff must recognise that sharing knowledge and skills enhances the roles of the respective professions.

3 The therapist working in a language unit must seek out other professionals who are relevant to the child at the time of the language unit placement, not only those on site or from education, and establish and maintain those relationships that are paramount to the holistic, multi-disciplinary, multi-agency approach to the child.

Skill Mix:

The speech and language therapist working in a language unit will normally be a speech and language therapist with specific responsibilities. If the therapist is a speech and language therapist with specific duties, she/he must have access to the senior therapist, so that collaboration can take place.

A therapist with specific responsibilities working in a language unit will have had experience of working with speech- and language-disordered children. She/he will have attended relevant post-graduate training and education courses, and may act as a point of reference for other speech and language therapists.

A therapist with specific duties working in a language unit will undertake post-graduate training in the update of identification of developmental speech and language difficulties and intervention programmes.

A speech and language therapist working in a language unit must be aware of current research and literature, and hold membership of relevant College Specific Interest Groups and professional associations e.g. NAPLIC.

Resource Requirements:

The speech and language therapist working in a language unit will require a full complement of equipment and test materials that can be used appropriately with all clients attending the unit, regardless of age, sex, race, and speech and language difficulty. Equipment should be safe, complete and regularly updated.

Accommodation:

Whilst the therapist working in a language unit may choose to work within the classroom for the majority of time, it is essential that the service has identified accommodation for one-to-one sessions, suitable for therapy and for formal assessment. This accommodation may be shared, but if so, the therapist must know when she/he is timetabled for access and when the accommodation will not be available. The therapist is responsible for ensuring that any accommodation provided by the education authority is safe and accessible.

NURSERY SCHOOLS
See section on Pre-School Facilities.

SPECIALIST OUT-PATIENT CENTRES

Definition/Description of the Location:

Specialist out-patient referral centres provide services to clients where a further opinion has been requested by the client, carer, speech and language therapist or other professionals, and for which an extra contractual referral (ECR) has been agreed between purchaser and provider authorities.

Aims/Principles of Service Delivery:

1 To acknowledge the right of every client referred to the speech and language therapy service to be referred on to and to attend a specialist out-patient centre.

2 To provide a speech and language therapy second opinion to every client referred to the centre.

3 To assess, diagnose and provide therapy and advice where indicated to such a client.

4 To ensure that the referring therapist/the client's local therapist is fully informed of all that is offered to the client, including details of appointments, assessments and interventions.

5 To recognise that the secondary referral may have been initiated by the client's local therapist/other professionals for a variety of reasons and where possible to identify those reasons and ascertain what all parties are expecting from the referral.

6 To work closely with other professionals within the centre, establishing and maintaining a holistic approach to client care.

7   To work closely with other professionals involved with the client, ensuring continuity of care, whilst acknowledging the roles and relationships that exist locally.

8   To recognise that implicit in the referral to the specialist centre is a request for access to all specialist skills available.

Referral:

1   Referrals to the specialist centre will normally be received via a medical service. The referral to speech and language therapy may come from a local therapist direct, from a local therapist via the general practitioner, from the general practitioner direct or from another professional involved in the client's care. **Referrals will be accepted from any source provided that the client's consent has been obtained.**

2   **The referral will be acknowledged to the referring agent, client/carer. Full liaison with the client's local speech and language therapist will take place prior to undertaking the assessment of the client.**

3   Referring agents should be informed of the need to give appropriate information when referring which describes the presenting speech and language problems.

4   **Referring agents should be given information on the referral procedures, on possible outcomes of referral and processes following referral.**

Assessment:

1   On receipt of the referral, the specialist centre will invite the client and carer to attend for assessment.

2   Where appropriate, the local speech and language therapist should be invited to attend the assessment with the client/carer.

3   Where it is inappropriate or not possible for the local speech and language therapist to attend the assessment, she/he should be requested to submit a full report.

4   If it is not possible for the local therapist to attend or submit a report, the specialist centre should attempt to discuss the referral/current findings with the local therapist.

5   **The assessment procedure will be pertinent to the apparent disorder, case history information and referral request.**

6   The assessment procedure will be inter-disciplinary, as appropriate, and the speech and language therapist will work closely with other team members.

7   Assessment may involve a range of formal and/or informal assessments as appropriate and may be continued outside the specialist centre location.

8   **Following assessment a management decision will be made and discussed with client/carer, referring agent, local speech and language therapist, and all other parties will be informed.**

9   The speech and language therapist at a specialist centre will need to consider whether speech and language therapy/intervention within the centre offers a model of care which will benefit the client to an extent above that which can be offered in local or other settings. Only if a client is considered to be able to make greater progress within a specialist centre and

funding has been agreed, should therapy be offered within that location. If intervention is to be offered in a local setting the speech and language therapist with specific responsibilities must ensure that recommendations made can be implemented.

10 Following assessment, a report will be written by the speech and language therapist.

11 **Following assessment, the management of the client's speech and language needs will be agreed by all parties. It is important that a single model of care is agreed upon and that the client/carer is fully aware of future management, primacy of management, care plans, appointments etc.**

Intervention:

1 Following the management decision, the method, timing and length of any intervention to be offered by the speech and language therapist at the specialist centre will be discussed and agreed with the client/carer.

2 For the client attending a specialist centre for intervention, the pattern of intervention will at times identify an inter-disciplinary approach as the most appropriate model of care.

3 **The expected nature and actual outcome of intervention will be fully recorded.**

4 At all stages during intervention, the client/carer should be fully involved in the decision-making process.

5 Appropriateness of intervention at a specialist centre following further referral should be re-assessed at the end of any contracted period of intervention.

6 Throughout the course of intervention the speech and language therapist should keep colleagues and members of the multi-disciplinary team and the client's local speech and language therapist informed of progress as appropriate.

Discharge:

1 The client may be discharged at any point following referral.

2 The decision to discharge will be taken, as appropriate, by the speech and language therapist and other members of the team involved in the client's care, following full consultation with the client/carer.

3 **A discharge report will be written and circulated as appropriate.**

4 When the client is discharged from the specialist centre it is likely that intervention may be continued at a local location. The speech and language therapist at the specialist centre will need to liaise with the local speech and language therapist to ensure continuing care and to ensure that the client/carer is informed about and prepared for any changes in the models of care.

Interface/Liaison with Other Professionals:

1 The speech and language therapist has a clear educative role towards other professionals within the multi-disciplinary team in representing the needs of the client with communication difficulties.

2 The speech and language therapist working in the specialist centre is required to work within an inter-disciplinary model of care, at times developing into a trans-disciplinary model of care.

3   The speech and language therapist will participate in multi-disciplinary meetings and case conferences as required.

4   The speech and language therapist in a specialist centre has a responsibility to liaise with local professionals involved with the client.

Skill Mix:

The speech and language therapist in a specialist centre will have specific responsibilities relevant to the particular client group.

Resource Requirements:

The speech and language therapist in a specialist centre requires a range of equipment and test materials that can be used with all clients, regardless of age, sex, race and speech and language diagnosis. Equipment should be safe, complete and finance made available for updating.

See general guidelines for accommodation and equipment (Chapter 8).

SUPPORTED LIVING/ GROUP HOMES

Definition/Description of the Location:

A service provided to clients living in homes of their own with the support of staff. The clients may have moved recently from their family homes or long-stay institutions. A range of therapeutic services may be provided to the clients.

Aims/Principles of Service Delivery:

1   To respect at all times the rights and dignity of clients referred to the service and to recognise that this location of service delivery is first and foremost the client's home.

2   To respect the client's home and his/her place within that home.

3   To deliver services within the client's home only when invited to do so by the client whenever possible.

4   To provide a service in the most appropriate and natural location for the client.

5   To assist the staff in building a communication environment that is conducive to the development of communication skills.

6   To contribute to the knowledge and skills of the staff, thereby enabling them to take into account the client's communication strengths and needs in their interactions with the client.

Referral:

1   **Referrals will be accepted from any source providing that the client's consent has been obtained.**

2   The speech and language therapist has a responsibility to discuss the referral with the client and key worker and where appropriate his/her family prior to actioning the assessment.

3   On receipt of the referral, the speech and language therapist will ascertain the reason for the referral, the keyworker involved and the expected outcomes of intervention.

4 A pre-assessment questionnaire may be completed by the appropriate staff, giving details of the client's perceived communication strengths and needs.

Assessment:

1 An assessment of the communication environment as it relates to the individual client will be carried out and the results communicated to the staff group as part of the total assessment findings.

This assessment may include assessment of environmental factors such as:

- noise levels;

- seating;

- opportunities to exercise communicative ability;

- choice through communication;

- the nature of the communication used by significant others in the home towards the client.

2 The client will be fully involved at all stages of the assessment process and the subsequent decision-making.

3 **At least one other person who knows the client well will be actively involved in the assessment.**

4 It is necessary to assess the staff's expectations of and aspirations for the client's communication performance, as their perceptions will be instrumental in planning intervention and deciding the appropriate level of staff training.

5 Assessment may take place in a range of settings in order to gain an overview of the client's strengths and needs in the fullest range of settings so that an accurate and comprehensive assessment result may be obtained.

6 Assessment procedures appropriate to the specific client group will be carried out.

7 **A profile of the client's specific communication strengths and needs and his/her personal communication environment will be drawn up and circulated for discussion to all staff concerned.**

Intervention:

1 All goals for intervention should be drawn up with the active participation of the home staff.

The home staff will be required to work closely with the speech and language therapist in implementing the communication programme. It is, therefore, important that they are involved in deciding which goals are appropriate for the client.

The client will be involved in this process wherever possible.

2 Due to the nature of communication it is imperative that the 'programme' of intervention is integrated into the client's regular activities. Speech and language therapy should not be seen as separate from the rest of the client's activities.

3 If a decision is made, based upon the assessment results and the client/staff views, to implement a programme, the speech and language therapist should enlist the support

of a 'keyworker' to implement the therapy goals. This person should be someone from the home staff who is in frequent contact with the client.

4 Intervention may take place on a one-to-one basis with the client, implementing through direct therapy a goal plan which states short- and long-term goals of intervention.

5 In addition to the above, intervention will integrate the goal plan into the client's everyday programme through the involvement of home staff and other home users.

6 Intervention may involve the setting up of specific therapy groups to develop and practise certain skills. At least one member of the home staff will be required to participate in these groups.

7 Whichever intervention programme is selected (it may be a combination) it is incumbent upon the speech and language therapist to make full use of the home environment in assisting the client to develop and use skills.

8 Goals will be functionally-based in order to be meaningful for the client and staff.

9 The speech and language therapist working with clients who are making full use of community facilities or who are engaged in work opportunities must be prepared to take the assessment results and goal plans into these environments.

10 **The goals of therapy will be rigorously monitored and updated accordingly.** It is important to gain the commitment of home

staff to a period of therapy, at the end of which goals may be re-evaluated and reset.

11 If the agreed goal plan has not been implemented consistently, it is unlikely to be successful and the efficacy of intervention may be called into question.

12 Intervention will usually require staff training by the speech and language therapist in either general communication concepts or more specific skills targeted at the actual goal plans in operation.

Discharge:

1 The speech and language therapist should seek to negotiate the termination of therapy with the client and keyworker when there is no evidence that the client is benefiting.

2 The speech and language therapist must retain the right to discharge on the basis of clinical judgement.

3 **A full report will be completed and circulated prior to discharge detailing:**

- a summary of the client's initial assessment;

- a summary of initial aims and objectives;

- progress since assessment;

- reasons for discharge.

- The process for re-referral should be made clear to the client and keyworker.

Interface/Liaison with Other Professionals

1 Speech and language therapists aim to provide intervention in a fully integrated manner contributing as part of the wider

team. Therefore, speech and language therapists working in a home should consider themselves part of the total home staff team whilst remaining aware of their unique contribution.

2 Speech and language therapists will participate in client reviews and planning meetings as appropriate.

The speech and language therapist working with clients who have moved out of another setting should seek to obtain all available information regarding previous speech and language therapy.

Skill Mix:

Speech and language therapists involved in supported living/group homes should have the necessary specialist/non-specialist skills appropriate to the client group they are serving.

Speech and language therapists engaged in supported living/group homes need to have undertaken training in:

- first aid and the primary management of emergencies e.g. epilepsy;

- management of challenging behaviour and personal safety.

Resource Requirements:

See general guidelines for accommodation and equipment (Chapter 8).

3

CLIENT GROUPS AND SERVICE PROVISION

This chapter describes the model of care offered by speech and language therapists to a range of client groups. It aims to provide 'guidelines' on good practice for speech and language therapists working with these client groups. A number of points have been highlighted and form 'standards' of good practice. These standards may be taken as indicators of good practice on a wider basis. They may be of particular interest to purchasing authorities and speech and language therapists engaged in drawing up quality indicators for service specifications.

The client groups listed in this chapter do not include individuals with complex multiple disabilities, who may experience communication difficulties attributable to combinations of physical disability, learning disability, language disorder, visual or hearing impairment, dual sensory impairment, or autism. The requirements of this client group may be subsumed in part under other client group headings, but it is acknowledged that these individuals have complex needs which may not be fully addressed in this text. Pre-school children and children with special educational needs do not appear separately in this section. This is because information on these children is provided in Chapter 2 and in other sections of this chapter.

This chapter includes guidelines on Counselling and AAC. Both these types of service provision have been included because they are relevant to a wide range of client groups. Guidelines on other areas of service provision which have relevance to a smaller range of client groups, such as Hypnosis and Endoscopy, are available from the College on request.

ACQUIRED NEUROLOGICAL DISORDERS

Cerebro-Vascular Accident

Definition/Description of Client Group:

Cerebro vascular accident is an acute disturbance of cerebral function of vascular origin, lasting more than 24 hours. The consequences include impairment of movement, sensation, visual and auditory processing and communication. The severity of these will be determined by the size and location of the disturbance.

Aims/Principles of Service:

1   To provide the most appropriate, effective, therapeutic and rehabilitative intervention to meet the communication and/or swallowing needs of clients who have experienced a cerebro vascular accident.

2   To take into account the medical, social, emotional and psychological needs of the client who has experienced a cerebro vascular accident.

3   To ensure that the client and carers become active partners in the therapeutic process.

4 To provide speech and language therapy within a multi-disciplinary setting.

5 To provide a service which is flexible in its management of in-patient and out-patient clients in order to maximise the skills and resources at its disposal.

6 To raise the awareness of relevant others regarding the potential communication needs of clients who have suffered a cerebro vascular accident.

Referral:

1 **An open referral policy will exist for clients with communication difficulties. In the case of in-patients, full consultation with medical staff in charge will take place prior to assessment.**

2 **Assessment will be carried out within two working days for an in-patient, within two weeks for an out-patient or domiciliary appointment.**

3 **Referrals will be acknowledged to the referring agent as appropriate.**

4 On receipt of the referral, liaison will take place with the multi-disciplinary team and medical colleagues where appropriate, to ascertain the stage of recovery and appropriateness of speech and language therapy.

Assessment:

1 Assessment may take place over several sessions and will seek to establish the presence and specific diagnosis of speech and language and/or swallowing disorder.

2 Assessment will take into account the following factors:

- physical health, including vision and hearing;
- psychological adjustment;
- motivation;
- insight and awareness;
- expectations;
- anxiety and presence of confusion;
- social/family environment.

3 Information gained will include:

- present medical condition;
- previous medical history;
- family history;
- current drugs;
- medical prognosis;
- present home situation;
- social needs;
- present family support;
- previous occupation;
- communication need;
- others involved with the client.

4 An interview with the client and his/her carers will seek to assess:

- language comprehension;
- language planning;

- expressive language;

- speech;

- reading and writing skills;

- use of gesture;

- eating and drinking skills.

and will identify where these skills are present, the extent to which they are used and to what effect.

5 **The assessment will utilise a range of standardised and non-standardised materials appropriate to the initial diagnosis.** The materials used should seek to gain maximum involvement of the client and his/her carers.

6 Qualitative and quantitative results from the assessment will enable the speech and language therapist to establish:

- type of disorder - by name with description and examples;

- severity of disorder and level of skills;

- other influencing factors affecting communication;

- the effects of the cerebro vascular accident upon the client's functional communication skills and psychological adjustment.

7 **The outcome of the assessment will be made known to the client/carer and relevant professionals, and recorded in the client's case notes.**

Intervention:

1 A management decision will be made after the preliminary diagnosis and will include one or more of the following:

- continuous assessment;

- review;

- intervention - direct, indirect, group or individual;

- access to non-professional support networks;

- referral to other agencies;

- advice/counselling;

- discharge.

2 If a client is offered therapy this will be in line with the guidelines for his/her specific disorder. It will, however, take into account the factors directly relating to the trauma effects of a cerebro vascular accident. This may necessitate close liaison and inter-disciplinary practice with colleagues in, for example, physiotherapy, occupational therapy and psychology.

Discharge:

1 **The reasons for discharge will be discussed with the client/carer and recorded in the casenotes.**

2 If appropriate the client should be made aware of relevant national societies/voluntary organisations and local groups.

3 **A full discharge report will be compiled and sent to relevant agencies.**

Interface/Liaison with Other Professionals:

1 Cerebro vascular accident may affect the physical, cognitive, emotional and social functioning of the client, and therefore close

multi- and inter-disciplinary co-operation is essential. The speech and language therapist can only deliver her/his services effectively where she/he does so in full consultation with other agencies and by taking into account their assessment and therapy plan for the client.

2   The speech and language therapist will liaise with medical and nursing staff in order to facilitate appropriate referrals.

It is the responsibility of the speech and language therapist to ensure that adequate feedback is given to the referring agent.

3   The speech and language therapist has a role in developing team members' awareness of the effects of cerebro vascular accident on communication and swallowing.

Skill Mix:

It is likely that a speech and language therapist holding a general adult caseload will be responsible for the initial assessment of the client who has had a cerebro vascular accident. Speech and language therapists in this situation must have access to a speech and language therapist with specific responsibilities for the particular disorder arising from the diagnosis. This access may be required in order to complete the full assessment and reach a firm diagnosis and/or in intervention planning/providing a second opinion.

Guidelines for speech and language therapists with specific responsibilities will follow guidelines on Skill Mix for Aphasia, Dysarthria, Dysphagia in Chapter 4.

Assistants:

See specific guidelines for Aphasia, Dysarthria, Dysphagia in Chapter 4.

See guidelines on skill mix (Chapter 9).

Resource Requirements:

1   Access to a wide range of standardised and non-standardised assessment material relevant to speech and language disorders potentially occurring as a result of cerebro vascular accident.

2   Access to a range of therapy materials, including professional journals.

3   Access to a range of AAC equipment for loan to clients pending full assessment at a specialist centre.

See general guidelines for accommodation and equipment (Chapter 8).

Dementia
(See also Elderly Section)

Definition/Description of Client Group:

Dementia is a chronic progressive deterioration of intellect, memory and communicative function as a result of organic brain disease. It is always of long duration, usually progressive and irreversible. It occurs predominantly within the elderly population, although it does occur in younger people.

The dementia syndrome in elderly people can be sub-divided on both clinical and neuropathological grounds into two main aetiological categories:

- vascular dementia - arising from impaired cerebral blood supply;

- Alzheimer-type dementia - arising from a primary degeneration of brain tissue.

Other dementia pathologies include:

- Lewy - body disease;

- Picks disease;

- Creutzfeld-Jacob disease.

Aims/Principles of Service Delivery:

1 To provide assessment and intervention of communication and swallowing function in clients presenting with dementia.

2 To deliver services with and through carers within the client's environment, as well as to the client.

3 To offer advice and support to carers in the client's environment.

4 To work within a multi-disciplinary framework - sharing goals of intervention, and, where appropriate, preparing joint goals with other professionals/carers.

5 To enable carers and other professionals to have a clear understanding of the communication strengths and needs of each client and provide the opportunity for the carer and other professionals to develop the appropriate skills in facilitating the client's communication.

Referral:

1 For clients with a swallowing problem, a written referral must be obtained (see Dysphagia section in Chapter 4).

2 **All referrals will be discussed with the multi-disciplinary team and relevant other professionals known to be involved with the client.**

3 **If a referral is from non-medical staff and indicates that a diagnosis of dementia has been made, the speech and language therapist must establish accurate medical information.** This may be via medical staff (consultant/GP) or via a client's medical notes.

4 Information should be obtained on time post-onset, the exact nature of the dementia, if known, and the nature of previous intervention provided by speech and language therapists or other members of the multi-disciplinary team.

5 Clients with dementia may be referred either from a hospital or community location.

Research indicates that clients with vascular or mixed type dementia are more likely to be in hospital when referred, whereas clients with Alzheimer's type dementia seem more likely to access services through the community.

Assessment:

1 Assessment should take place in a variety of environments if possible and particularly in a client's day-to-day environment.

2 Assessment may include:

- observational analysis;

- discussion with significant others in the client's environment;

- repeatable informal assessment;

- repeatable formal assessment;

- a limited number of specific communication assessments for clients with dementia are available. These should be used if possible, and supplemented by aphasia assessments, if appropriate.

Assessment should consider the following:

- the client's functional communication skills;

- the client's communicative needs;

- the appropriateness of the environment in facilitating the client's communication abilities;

- the client's motivation and the motivation of others within their environment for speech and language therapy intervention;

- the client's communicative strengths and weaknesses and whether there would be any effective way of improving the client's overall communication skills/effectiveness;

- the client's swallowing function, if appropriate.

3   Assessment will involve a detailed case history from carers in the client's life.

4   Clients should be referred to other agencies as appropriate.

Intervention:

1   Due to the progressive nature of dementia, the speech and language therapist must outline specific aims of intervention. **Goals set will be realistic, will be regularly evaluated and will be carried out within a defined time-span. They will be recorded in the case notes.**

2   **Time must be allocated for sharing and explaining the goals of intervention with significant others and for establishing together how these goals can be achieved in an everyday context.**

3   The speech and language therapist must take into account the carer's perceptions of the client's communication difficulties and also the carer's concerns. It may take time to adequately explain what speech and language intervention is aiming to achieve. It is important that the carer's expectations are realistic (i.e. the dementia will not improve) but equally that the carer understands the value of intervention (i.e. by shaping the carer's communicative skills, working on the client's environment etc.).

It is important that carers remain involved and participate in the intervention process.

4   There may be great benefits in working jointly with other professionals, particularly when there are shared goals of intervention, such as in group intervention.

5   The multi-disciplinary team should be kept informed of speech and language therapy intervention via either verbal discussion, written reports, case conferences, as appropriate.

6   Whilst individual face-to-face contact with a client may occasionally be the most appropriate form of intervention, it will not

be so for the majority of clients. Due to the nature of dementia, intervention will typically:

- involve carers and educate them in facilitating a client's communicative abilities;

- be based in the client's everyday environment;

- concentrate on functional communication skills;

- work on interactions that naturally occur in a client's life;

Group interaction may often be an appropriate method of therapeutic intervention.

7   Speech and language therapists must evaluate whether any intervention for swallowing difficulties (for example, use of compensatory strategies or manoeuvres) is appropriate. (See Chapter 4 for details).

Discharge:

1   The efficacy of intervention must be closely evaluated, so that clients not/no longer benefiting from therapy either have the goals of intervention redefined or are discharged.

2   Since a major role of intervention will be to enable others in the client's environment to facilitate the client's communicative abilities effectively, this should be an indicator regarding discharge.

3   **A discharge report will be prepared and submitted to other staff/agencies as appropriate.**

Interface/Liaison with Other Professionals:

1   Wherever possible the speech and language therapist should work within a multi-disciplinary team.

2   Close multi-disciplinary working should involve discussion of individual professional goals and establishing joint goals/care plans.

Skill Mix:

See guidelines for the elderly population.

Resource requirements:

Access to a wide variety of assessment and therapy materials.

See general guidelines for accommodation and equipment (Chapter 8).

Neurosurgery

Definition/Description of Client Group:

Neurosurgical intervention may take place in a variety of cases following traumatic injury, vascular or space occupying lesions. It is recognised that intervention for these clients may follow the general model of care for a defined client group e.g. head injury, stroke.

Aims/Principles of Service Delivery:

1   To work within the framework of the multi-disciplinary team and thereby provide a co-ordinated approach to all phases of the management of neurosurgical clients.

2   To provide information and advice to other professionals regarding the results of speech and language therapy assessment and intervention.

3   To provide appropriate assessment and management of neurosurgical clients, in consultation with the neurosurgical medical staff.

4   To provide advice and support to carers.

Referral:

1   **All referrals will be discussed with the neurosurgical medical staff regarding the appropriateness of speech and language therapy intervention.**

Assessment:

1   Pre-operative speech and language therapy assessment of clients may be appropriate and must be fully discussed with the neurosurgical team.

2   **Post-operative assessment will be carried out only when the client is sufficiently medically stable and when agreed by neurosurgical medical staff.**

3   Post-operative complications may affect speech and language therapy assessment and management, and therefore must be taken into consideration. These complications may include oedema, chest conditions, epilepsy.

4   Assessment may include a client's need of AAC equipment, whether temporary or permanent.

Intervention:

1   The appropriateness and timing of speech and language therapy intervention will need to take into consideration factors such as:

- the client's level of consciousness;

- the information shared by the neurosurgical team;

- the neurosurgeon's opinion regarding the client's prognosis.

2   **Consultation with the neurosurgical team or medical staff must be maintained throughout the speech and language therapist's involvement with a client.**
This will involve the speech and language therapist gaining accurate medical information (sometimes on a daily basis) from the medical and nursing staff.

3   Intervention may involve joint goal planning with other professionals.

4   The goals of speech and language therapy intervention should be shared with the neurosurgical team and where appropriate other members of the team should be encouraged to continue work on these goals within an everyday context.

5   Clients may frequently present with deficits in attention control and memory. These deficits will have implications for the nature of intervention.

6   The speech and language therapist will provide advice and support to carers. This will involve the sharing of clearly-defined goals of intervention.

7   Medico-legal reports may be required from the speech and language therapist,

when working with certain clients e.g. head-injured clients. (See Chapter 6).

Discharge:

1 **Discharge from speech and language therapy will be fully discussed with the neurosurgical team.**

2 **The reasons for discharge will be explained to the client and/or carers and the process for re-referral explained.**

Interface/Liaison with Other Professionals:

1 Close liaison will be maintained with the neurosurgical team and other professionals working with the client.

2 All referrals to other professionals will be discussed with the neurosurgical team.

3 In order to plan relevant and functional therapy, it may be necessary for the speech and language therapist to liaise with people in the community such as:

■ client's employer;

■ home tutor;

■ day centre staff.

Skill Mix:

A speech and language therapist with specific responsibilities working in the area of neurosurgery will have:

■ an up-to-date working knowledge of the types and uses of endotracheal tubes and ventilation systems available;

■ an understanding of the effects and

possible hazards of such tubes in situ (e.g. effects on the respiratory status, phonation);

■ an understanding of the scales used to measure conscious states e.g., the Glasgow Coma Scale (Teasdale and Jennet, 1974);

■ a knowledge of post neurosurgical complications e.g. oedema, cranial nerve palsy, and their effects on speech and language therapy intervention;

■ an understanding of investigative procedures that may be carried out (such as four vessel angiography, brain scanning) and the effect of these investigations on the physical, cognitive and emotional state of a client;

■ attended appropriate post-qualification multi-disciplinary training.

Speech and language therapists with specific duties require induction and close on-site supervision by a speech and language therapist with specific responsibilities in neurosurgery.

Assistants:
See guidelines on skill mix (Chapter 9).

Resource Requirements:

Materials available on the wards.

Opportunities to attend post-graduate uni/multi-disciplinary education training events.

See general guidelines for accommodation and equipment (Chapter 8).

Progressive Neurological Disorders

Definition/Description of Client Group:

The term progressive neurological disorders refers to disorders of the nervous system which are on-going and deteriorate over time. Common disorders include Parkinson's Disease, Motor Neurone Disease, Multiple Sclerosis, Huntingdon's Chorea and tumours of the central nervous system.

The model of care described in this chapter is relevant to adults and children with progressive neurological disorders and/or terminal illnesses.

Aims/Principles of Service Delivery:

1 To promote and encourage early referrals of clients with progressive neurological disorders, through education of relevant medical staff and other professionals.

2 To provide structured management programmes, to ensure clients are able to receive therapy advice and/or support throughout the progression of the disorder.

3 To maximise a client's communication potential within his/her environment and to enable maintenance of communication skills for the longest possible duration.

4 To provide ongoing assessment and management of swallowing disorders.

5 To provide information and advice to clients, carers and other professionals regarding the use of AAC equipment.

6 To keep clients, carers and other professionals informed regarding the nature of the client's communication and/or swallowing difficulties and the ongoing goals of intervention.

7 To maintain close liaison with other professionals and voluntary agencies.

8 To assist the client's carers in communicating with the client in a positive way throughout the progression of the client's illness.

Referral:

1 **On receipt of referral, the speech and language therapist will establish from the referring agent if the client/carer is aware of the diagnosis and prognosis.**

2 If the client/carer is unaware of the diagnosis/prognosis, then the difficulties of carrying out an intervention programme should be fully discussed with the relevant medical staff.

3 **Prior to assessment, accurate information will be gathered on the client's medical and social history.**

4 In the case of children, the child's pre-trauma speech and language development should be ascertained.

Assessment:

1 Assessment will include:

- a detailed case history;

- assessment of the client's speech and language skills (the assessment should be repeatable, so that any deterioration can be clearly identified over time);

- informal/formal assessment of swallowing;

- an assessment of the client's environment and of his/her communication needs (current and future).

2 Care should be taken not to assume the client's/carer's understanding of the situation, and the client/carer should be given time to explain their understanding and perceptions of the disorder.

3 The speech and language therapist may consider it appropriate to refer on to other agencies following assessment (e.g. social worker, physiotherapist, support group).

Intervention:

1 The progressive nature of these disorders means that for many clients with communication and/or swallowing difficulties their needs will change over time and there will be a need for renewed therapy aims.

For this reason, a structured management programme is required to ensure that clients are able to receive long-term help.

2 Structured management programmes may include:

- regular therapy;

- intensive therapy either individually or in groups run on a periodic basis, with review appointments in the interim;

- the use of review appointments for ongoing advice and support.

With more rapidly progressing disorders,

such as Motor Neurone Disease, review appointments may need to be more regular if the client's communication/swallowing difficulties are changing rapidly.

3 Therapy may involve the teaching of compensatory strategies to improve verbal communication. The use of audio or video tape may be useful to encourage self-monitoring of communicative competence.

4 **The aims of a therapy programme will be clearly explained to the client/ carer, especially in regard to the long-term maintenance role of intervention.**

5 Clients presenting with dysphagia should receive intervention as laid down by the guidelines on dysphagia (see Chapter 4).

6 When many professionals are involved with a client, it may be appropriate for a key worker to be nominated who can act as a co-ordinator for the multi-disciplinary team. It may be appropriate in some circumstances for the speech and language therapist to take on this role.

7 During the course of the disorder, some clients may require communication aids. The speech and language therapist will be able to advise the client, carer and other professionals on the type of aids available and the most suitable aid for the client's needs, accessing advice from specialist sources as appropriate.

8 The speech and language therapist has an important role to play in facilitating an understanding on the part of the client's carers of the nature of the client's communication disorder. Carers may be unsure as to the client's comprehension skills and may need reassurance regarding the best

way to communicate and interact with the client.

9 **Clients and carers will be kept informed of current literature that is available, and will be given relevant information on voluntary agencies and support groups as required.**

10 The provision of domiciliary visits may be appropriate for some clients, particularly for those clients whose condition has reached an advanced stage.

Discharge:

1 **Clients with communication and/or dysphagic problems associated with progressive neurological disorders, will have access to speech and language therapy services as required throughout the course of the disorder.**

2 Discharge from speech and language therapy may occur at the client's request, or if therapy is no longer deemed beneficial. However, clients and carers will be encouraged to contact the speech and language therapy service if further difficulties arise which may be amenable to speech and language therapy intervention.

Interface/Liaison with Other Professionals:

The child or adult with a progressive neurological disorder may experience a range of difficulties and it is, therefore, likely that a range of professionals may be involved with the client. It is vital that the speech and language therapist works as part of this multi-disciplinary team. The speech and language therapist may work in close conjunction with a range of agencies including education,

social services and voluntary groups.

Skill Mix:

Speech and language therapists working with clients with progressive neurological disorders will require skills specific to the disorder with which the client presents e.g. dysphasia, dysarthria and dysphagia. (See Chapter 4 for guidelines relating to specific disorders). In addition to these skills, speech and language therapists working with this population, must have a clear understanding of the nature of progressive disorders and the potential effects upon the client's physical, cognitive and emotional state.

Therapists will also require an understanding of the benefits to be gained from the use of AAC equipment and the systems for obtaining such equipment.

Speech and language therapists who are inexperienced with this group of clients are advised to work as part of a department with other colleagues, and all therapists should have access to a support network.

Resources:

See general guidelines for accommodation and equipment (Chapter 8).

Traumatic Brain Injury

Definition/Description of Client Group:

Traumatic brain injury describes injury to the brain caused primarily by physical trauma. Traumatic head injury is a broader term which also includes soft tissue injuries and lacerations which may or may not be accompanied by brain damage. Closed head injury describes trauma which does not result in opening of the skull, and typically gives rise to diffuse damage. Open head injury or penetrating injury tends to give rise to more focal damage.

These injuries may range from minor to very severe. Length of coma/unconsciousness (unconsciousness being defined as an alert state scoring nine points or less on the Glasgow Coma Scale (Teasdale and Jennet, 1974), and post-traumatic amnesia (the time interval between the injury and the reinstatement of continuous day-to-day memory, as assessed clinically) are generally taken as measures of severity of the injury.

The descriptions of severity are as follows:

- **very severe brain injury:** an injury causing unconsciousness for forty eight hours or more, or a post-traumatic amnesia of seven days or more;

- **severe brain injury:** an injury causing unconsciousness for six hours or more, or a post-traumatic amnesia of twenty four hours or more;

- **moderate brain injury:** an injury causing unconsciousness for more than fifteen minutes but less than six hours, and a post -traumatic amnesia of less than twenty four hours.

- **mild brain injury:** an injury causing unconsciousness for fifteen minutes or less.

Other aetiologies: similar disorders may result from toxic or anoxic states and cerebral inflammatory disorders.

Aims/Principles of Service Delivery:

1   To provide a service appropriate to clients with communication disorders. These may include disorders of speech, language, cognition and social skills.

2   To provide a service appropriate to clients with swallowing disorders.

3   To advise and support carers/employers, as appropriate, on helping and coping with the client's communication deficits.

4   To work with an inter-disciplinary approach in order to meet as far as possible the totality of the client's needs rather than focusing on a specific deficit in isolation.

5   To ensure flexible access to a range of acute, rehabilitation and community services, some of which may specialise in brain injury.

6   To support, advise and actively involve the client's carers in all stages of the rehabilitation process.

Referral:

1   **Open referral will exist, except in the acute phase of management, or in the case of a client with a swallowing disorder, where a medical referral will be required.**

Assessment:

1   The assessment of clients with traumatic brain injury should be an ongoing procedure throughout the recovery phase. It should focus on the client's abilities, specific

communication needs and the communication environment.

2 The client's level of ability requires full assessment.

The following areas need to be considered and the speech and language therapist shares responsibility for the assessment of the client's abilities:

- behaviour,
    e.g. ability to cooperate;
          disinhibition;
          aggression;
          passivity;

- relevant physical status,
    e.g. head and trunk control;
          upper limb function;
          oral movement;

- self care,
    e.g. eating and drinking;
          oral (and general) hygiene;
          presentation;

- cognition,
    e.g. orientation/confusion;
          attention;
          memory;
          reasoning;
          planning/organisation;
          initiation;
          flexibility;
          executive ability;
          insight;

- sensory status/perception,
    e.g. visual ability;
          auditory ability;
          oro/facial sensation;
          unilateral neglect;

- emotional/psychosocial condition,

    e.g. emotional adjustment;
          lability;
          depression/euphoria;
          motivation;
          social skills;
          ego-centricity;
          reduced stress tolerance.

3 The speech and language therapist has specific responsibility for assessing the following areas:

- communication,
    e.g. expressive language
          (written and spoken);
          receptive language
          (written and spoken);
          specific acquired dyslexia;
          speech;
          non-verbal communication;
          social communication;

The need for an augmentative/alternative means of communication.

- swallowing.

4 In traumatic brain injury a language disorder may include some typically dysphasic symptoms, but language may also be disrupted by deficits in associated cognitive functioning. Right hemisphere language functioning, pragmatic, idiomatic and inferential ability will also require assessment.

5 It is important to research the client's level of functioning prior to trauma, particularly in the case of a child with traumatic brain injury. In this case the overall language profile will depend not only on the site and extent of damage, but also on the language development prior to onset.

6 Relevant social history should be obtained. There should be continued appraisal of the client's immediate and future communication needs throughout the recovery period.

Intervention:

1 The speech and language therapist may identify persisting cognitive difficulties in the course of making a differential diagnosis. It may, therefore, be necessary to make appropriate onward referrals.

2 **Speech and language therapy assessments and recommendations will be reported to the team, and discussed with client and carers, as appropriate.**

3 Intervention may include therapy for specific communication disorders and/or eating/swallowing difficulties.

Methods of delivery may include:

- intensive individual therapy;

- regular individual therapy;

- group therapy;

- generalisation of skills into other environments and everyday functional activities;

- joint sessions with professionals from other disciplines in order to share skills;

- specific intervention programmes may be devised by the speech and language therapist to be carried out by trained care staff, assistants or volunteers. These programmes must be regularly monitored, reviewed and updated by the speech and language therapist;

- regular review assessments with provision to offer:

  - further therapy in response to changes in the client's ability or in the demands made by his/her environment;

  - periodic therapy for maintenance of gains made during rehabilitation;

  - re-evaluation of AAC equipment in the light of the client's changing abilities, needs or the availability of new AAC equipment.

4 If appropriate, re-referral for further speech and language therapy must be available as clients are transferred from one setting to another. The client and carers must be informed of the opportunity for re-referral and of how to achieve this.

Discharge:

1 The decision to discharge will be a team decision taken after full discussion with the client/carers. **On discharge from the service, a full report will be compiled and circulated to all relevant parties.** It may be appropriate for this to be an individual or a component of a multi-disciplinary team report.

2 It is essential to have good liaison between hospital, unit and community-based teams in order to ensure that follow-up care and total management is effective.

Interface/Liaison with Other Professionals:

1 Due to the diffuse nature of traumatic brain injury and the multiple difficulties which may arise from it, it is necessary for the speech and language therapist to work within a multi-disciplinary team.

2   In order to plan relevant and functional therapy it may be necessary for the speech and language therapist to liaise with people in the community. These may include the client's employer, as well as community health, social, educational and voluntary services.

3   A speech and language therapist may be an appropriate team member to operate as a 'keyworker' providing the consent of the client has been obtained.

Skill Mix:

A speech and language therapist with specific responsibilities working with this client group should have post-graduate training to develop specific skills and expertise in this area. Further opportunities should also be taken to attend multi-disciplinary courses/conferences to develop knowledge and expertise in associated areas that are not generally covered in sufficient depth in undergraduate training. These areas include: memory, drug effects, physical handling, nutrition, perception, cognition, medico-legal affairs and inter-disciplinary models of care.

Speech and language therapists with specific duties working with this client group should work with the support and guidance of a colleague with specific responsibilities or have the ability to refer to specialist colleagues in related fields. Membership of the appropriate College Specific Interest Group is advised for all therapists working with this client group.

Assistants:

The role of the assistant to the speech and language therapist will be dependant upon the client's stage of recovery, degree of adaptation to his/her disability and general behaviour. Fully supervised assistants may have a role in the delivery of direct individual therapeutic programmes, which have been designed and initiated by the therapist. It may be that a consistent behavioural approach is required during their administration. Speech and language therapy assistants may also be helpful in the transport of clients, preparation of equipment and administration duties.

See guidelines on skill mix (Chapter 9).

Resource Requirements:

The speech and language therapist needs to work within an inter-disciplinary team and therefore requires time for liaison and appropriate clinical and office accommodation. She/he will also require access to a range of assessment and intervention materials including biofeedback devices.

See general guidelines for accommodation and equipment (Chapter 8).

AUGMENTATIVE AND ALTERNATIVE COMMUNICATION (AAC)

Definition/Description of Client Group:

Augmentative/alternative communication refers to methods of communicating which supplement or replace speech and handwriting. The term refers to a function, not to any specific communication systems or methods. In practice, augmentations and alternatives to speech often overlap and go together, but it should be recognised that they are not interchangeable terms.

Communication itself may be defined as the transmission and reception of meaning between one individual and another, or between an individual and a group - where 'meaning' is taken to include social and affective intentions and reactions, as well as propositional content. The mode or medium of the exchange (speech, non-verbal signals, symbols, signs, writing, electronic code etc.) does not alter this definition of the central essence of communication.

There are, however, severely communication-impaired or non-speaking individuals for whom augmentations and alternatives to speech are necessary in order to give access to the basic functions of everyday life. This population may be defined as those individuals whose speech is severely impaired and who require special techniques, materials or devices for communication to replace or supplement speech. This broad definition would include people with deafness or hearing impairment, many of whom use aids to communication in the form of hearing aids, and many of whom use manual signing and technological tools as alternatives to speech.

Such special aids and strategies are often referred to as 'Augmentative Communication Systems' in that they are designed to supplement whatever oral speech abilities the individual does have. The term 'Augmentative Communication System' refers to the totality of an individual's functional communication behaviour, and would normally include:

- a communication medium, for the transmission of meaning. This might be 'unaided' (e.g. natural gesture, facial expression, eye-pointing, manual signs) or 'aided' (e.g. requiring some physical object such as a symbol chart, or electronic device).;

- a means of access to the communication medium, e.g. ability to use a keyboard or a switch, ability to scan and select from an array;

- a symbol set or system, which is a means to represent meanings, ideas and concepts e.g. traditional orthography, Blissymbols, Rebus, Picture Communication Symbols, British Sign Language, Paget-Gorman Signed Speech;

- interaction strategies necessary for success in exchanges with communication partners e.g. the ability to initiate conversations, to maintain conversations by turn-taking behaviour and use of questions and to repair conversation breakdowns.

The service to clients using augmentative/ alternative communication falls into two distinct but related parts:

- the service provided by the local therapist with specific duties who needs to consider the use of augmentative/alternative communication when planning intervention for a client;

- the service provided by the speech and language therapist with specific responsibilities who may operate on a regional or supra-regional basis. She/he will be able to offer specific advice and support regarding the use of augmentative/alternative communication and will act as a resource for the speech and language therapist with specific duties.

Aims/Principles of Service Delivery:

1   To work as a member of an inter-disciplinary team, promoting more effective communication and equality of opportunity for individuals with severe communication impairments.

2   To promote access to opportunities for development and self-fulfilment, access to autonomous action and participation in community life, when the potential for securing such basic human rights and freedoms is compromised by a severe communication difficulty.

3   To recognise that, "Given the state of the art regarding development and use of communication techniques, there is no non-speaking person too physically handicapped to be able to utilise some augmentative communication system. Therefore, the speech and language professional is now faced with increasingly diverse programme and treatment options for non-speaking persons and she/he must develop the competency necessary to serve these clinical needs." (ASHA 1981)

4   To take part in the education of colleagues, the community and the general public regarding augmentative communication in general as well as specific client's needs.

5   To take account of the technological advances which have made communication equipment flexible, broadened the application of equipment and made it useful to a wider spectrum of non-verbal people.

6   To respond to the growing awareness of the needs of severely communication-impaired individuals, and to increases in the demand for services brought about by recent social trends and government policies which reduce the emphasis on long-stay institutional care.

7   To highlight the need for 'care in the community' and 'independent living' which must include consideration of day-to-day communication needs.

8   To demonstrate that communication needs will not be met by technological aids alone but by aids plus skilled support and intervention.

Referral:

1   **Specialist centres will accept enquiries and referrals from any source including people with communication difficulties, carers, education, health and social services professionals.**

2   There may be a pre-referral enquiry stage where the client's needs are identified and information sought from a speech and

language therapist. Specific information about augmentative/alternative communication may be supplied by a specialist centre to a locally-based speech and language therapist on issues such as:

- who can benefit;

- available options;

- procedures for obtaining AAC equipment.

3 When an initial referral is made to speech and language therapy, this would usually be to a local service. The local speech and language therapist might seek to establish a joint assessment process with colleagues with special competence in augmentative/alternative communication. In certain circumstances, the assessment process may result in onward referral to a specialist centre for augmentative/alternative communication. This may involve Regional, National or Voluntary Sector resources in health or education sectors.

4 **At all stages of referral and assessment, speech and language therapy services will establish and maintain a full exchange of information.**

5 Acceptance of a referral, leading to a full augmentative/alternative communication assessment and action plan will carry significant long-term resource implications with regard to:

- funding of staff time/supplementary staff cover;

- funding for specialist training for staff;

- funding for the purchase of augmentative/alternative communication materials and equipment ('low technology' and/or 'high technology');

- arrangements for insurance, maintenance and phased replacement of equipment;

- funding for peripheral equipment, e.g. wheelchair mountings etc., and fixing arrangements;

- provision for regular follow-up and evaluation.

Speech and language therapists need to be aware of the forthcoming demands on resources and to plan with these in mind.

Assessment:

1 Background information will be collected from a wide range of sources, for example, clients, carers and professionals from several disciplines. This would cover:

- medical history;

- educational history and cognitive skills;

- physical and sensory condition and skills;

- functional communication and language skills;

- previous use of augmentative/alternative communication;

- the client's own view of his/her communication problems;

- the communication environment(s) of the client.

2 As part of this process, contact will be made with the full range of other

professionals and agencies involved with the client. This will also contribute to the development of good working relationships.

3 The speech and language therapist will undertake an observation of the client's current communication and interaction skills.

Such observations will include observation of the client in his/her usual environment, wherever possible.

Such observation will include not only the communication behaviour of the client him/herself, but also that of communication partners.

4 Assessment should include contributions from an inter-disciplinary team. Procedures should link AAC assessment to the statutory assessment and review procedures for special educational needs and/or for local social services/'care in the community' where these apply.

5 Assessment should include an identification of the client's own wants and needs with regard to communication.

6 Assessment should include identification of the demands of the client's environment, e.g. educational curriculum.

7 In augmentative/alternative communication, standardised assessment tools need to be applied with extreme caution. They must be supplemented by relevant, non-standardised techniques.

8 Assessment: the following areas will be considered by speech and language therapists:

- medical diagnosis/condition/prognosis (plus details of medication);

- current use of augmentative/alternative communication system(s);

- linguistic skills;

- social interaction skills;

- cognitive skills;

- visual and auditory perceptual skills;

- motor skills (effective, consistent, physical 'control sites'), in conjunction with an occupational and/or physiotherapist;

- seating and positioning in conjunction with an occupational therapist;

- communication opportunities.

9 Reassessment will be necessary at regular intervals.

Intervention:

1 **The speech and language therapist will use the assessment information to create a communication intervention programme to meet the client's needs.**

2 **Conclusions and a 'plan of action' for future management, will be mutually agreed by all members of the assessment team.**

3 It is important that one named person takes on the central role of initiating and co-ordinating assessment and intervention amongst what may be a large and perhaps geographically fragmented group. In many cases, it is likely that the speech and language therapist will be the individual who best fulfils the requirements of team co-ordinator, as the individual best equipped to

evaluate communication needs and abilities and the suitability of augmentative systems.

4 Goals set will give equal consideration to a variety of modes of augmentative/alternative communication and their use in combination, e.g. signing and picture board and electronic device.

5 The 'plan of action' will normally include the identification of:

- specific named key helpers;

- specific tasks for each helper;

- specific targets for each task;

- specific record-keeping techniques;

- explicit estimates of the time and personnel required for implementation.

The 'plan of action' will embody:

- a functional, interactive approach;

- a requirement that its contents be widely disseminated throughout the client's communication environment;

- recommendation of a specific augmentative/alternative communication system, hardware and software, mounting equipment, software development etc.

6 The speech and language therapist has responsibility for advising and counselling the client/carer regarding non-speech communication.

7 The speech and language therapist is responsible for liaising with professionals from other disciplines and with the carers, and for integrating augmentative

communication procedures into a variety of settings.

8 **The speech and language therapist will evaluate the progress achieved by the 'plan of action' within the specified time period.** This may include:

- identifying functional communication gains;

- identifying and rectifying reasons for failure to achieve progress;

- identifying changes in circumstances;

- initiating and progressing requests for funding, including joint funding where appropriate;

- re-assessing and developing a new 'plan of action' or leaving the client on active review.

9 Throughout the long-term implementation of an augmentative/alternative communication programme, intervention may include:

- one-to-one therapy;

- group work;

- the involvement of familiar/unfamiliar communication partners in a range of different situations;

- the introduction and development of communication strategies;

- team-teaching in classroom/nursery/day centre;

- creation of new communication opportunities.

This work will not be conducted entirely by

speech and language therapists, but will need to involve the "significant others" in the client's life.

10 The speech and language therapist has a central role in providing training for the 'significant others' in the client's life.

11 Speech and language therapists working in an educational setting or with a school-/college-aged individual, will liaise with relevant professionals at every stage of curriculum planning, development and delivery, in order that the use of augmentative/alternative communication becomes an integral part of the individual's daily programme.

The augmentative/alternative communication user will be especially vulnerable at times of change in the educational process, e.g. transition from nursery to primary school. The speech and language therapist will need to ensure that carers and other professionals in any new placement understand and accept the client's communication system, including use of all appropriate channels of information, e.g. video material and communication passport. The speech and language therapist will have an important role in ensuring continuity and transfer of information in these situations.

12 The role of the speech and language therapist and teachers with an augmentative/alternative communication user will interlink and overlap, e.g. in the development of reading, spelling and the creative use of language.

13 In many cases, the process of therapy will include an integration of different approaches at different stages. During intervention, the speech and language therapist may use

therapy materials and tools such as: pictures, toys and tape-recorders; non-aided augmentative systems such as signing; 'low tech' aided augmentative systems such as picture, word or Bliss boards; and new 'high tech' tools, including computer-based therapy aids such as Visispeech, and electronic augmentative devices such as those offering speech or text output.

14 The therapist will, at different times, be making use of both long-established and new theories and approaches. Using augmentative communication as a therapeutic approach may often involve a change of theoretical stand-point and of philosophical attitude, rather than any tangible or visible change of materials or methods of therapy. The same materials may be used, but in different ways; the same techniques may be taught, but with different purposes. Teaching communication augmentation may mean teaching a set of strategies as much as, or more than, using equipment.

Discharge:

1 **Discharge from a specialist centre may be to the local speech and language therapy service. A full written report will accompany this action.**

2 The management of the client requiring an augmentative/alternative communication service, should be viewed in the long term. Regular and long-term review is required as new technology develops and the client's needs change.

3 **The decision to discharge will be communicated to the inter-disciplinary team and the process of re-referral made explicit.**

Interface/Liaison with Other Professionals:

Speech and language therapy interacts with a number of other professions in the diagnosis, assessment and management of individuals with severe communication impairment. A holistic approach is essential if speech and language therapy intervention is to have a successful outcome. Speech and language therapists must expect to work as part of an inter-disciplinary team which is likely to include occupational therapists, physiotherapists, teachers, psychologists, doctors, bio-engineers, technicians, social workers and others. It is vital that communication-impaired individuals, their carers, friends and helpers are also considered part of the team.

Where appropriate, the speech and language therapist has a central role in liaising with teachers, to ensure a co-ordinated approach to the development of literacy skills and written communication skills.

The speech and language therapist will liaise with medical and paramedical professionals to ensure optimum seating and positioning conditions, so that the most effective functional use of any augmentative system is achieved.

Therapists and managers should recognise that the most helpful and appropriate training resources in the field of augmentative communication may lie outside the speech and language therapy profession and special cross-disciplinary arrangements may be required for access to these. Membership of inter-disciplinary professional associations such as ISAAC (International Society for Augmentative and Alternative Communication) is to be encouraged.

Skill Mix:

Central to the notion of high standards of professional competence and conduct is the concept that speech and language therapists should only provide services which they have been properly trained to provide. Therapists are able to make an assessment which will recognise whether or not a specific client might benefit from augmentative/alternative communication and whether or not they themselves have the skills and resources to provide adequate therapy for the client. Therapists may then seek consultation and refer to appropriate other agencies, for example, one of the Communication Aid Centres, ACE centre, CALL Centre, one of the ACCESS Centres or to similar units which may be developed in the future. The referral may be to a speech and language therapist with specific responsibilities, or to a specialist member of another profession.

Speech and language therapists with specific responsibilities must have the following:

- an understanding of the importance of positioning, seating, mobility, style of teaching and learning, motivation etc. in the development of a communication system for non-speaking clients and collaboration with other disciplines as appropriate;

- a working knowledge of the provisions and funding procedures for augmentative/alternative communication systems;

- an awareness of the implications of using augmentative/alternative communication systems, including the attitudes of clients and their carers, and how this may influence acceptance and eventual success or failure of systems recommended;

- clinical experience and relevant post-graduate training pertaining to non-speaking clients.

Speech and language therapists who do have knowledge of augmentative communication techniques and technology should endeavour to share information and expertise with other speech and language therapists, clients, carers, professionals from other disciplines and other agencies.

Speech and language therapists with specific duties:

All speech and language therapists involved in the delivery of an augmentative/alternative service should have knowledge of:

- assessment procedures for determining if a client is suitable for augmentative communication, and knowledge of appropriate system characteristics;

- assessment of pre-linguistic and non-linguistic communication strategies;

- knowledge of currently available augmentative communication systems and techniques, both unaided and aided;

- understanding of the processes of augmentative communication use in interaction between speaking and non-speaking people, and between two or more non-speaking people;

- development and evaluation of therapy programmes aimed to teach non-speaking people to achieve communicative competence through the medium of augmentative communication.

Close liaison of speech and language therapists with specific responsibilities may be necessary in order to ensure the above.

Assistants:

Speech and language therapy assistants may have a role in the implementation of an augmentative/alternative communication programme.

See guidelines on skill mix (Chapter 9).

Resource Requirements:

Departmental budgets should reflect the need to hold and update a 'bank' of communication aids for assessment , trial and long-term loan (ICAC 1995), and to provide for the creation and implementation of 'low-tech' AAC systems as well as the configuration and implementation of 'high-tech' AAC systems.

Budgets must also make provision for access to technical support for maintenance and repair of AAC equipment.

Speech and language therapy resources for AAC should also reflect the importance of procedural and practical links with other services. These would include joint assessment with other professionals, a system of referral to an appropriate specialist assessment centre, links between AAC assessment and therapy and the statutory assessment and review procedures relating to special educational needs, local social services and community care, and links with local services providing assistive equipment/technology for people with disabilities.

See general guidelines for accommodation and equipment (Chapter 8).

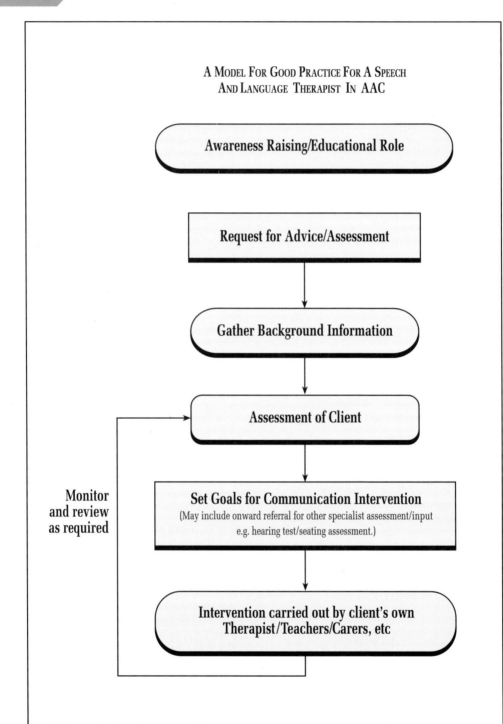

A MODEL FOR GOOD PRACTICE FOR A SPEECH
AND LANGUAGE THERAPIST IN AAC

Awareness Raising/Educational Role

Request for Advice/Assessment

Gather Background Information

Assessment of Client

Monitor
and review
as required

Set Goals for Communication Intervention
(May include onward referral for other specialist assessment/input
e.g. hearing test/seating assessment.)

Intervention carried out by client's own
Therapist/Teachers/Carers, etc

THE AUTISTIC CONTINUUM

Definition/Description of Client Group:

Autism is a pervasive developmental disorder characterised by impairment in social interaction and communication, and restricted, repetitive behaviour (WHO, 1994).

Language development is delayed and often disordered. Communication impairments include a lack of social use of language, little flexibility in language expression, limited conversational exchange, lack of emotional response to the overtures of others, impaired use of intonation and accompanying gesture to aid communication. A high proportion of children with autism also have intellectual impairment.

Current research suggests that autism should be viewed as existing on a continuum. Asberger's syndome is often described as a milder form of autism. It shares many of the features that typify autism in terms of social and communicative impairments, but there is no general delay in language or cognitive development. Speech and language therapy involvement with such children would not be qualitatively different from that of children with autism.

This section focuses on speech and language therapy services for children with autism. However, much of the information will also be of relevance to services for adults.

Aims/Principles of Service Delivery:

1 To ensure early identification of autism through multi-disciplinary assessment.

2 To establish the exact nature of the child's communication skills and needs in terms of development and his/her use of language.

3 To enable all those in contact with the child to have an understanding of his/her specific communication stengths and needs.

4 To work within a multi-disciplinary framework to disseminate detailed information to other professionals.

5 To enable the child and his/her carers to benefit from the advice and support of other professionals/agencies as appropriate.

6 To enable all those involved with the child to provide the optimum communication environment.

7 To support carers through the impact of the diagnosis of autism.

Referral:

1 **An open referral system will operate.**

2 If a referral indicates the presence of autism, the speech and language therapist will ascertain whether the carers are aware of the diagnosis prior to assessment.

3 **All relevant information from other professionals will be gained prior to the interview with the carers.**

4 A therapist with specific duties may pass the referral on to a speech and language therapist with specific responsibilities at any stage in the course of referral, assessment, diagnosis and therapy.

Assessment:

1 Assessment will focus on language

development and social development.

2   The aim of an assessment will be to obtain a profile of the child's skills. Areas of investigation may include:

■   a developmental history;

■   language (semantic, pragmatic and phonological skills);

■   social interaction;

■   symbolic understanding;

■   observation of behaviour.

3   It is important that the speech and language therapist is aware that she/he may be the first professional to be involved with the child and, hence, to observe the presence of autistic features. Therefore, she/he should have access to the advice of a therapist with specific responsibilities and request the involvement of the multi-disciplinary team.

4   It is essential that the label "autism" does not prevent the recognition of additional features such as a learning disability during assessment procedures.

5   **The speech and language therapist will write a detailed report for distribution to other professionals who are also considering the child's future needs.** The aim of the report must be to describe the behaviour and characteristics of the child, and to clarify the often contradictory nature of his/her difficulties.

6   The actual terminology used and the need for diagnostic labelling of a child will be dependent upon many factors and, whenever possible, the decision regarding final diagnosis will be made by the multi-

disciplinary team. It is incumbent upon the speech and language therapist, however, to clarify the nature of the child's problems so that carers are aware that difficulties are not confined to communication alone. The aim should be to enable carers to have a better understanding and acceptance of the child's difficulties regardless of the presence or absence of the label 'autism'.

Intervention:

1   If appropriate, a recommendation should be made that the child attends nursery or play group, where staff are aware of the specific needs of a child with autism.

2   The speech and language therapy input should be based on theoretical knowledge and detailed understanding of the child.

3   As a child with autism has a disorder of communication, the speech and language therapist, because of her/his theoretical knowledge of language breakdown and remediation may co-ordinate the intervention process with other team members. Direct intervention, either individually or in a group situation, may be appropriate or ongoing assessment may be required in order to enable the therapist to plan a suitable intervention programme.

The speech and language therapist is able to offer an integral approach to the development of communication by providing language/social skills training relevant to the child's overall level of development.

4   The child with autism experiences difficulty in acquiring and using appropriate language skills in a social context. It is therefore essential that the speech and language therapist applies the indirect

model of intervention, in order to provide opportunities for generalising skills in a variety of functional settings.

The speech and language therapist recognises the influence of those who interact with clients in their everyday experience. It is these individuals who are the major influence on the skills which the child acquires. Therefore, these carers, e.g. nursery staff, teaching staff, parents, are central to therapy input.

5   It is important to focus on the most relevant experience for the child. Many children with autism rely heavily upon the notion of 'significance', so the carer will be the appropriate channel of therapy as it is the carer who will hold most significance for the child. The role of the therapist is to identify the most appropriate intervention channel and direct the 'task' of therapy accordingly.

6   **Intervention will be accompanied by clearly defined aims and objectives of therapy which will be discussed and agreed with the carer.**

7   The speech and language therapist must facilitate the implementation of indirect therapy through clear channels of communication and written information. Adequate support must be available to carers/teaching staff in order that all programmes are consistently administered.

8   The speech and language therapist is required to review regularly the effectiveness of the intervention programme.

Discharge:

1   **The decision to discharge a child from speech and language therapy will be taken after consultation with the child's carers and other involved professionals.**

2   The decision to discharge will be taken by the speech and language therapist responsible for the child's care in the light of progress achieved.

3   Carers and other professionals will be informed of the process of re-referral.

Interface/Liaison with Other Professionals

1   Speech and language therapists are advised to work as part of a multi-disciplinary team. The team may include:

- clinical psychologist;

- educational psychologist;

- teacher;

- special education assistants;

- nursery nurses;

- paediatricians.

Skill Mix:

Speech and language therapists with specific responsibilities managing clients with autism will have had experience of the client group of usually not less than two years, in a range of settings, with the support of a senior experienced colleague.

Speech and language therapists will have a working knowledge of current research pertaining to this client group and act as a resource for speech and language therapists with specific duties treating clients with autism.

Speech and language therapists must be able, if required, to show evidence of an up-to-date knowledge of advances in the field and in post-graduate education and development.

It is recommended that speech and language therapists should be members of the College Special Interest Group for Autism and the National Autistic Society.

Speech and language therapists with specific duties, i.e. those holding a generic caseload or a dedicated caseload with the support of a speech and language therapist with specific responsibilities are recognised as being able to treat clients presenting with autism.

However, this must be with the ability to refer to colleagues with specific responsibilities or to College advisers in autism. Such staff are encouraged to join College Special Interest Groups and relevant organisations in order to ensure delivery of the highest quality standards of care for clients.

Assistants:
Speech and language therapy assistants are considered to have a role to play in administering communication programmes devised by the speech and language therapist.

The importance of the natural environment and the 'significant others' in the therapeutic process creates a particular requirement for effective communication between the speech and language therapy staff and others in the child's life. The speech and language therapist's assistant has an important role in maintaining liaison between other professionals/carers and the speech and language therapist.

See guidelines on skill mix (Chapter 9).

Resource Requirements:
See general guidelines for accommodation and equipment (Chapter 8).

CEREBRAL PALSY

Definition/Description of Client Group:
Cerebral palsy is a persistent disorder of movement and/or posture due to a non-progressive lesion of the brain, acquired during rapid brain development. There is a continuum of severity from mild to severe and changes may occur over time.

There are three main types of cerebral palsy:

- athetosis - slow writhing involuntary movements which are increased by excitement, insecurity, cognitive demands and the need to make voluntary movements;

- spasticity - stiff, laboured movements. Abnormal postures are held by tight spastic muscles;

- ataxia - inability to co-ordinate voluntary movements which may be poorly-timed, graded and directed.

Any of these types of cerebral palsy may co-occur and one or more limbs may be affected by spasticity e.g. hemiplegia, diplegia, quadriplegia. Cognitive and sensory impairments may be associated with this disorder, but there is no relationship between the degree of physical impairment and cognitive ability.

Clients with cerebral palsy may present with multiple difficulties in the areas of voice (e.g. resonance) and speech (e.g. dysarthria, dyspraxia, fluency and prosody), language and communication, literacy, feeding, drooling and swallowing. The impairments which cause these difficulties may be motoric, sensory, cognitive, linguistic or social. Failure to address the problems of people with cerebral palsy will have marked consequences for their success in the social, educational and vocational aspects of their lives. The speech and language therapist will need to take account of these factors when planning assessment and intervention.

See Chapter 4 for further information on the following:

- developmental speech and language disorders;

- written language disorders (developmental);

- developmental dysarthria;

- dysphagia ;

- eating and drinking difficulties in children.

Aims/Principles of Service Delivery:

1 A speech and language therapist with specific responsibilities should be available to all clients with cerebral palsy who present difficulties in the areas of speech, language,

communication, feeding, swallowing and drooling.

2 Access to generic services should be sought wherever this is appropriate for the assessment and treatment of disorders which are not primarily related to cerebral palsy.

3 Service delivery should be carefully planned and should maintain consistency from infancy onwards. Intervention may be indirect as well as direct, and environmentally focused as well as individually focused. The frequency and duration of intervention will vary with changes in the circumstances of the client.

Aims of Service Delivery:

1 To promote the development and use of effective systems of language and communication. These may include:

- use of non-verbal modes such as eye gaze, gesture, facial expressions etc.;

- use of AAC systems: manual signs or symbols such as pictures, graphic symbols or written words presented in the form of communication books or boards;

- accessing a graphic communication system;

- use of assistive technologies which involve access to a speech output device and/or computer software.

2 To promote the social, cognitive and motor skills which contribute to effective communication, e.g. mobility, environmental controls, cause and effect etc.

3 To ensure that clients receive adequate

nutrition. Clients should be able to take nourishment in ways that are safe, comfortable and dignified.

4 To provide information and advice regarding the management of drooling.

5 To offer information, support and advice regarding therapy procedures to speech and language therapists with specific duties directly responsible for the follow-up of clients.

6 The speech and language therapist should be involved in exchanges of information and knowledge with professionals and carers involved with the client.

7 To ensure that clients with cerebral palsy continue to have access to speech and language therapy when needed.

Referral:

1 **An open referral system will operate.**

2 Referral to the speech and language therapist with specific responsibilities should occur at the point when cerebral palsy is diagnosed, if the client has not already been referred e.g. feeding difficulties in neonates.

3 Referral to other professions should be made when necessary, e.g. opthalmologist, dietician, gastroenterologist, audiologist, social worker, clinical and/or educational psychologist etc.

4 Referral to a specialist centre should always occur if it is considered that assistive technology is of potential benefit to enhance the communication, educational, social and

vocational opportunities of the client.

5 Referral to a specialist centre may also be appropriate for specialist advice regarding the design and use of 'low tech' AAC systems e.g. communication boards.

Assessment:

1 Assessment must take place within an inter-disciplinary and co-ordinated team approach to provide a joint overall management and intervention plan.

2 Assessment procedures will vary at the discretion of the speech and language therapist and will include informal and formal assessments. (Formal tests results should be viewed with caution due to the specific and complex nature of cerebral palsy.) The assessment protocol will usually include:

- a full case history (including information on type of cerebral palsy), information given by carers and other professionals;

- information regarding medication taken by the client and its side effects (if any);

- information regarding hearing and auditory perceptual skills;

- informal assessments of the client's use of communication skills with a variety of partners;

- information regarding vision and visual-perceptual skills;

- where possible, repeatable and measurable assessments of prelinguistic skills, receptive and expressive language and speech production;

- assessment of the oral-motor co-ordination contributing to drooling, eating, drinking and swallowing skills. The feeding assessment should also include nutritional status, the social and sensory aspects of mealtimes;

- an assessment of the appropriateness of aided communication systems;

- **clients/carers should be informed of, and involved with, the assessment and therefore the results and should be included in decisions regarding their future management;**

- assessment of the factors in the environment which support or inhibit the client's effective functioning.

3 Assessment will take account of the client's communication environments including the range of communication partners and any relevant disabilities these partners may have.

4 Attendance of local professionals at assessment at specialist centres is essential e.g. speech and language therapist, teacher, co-ordinator.

Intervention:

1 The speech and language therapist's major consideration will be the client and/or associated concerns of the client's carers.

2 Where many professionals are involved with a client, a co-ordinator needs to be nominated. It may be appropriate for the speech and language therapist to take on this role in some instances.

3 Referral to a specialist centre may take some time and it is inadvisable to delay

intervention because of this. The speech and language therapist should plan intervention programmes which can realistically be implemented in the interim.

4 The speech and language therapist with specific responsibilities must ensure the efficient and effective transfer of information (including personal profiles such as video material and 'communication passports') and continuity of care during any transition period.

5 Intervention must take place in the context of an inter-disciplinary framework and will, at all times, take into account the client's management by all members of the team.

6 Access to mobility and environmental control systems must be co-ordinated with access to other technologies, the ultimate aim (where appropriate) being an integrated system. Consultation with other team members (occupational therapist, physiotherapist and rehabilitation engineer) is essential to achieving this aim.

7 Effective intervention will involve the development of strategies to provide an environment which is supportive of the client's system of communication and nutrition.

8 Effective intervention will involve the provision of training to carers and peer groups to develop appropriate strategies for communication and/or feeding. For example, effective intervention for an adult may involve the speech and language therapist going into the client's workplace and teaching others how best to communicate appropriately with a physically disabled person.

Discharge:

1 **Team members, the client and carer should be involved in the decision to discharge a client.**

2 The procedure for re-contacting the speech and language therapy department should be made clear to the client and carer.

3 Discharge from a specialist centre may be to the local speech and language therapy service. **A full written report should accompany this action.**

4 The management of the cerebral palsy client should be viewed over the long term. As new technologies and techniques develop and the client's needs change, the opportunities for regular and long-term review need to be made available.

5 The co-ordinator should be aware that re-referral may be necessary during major life transitions and therefore contact should be made with the speech and language therapist for a re-assessment of the client's needs e.g. community care assessments.

6 The decision to discharge should be communicated in writing to all the members of the team and the process of re-referral made explicit.

Interface/Liaison with Other Professionals:

1 A co-ordinated team approach should be provided for the client which encompasses health, education and social services, and employment.

2 The speech and language therapist should be a key member of the inter-disciplinary team involved with the individual and should liaise closely with other team members in areas such as:

- assessment;
- planning;
- intervention;
- staff training.

3 The speech and language therapist needs to be involved in the community care assessment procedures for clients. This should be highlighted within the transition plan when a young person is leaving education.

Skill Mix:

It is recommended that clients with cerebral palsy are not seen as part of a generic caseload without the support of speech and language therapists with specific responsibilities e.g. cerebral palsy, AAC, learning disabilities, dysphagia/eating and drinking.

The speech and language therapist with specific responsibilities will have:

- undertaken a range of post-graduate training courses in neurology, feeding, AAC, technology and assessment, learning disabilities, sensory disabilities, dysarthria, drooling, and disability issues;

- an understanding of the importance of positioning, seating, mobility, style of teaching and learning, motivation etc. in this client group;

- relevant clinical experience.

Assistants have a role to play in preparing materials and assisting the speech and language therapist in carrying out individual and group programmes.

Resource Requirements:

The UK advice co-ordinator, regional co-ordinators, Specific Interest Groups, SCOPE, Disabled Living Foundation and specialist centres can together provide information regarding specialist equipment for eating and drinking, seating and mobility, signs and symbol systems, voice output communication aids, computer software, aids for daily living and environmental control systems.

Budgets should enable speech and language therapists to travel to specialist assessment centres with clients and for any subsequent training e.g. programming different speech output devices for clients.

Funding for communication aids should be made available for clients who require them.

Appropriate resources and sufficient time are essential for the following:

- assessing, supplying and using assistive feeding devices;

- the continuous monitoring of feeding status and the training of relevant carers in feeding;

- enabling the speech and language therapist to assess, design and implement the introduction of the aided communication system;

- training carers/staff and the client in the communicative and technical use of the AAC equipment;

- the continuous development and ongoing evaluation of AAC equipment.

CLEFT LIP/PALATE AND VELOPHARYNGEAL ANOMALIES

Definition/Description of Client Group:

This section refers to children and adults born with a cleft palate, other craniofacial anomalies and associated syndromes, and velopharyngeal disorders of a structural or functional nature.

Aims/Principles of Service Delivery:

1 To offer a service from infancy to those with a cleft lip and/or palate. This is in order to monitor speech and language development and initiate early intervention for communication disorders and feeding difficulties which often occur in this population.

2 To offer a service which provides differential diagnosis of problems reflective of velopharyngeal dysfunction in the non cleft population.

3 To offer information, support and advice regarding intervention procedures to speech and language therapists with specific duties directly responsible for the follow-up of clients.

4 To provide clients with a co-ordinated team approach including plastic, maxillo-facial, ENT or paediatric surgery, as appropriate.

Referral:

1 **To offer an open referral service to infants**

born with a cleft lip and/or palate.

2 To provide facilities for joint consultation between the staff involved with the client and the speech and language therapist.

3 To offer open access to speech and language therapists seeking a second opinion and/or advice on disorders reflective of a cleft and/or velopharyngeal dysfunction.

Assessment:

1 At first contact with the client, screening will determine suitability for full assessment and intervention.

2 Infants referred with a feeding difficulty will receive a full assessment appropriate to their needs. Early communication development should be monitored, and advice given as appropriate.

3 Clients at that time, or subsequently, will receive a full assessment which would usually include:

■ full case history;

■ acoustic and perceptual evaluation including objective measurement of airflow through nasal anenometry or nasometry.

4 Clients/carers should be informed of the assessment results and encouraged to participate in the decisions regarding their future management.

5 **A management plan, detailing aims and objectives of therapy, expected duration and appointment procedures, will be drawn up in conjunction with the clients and their carers and recorded in the case notes.**

6 On the basis of the assessment, referral to other agencies may be appropriate after consultation with the consultant in charge and should be made with the client's/carer's consent.

7 Following assessment, therapists should report back to the referring agent, the plastic/maxillo-facial team and the client's general practitioner.

8 Videofluoroscopy and nasendoscopy should be made available as appropriate.

Intervention:

1 Speech and language therapists will be part of a multi-disciplinary team. The speech and language therapist in the team will have as her/his major consideration the client's/carer's own priorities and concerns.

2 Intervention will at all times take into account the totality of the client's therapy from all members of the multi-disciplinary team. This may include the client's surgical intervention, orthodontic treatment, or the ENT consultant's treatment plan.

3 In order to implement a speech and language therapy programme effectively, the speech and language therapist will need to liaise closely with those in frequent contact with the client. This will include the local therapist, if two therapists are involved, carers, teaching and nursery staff where appropriate.

4 Intervention may take place at any stage in the development of a child with a cleft and/or velopharyngeal dysfunction, or an older child or adult referred for therapy.

Clients are likely to have several episodes of therapy throughout their history. It will at times be appropriate for clients to be held on long-term review for future follow-up.

Discharge:

1 **Discharge will be at the discretion of the therapist in full consultation with the client/carer, and in consultation with the multi-disciplinary team.**

2 For clients born with a cleft or a velopharyngeal dysfunction who have identified disorders of resonance, further changes may take place during adolescence and early adulthood. These may require follow-up.

3 The process for re-referral or ongoing access to therapy must be made clear.

Interface/Liaison with Other Professionals:

1 Liaison is most successful where joint clinics between surgeon, orthodontist, ENT and speech and language therapist are held and where there is clarity in the respective roles of each team member.

2 The speech and language therapist is advised to be aware of the range of professionals who may potentially play a part in cleft/velopharyngeal anomalies therapy: they may include, for example, colleagues in the fields of psychological medicine, counselling and social work.

Skill Mix:

It is recommended that speech and language therapists engaged in cleft/velopharyngeal dysfunction therapy should where possible work as part of a department with

professional accountability to a senior speech and language therapist.

Speech and language therapists with specific responsibilities for cleft/velopharyngeal dysfunction should be the main channel of service delivery. It is recommended that clients with cleft/velopharyngeal dysfunction disorder are not seen as part of a generic caseload without the support of such a speech and language therapist.

Speech and language therapists with specific responsibilities for clients with cleft/velopharyngeal dysfunction must have undertaken:

■ a period of work experience fully supervised by a therapist with specific responsibilities for cleft/velopharyngeal dysfunction.

All speech and language therapists with specific responsibilities should be familiar with:

■ the use of instrumentation in vocal examination;

■ the use of objective measures in the assessment of cleft/velopharyngeal dysfunction;

■ counselling skills.

Therapists engaged in active counselling as a key therapy approach must have access to case supervision outside of the line management structure.

Speech and language therapists with specific responsibilities for clients with cleft/velopharyngeal dysfunction will be members of the College Specific Interest

Group for cleft/velopharyngeal dysfunction.

Speech and language therapists with specific duties, i.e. those clinicians holding a generic caseload or a dedicated caseload with the support of a speech and language therapist with specific responsibilities are recognised as being able to provide therapy for clients presenting with cleft/velopharyngeal dysfunction disorders.

However, this must be with the ability to refer to colleagues with specific responsibilities or to College advisers in cleft/velopharyngeal dysfunction disorders. Speech and language therapists with specific duties working independently will be required to give evidence to the College of their capability to obtain peer and case supervisory support. Such staff are encouraged to join College Specific Interest Groups and relevant organisations in order to ensure the delivery of the highest quality standards of care for clients.

Assistants:

Assistants should be involved at the discretion of the speech and language therapist. There may be a limited role for assistants in this area, as much of the work of the speech and language therapist involves the delivery of ongoing assessment as well as intervention. In addition, the medical condition of the client requires careful monitoring in view of the potential for laryngeal disease. Taken together, these factors restrict the use of assistants in direct intervention with clients.

See guidelines on skill mix (Chapter 9).

Resource Requirements:

Speech and language therapists working with this client group require access to the objective assessment facilities as outlined under assessment.

See general guidelines for accommodation and equipment (Chapter 8).

COUNSELLING

Counselling is the mechanism through which an individual is assisted to make a decision from the many choices available.

Counselling can be defined as:-
"A process through which one person helps another by purposeful conversation in an understanding atmosphere".

The process of counselling is designed to establish a helpful pathway in which the individual being counselled can express his/her thoughts and feelings in order to clarify the situation, come to terms with a new situation or see a difficulty more objectively. The individual is thereby enabled to approach the particular aspect of his/her life with less anxiety and tension.

Counselling is concerned with an individual's growth and awareness. It underlines and enforces a client's autonomy. It involves the application of active listening, responding and support by the counsellor and disclosure, trust and an identified need by the counselled.

Counselling is part of the speech and language therapist's repertoire of clinical skills. The extent to which a counselling approach is adopted will depend on the needs of the particular client in the therapeutic process.

During the course of therapy the therapist aims to create an atmosphere that allows the client to come to terms with his/her difficulties. This will, in many circumstances, involve the therapist in a process of enabling the client to gain a greater understanding of the nature of the difficulties, expectations of therapy and an understanding of the likely outcome of therapy. Speech and language therapists will often be working with clients in unfamiliar and distressing circumstances. Due to the interpersonal nature of the relationship that develops between the therapist and the client it is likely that the client will share his/her anxieties with the therapist and this will need to be managed sensitively.

Guidelines

1. All speech and language therapists should have undertaken basic training in counselling, listening and communication skills.

2. Counselling should be part of a holistic approach to intervention for a primary communication disorder.

3. Where speech and language therapists are working with clients in distressing circumstances, they should have access to support.

4. Where counselling skills are used as a main therapeutic approach, it is vital that:-

- the focus of therapy is explained and agreed with the client at the outset of

the contract .

- the speech and language therapist has undertaken postgraduate counselling skills courses.

- the speech and language therapist should be able to access case supervision and support.

5. Therapists using counselling skills as a primary method of intervention must ensure that their manager is fully aware of their practice and that this is reflected in their job description.

6. If advanced postgraduate counselling skills are an essential criteria for the job, then the grade as well as the job description should reflect this responsibility.

7. Where a speech and language therapist is working as part of a team, relevant information gained during counselling should not be passed on without the client's full consent.

8. All speech and language therapists should be aware of the limits of their competence as counsellors and should refer on if necessary.

DEAFNESS/ HEARING IMPAIRMENT

Definition/Description of Client Group:

This section refers to children and adults with congenital or acquired deafness who have an educationally and/or socially significant hearing loss. It is acknowledged that individuals may prefer alternative terms e.g. partially hearing, hard of hearing, hearing impaired, deaf, but for the sake of uniformity 'deaf' has been used throughout these guidelines.

A new subsection on services to clients with cochlear implants is included at the end of this section.

Aims/Principles of Service Delivery:

1 To provide an integrated service in conjunction with all other relevant agencies to clients referred to speech and language therapy.

2 To facilitate the early referral of all deaf clients and to provide a specialised service to meet their needs.

3 For school age children, to work within the educational context.

4 To provide a responsive and effective service for adults referred to the service.

5 To assist in facilitating the communication skills of children and adults referred to the service and to carry out specific work as appropriate.

6 To initiate and contribute to workshops for staff and carers on topics related to communication.

7 To contribute to the formulation and implementation of policies pertaining to communication written by other agencies e.g. education and social services.

8 To integrate the work of the speech and language therapist with the policies of other agencies, in particular the local education authority in the case of children, adult education and voluntary groups in the case of adults.

Referral:

1 **An open referral system will operate.**

2 Where appropriate, joint clinics with the audiology service will contribute to the effectiveness of the referral procedure.

3 Appropriate referrals will be facilitated through clearly defined channels of communication particularly with medical colleagues, health visitors, audiologists, teachers of the deaf, hearing therapists, educational psychologists and social services personnel.

4 **A clear referral procedure will be available to all potential referring agents.**

Assessment:

1 The assessment of the communication skills of a deaf child or adult may take place in a range of locations. In certain locations, for example, assessment clinics, it may take the form of an initial screening procedure, followed by an in-depth assessment of the client's communication strengths and needs. Where appropriate, assessment may be carried out jointly with a deaf co-worker.

2 At the time of the assessment, information will be gathered in the following areas as appropriate:

■ audiological information, e.g. type of hearing loss, pure tone audiogram, and/or speech-aided thresholds if available;

- audiological equipment, e.g. type of aids, mon/binaural fitting, use of radio aid, cochlear implant, vibro-tactile aid;

- relevant medical information;

- a note of other professional agencies involved;

- preferred mode of communication e.g. oral/aural; British Sign Language; gestural; cued speech; manually coded English systems (Makaton, sign supported English, signed English, Paget Gorman etc.).

3 The assessment of communication skills and the development of spoken language may take the form of observation, subjective description and the objective evaluation of hearing, spoken and sign language development. The assessment procedure will take into account the age, hearing status and case history of the client. The actual procedure will differ depending on whether a child or an adult is referred.

The assessment procedure will normally include:

- a detailed case history;

- full audiological details;

- assessment of the client's receptive skills;

- assessment of the client's expressive skills.

4 Where the speech and language therapist is also trained in audiology it may be appropriate for her/him to carry out audiological assessments.

5 In assessing receptive and expressive skills the speech and language therapist will consider spoken, signed and written language forms as appropriate, including for example:

- airstream mechanisms;

- voice (quality, pitch level and range, loudness);

- resonance;

- phonetic and phonological analysis (segmental and non-segmental);

- vocabulary level;

- syntactic analysis;

- semantic and pragmatic aspects of communication;

- social skills.

6 An audio or video recording will normally be made during the assessment.

7 Assessment will include a consideration of the client and carer's expectations of therapy.

8 **The client and carer will be involved throughout the assessment process and will be kept fully informed of assessment results.**

9 **A written report will be compiled and shared with the client and carer and relevant professionals.**

Intervention:
General:

1 **Following the assessment, the therapist will plan a programme of intervention as appropriate.**

2 **When appropriate, this plan will be fully discussed with the client, carer and other professionals involved.** The speech and language therapist's role may then be advisory, in which case she/he would give advice and guidance to carers, care staff, educational staff and others on relevant communication issues.

3 The speech and language therapist may have a direct role in the form of regular intervention, involving direct therapy and liaison with other team members.

Children:

1 If specifically requested to take a referral, the speech and language therapist may be one of the first professionals involved in the management of the baby who is 'at risk' of a hearing loss. The speech and language therapist may be asked to advise parents and other professionals about encouraging the child's communication development, including early interactive skills, intentional communication, early language and developing listening and voice skills.

2 Where teachers of the deaf are involved from the time of diagnosis, the speech and language therapist and teacher will normally work together, reinforcing each other's work. It is vital that close liaison exists between them in the management of deaf children and their carers.

3 The speech and language therapist and teacher of the deaf will continue to work together during pre-school, nursery and school years. Intervention may take place at home, or in schools, nurseries or health centres.

4 Other members of the paediatric hearing assessment team will provide crucial input and the child's general progress will be carefully monitored at all times.

5 Where assessment indicates that speech and language therapy intervention aims to increase communication and language development, a therapist will contribute to the planning of the child's communication programme with the teacher of the deaf. The speech and language therapist will carry out agreed work related to this programme as appropriate. This input could be on an individual and/or group basis and may be undertaken with the teacher.

6 Communication programmes will be monitored and updated by the speech and language therapist as necessary, in conjunction with the teacher of the deaf.

7 The speech and language therapist will contribute to full assessments, re-assessments and reviews of statements of Special Educational Needs/Record of Needs (Scotland).

8 In the case of children in mainstream schools, the speech and language therapist may offer support to the mainstream teachers and assistants in relation to communication assessment, advice on specific aspects of communication and help with the planning of individual work on communication skills.

Individual work with the child may be carried out in part by the speech and language therapist, although this work will usually be carried out by the mainstream teacher, assistant or peripatetic teacher.

9 The speech and language therapist may offer training to other professionals involved

in delivering services.

10 The speech and language therapist will contribute to the formation and development of school policies regarding communication and language issues.

11 Where appropriate, the speech and language therapist will organise or contribute to workshops for carers on aspects of speech, language and communication.

12 Where appropriate, the therapist will assist carers in improving their communication skills.

13 The speech and language therapist will attend and contribute to meetings and case conferences where the management of individual children is discussed and planned.

Adults:

1 Intervention with adult clients may involve individual or group therapy aimed at improving communication. Therapy may, for example, focus on communication skills and strategies, English language use, speech intelligibility, speech conversation, and other issues in relation to social skills and employment opportunities. In the case of acquired deafness, adjustment to the new hearing status will also be addressed.

Where possible, the speech and language therapist should liaise with the hearing therapist and audiology/ENT department.

2 The speech and language therapist may be involved in evening classes and voluntary groups working with deaf people.

Discharge:

1 Discharge will be at the discretion of the speech and language therapist responsible for the adult/child in full consultation with the client and/or carers. Where the therapist is part of a multi-disciplinary team there will be full consultation prior to the decision to discharge.

2 In the case of adults, the client may wish to discharge himself/herself before the programme of therapy is complete.

3 **Upon discharge a report will be written and circulated to relevant professionals as appropriate.**

4 The process for re-referral should be made clear to all clients, carers and relevant professionals.

5 If the client is transferred to another speech and language therapist, relevant information should be forwarded.

Interface/Liaison with Other Professionals:

The speech and language therapist has an important role in contributing to the educational, audiological and social needs of the client. In order to ensure an integrated, holistic and successful programme of therapy, it is essential that the speech and language therapist establishes her/his role within the relevant multi-disciplinary team.

It is the therapist's responsibility to identify key individuals associated with the client, e.g. carers, teacher of the deaf, deaf assistant etc., and then to ensure that all assessments and intervention programmes are fully discussed with these people. It may be necessary to agree joint intervention goals in order to achieve maximum support and carry over.

Skill Mix

Speech and language therapists with specific responsibilities for this client group will have:

- two years generalist speech and language therapy experience;

- qualification in the post-graduate Short Courses 1 and 2;

- qualification from the Council for the Advancement of Communication with Deaf People, British Sign Language: Stage I/Stage II (preferred)

- knowledge of the deaf community, deaf culture and deaf education.

In addition, it is desirable that the speech and language therapist will have completed the Advanced Clinical Studies Course in Speech and Language Therapy with Deaf People.

Speech and language therapists with specific duties, i.e. those holding a generic caseload or a dedicated caseload with the support of a speech and language therapist with specific responsibilities, are recognised as being able to manage deaf clients, providing that they can refer to colleagues with specific responsibilities.

All therapists should have access to other therapists working in the specialism through College Special Interest Groups and training days.

Assistants:

Speech and language therapy assistants may assist the speech and language therapist in undertaking specific individual work or group therapy. Assistants may also be employed in general administrative tasks as directed by the therapist.

See guidelines on skill mix (Chapter 9).

Resource Requirements:

See general guidelines for accommodation and equipment (Chapter 8).

Cochlear Implant Teams

This section describes good practice for speech and language therapists providing services to clients requiring cochlear implants to assist their hearing.

1   All cochlear implant teams should include an appropriately qualified speech and language therapist.

2   The speech and language therapist assesses, advises, monitors and evaluates clients' communication skills, both before and after implantation.

3   The speech and language therapists works with the client directly at the implant centre, at home, at school or in a local clinical setting. Liaison and advisory work with carers and with other professionals should occur throughout. Liaison is most successful when there is clarity in the respective roles of each team member.

4   The exact protocol of service provision is team and client dependent, as it is integrated within the working styles of the full team.

Levels of provision of speech and language therapy advice and intervention should be published by the team.

5 Liaison with local speech and language therapists is vital to ensure that a programme of therapy is fully implemented.

6 Levels of local provision for deaf clients should not be compromised by the presence of a speech and language therapist working with the cochlear implant team.

THE ELDERLY POPULATION

Definition/Description of Client Group:

This client group includes adults over the age of sixty five with a specific or generalised communication disorder and/or swallowing disorder. Such disorders would arise as a result of cerebro-vascular accidents, head injury, tumour, organic disease, including Parkinsonism, Motor Neurone Disease and the dementias.

Aims/Principles of Service Delivery:

1 To provide a timely, effective and appropriate service to elderly people with communication and/or swallowing difficulties in the context of multi-disciplinary rehabilitation.

2 To provide an integrated service to the elderly population with communication and/or swallowing difficulties, in a range of locations.

3 To identify specific areas of communication and/or swallowing difficulty.

4 To assist the medical team in the overall diagnosis of the client's disorder.

5 To ensure that the communication and/or eating and drinking needs of the client are fully considered in their day-to-day management.

6 To provide guidance and support to staff and carers on how to maximise their interaction with clients during everyday activities and how to ensure optimum use of communication and safe swallowing.

7 At all times to respect the rights and dignities of the elderly person, valuing them for the life experience they hold.

Referral:

1 **An open referral system will operate. Written referral is required for clients with swallowing problems.**

Assessment:

1 The aim of the assessment is to establish a clear picture of the client's communication and/or swallowing strengths and needs in order to establish whether or not intervention is appropriate. With this client group, particular care needs to be taken in the differential diagnosis of dementia and dysphasia.

2 The assessment will be carried out after the full case history has been taken. **The assessment procedure and results will be recorded in the case notes.**

3 There should be:

- screening and in-depth observational assessment of communication and communication needs, as appropriate.

- informal assessment of:
  - cognitive skills;
  - motivation;
  - insight.

4 In-depth assessment of the elderly person's communicative environment will be necessary in order to identify any factors within the environment which may be adversely affecting the client's communication skills.

5 Joint assessment may be carried out with other members of the multi-disciplinary team.

6 It may be necessary to liaise closely with the multi-disciplinary team in order to establish a clear picture of the client's communicative functioning within an everyday context.

7 If required, a full assessment of the client's eating and swallowing skills will be undertaken.

8 Particular attention should be paid to sensory deficits and the way in which the various pathologies may be interacting with each other.

9 Referral to other agencies/professionals may be considered particularly in relation to:

- vision;

- dentition;

- hearing.

10 **A written report stating recommendations will be forwarded to the relevant professionals.**

11 Written information will be available to the client and his/her carers.

12 Reassessment may take place at any point in the therapeutic process and used as a basis for:

- terminating therapy;

- extending the period of therapy;

- agreeing a different pattern of therapy.

13 **All client/carers will be made aware of available literature pertaining to their specific diagnosis.**

Intervention:

1 The model of intervention for elderly clients will vary with the location of delivery and the specific impairments and needs identified.

In general, the model of care will fall into two categories:

- clients with an acute onset of communication and/or swallowing difficulties may follow a rehabilitative model of care consisting of a direct communication therapy programme with a working hypothesis - assessment - treatment methodology.

Intervention may include written goals and advice relating to the communication and/ or swallowing problem. It may include psychosocial goals for the client, carers and team members.;

- clients with long-term, progressive and potentially irreversible communication difficulties where intervention will focus on the client's functional communication and/or swallowing difficulties by considering their interaction with others in their everyday setting.

2 The speech and language therapist will contribute to the care plan in a written form.

3 **In every case of intervention, written goals of therapy will be formulated and recorded in the client's notes.**

4 Management plans specifically aimed at effecting a change in the environment in order to maximise a client's opportunities and needs for communication are to be shared with relevant carers and staff and the appropriate training and support offered.

5 Clients with progressive neurological disorders and their carers are to be made aware of relevant societies providing advice and support.

Discharge:

1 Due to the ongoing nature of the difficulties that present in a large number of elderly people, discharge criteria can be difficult to establish. It is therefore important that **from the onset of therapy clear written goals with specified timescales will be defined and regularly reviewed.**

2 This is particularly important, in the case of elderly clients presenting with chronic, progressive disorders, when the efficacy of maintenance/functional therapy must be closely evaluated.

Maximum use should be made of carers in the client's life, as it is through their relationship with the client that the most effective therapy may be delivered.

3 When discharge occurs, carers and staff should be familiar with strategies for continuing the emphasis on functional communication within the client's environment.

4 Client/carers should be informed of the process for re-referral.

5 **A discharge report will be completed and distributed to all relevant parties.**

6 **Clients and their families will be made aware of support networks available after discharge from active therapy, including social stroke groups, self-help groups and societies.**

Interface/Liaison with Other Professionals:

1 The speech and language therapist should, where possible, work as a member of a multi-disciplinary team and liaise closely with other team members for:

- assessment;

- planning;

- intervention;

- staff training.

2 The speech and language therapist will be required to participate in staff training and education sessions.

3 The speech and language therapist may be required to participate in case conferences and planning meetings regarding all aspects of the client's life.

Skill Mix:

Specialists posts for this client group are a relatively recent development. The College supports the establishment of such posts for the elderly to develop the speech and language therapy service to this client group.

A speech and language therapist with specific responsibilities will:

- have had a period of work experience with elderly clients, supported by a senior colleague;

- have undergone post-graduate clinical training in subjects specific to the elderly population;

- participate in staff training.

Where services are provided by less experienced speech and language therapists, the therapist will have the ability to obtain the advice and support of a colleague with specific responsibilities in the care of the elderly.

Assistants:

The role of assistants with this client group may include preparation of equipment, movement of clients, and where appropriate, engaging in supervised individual and group therapy.

See guidelines on skill mix (Chapter 9).

Resource Requirements:

Access to a speech and language therapist with specific responsibilities appropriate to the client's diagnosis and presenting disorders.

See general guidelines for accommodation and equipment (Chapter 8).

ENT SERVICES

Head and Neck Injury (including associated surgical procedures)

Definition/Description of Client Group:

This client group include those clients with a deficit in either function or structure of the articulators, contributing to deficits in the voice, speech and/or swallow mechanism as a result of trauma, cancer, viral infection or congenital abnormality. The clients may have undergone surgical intervention, radiotherapy and/or chemotherapy.

Aims/Principles of Service Delivery:

1 To provide a specialist service to clients referred to speech and language therapy which takes into account their medical condition.

2 To provide clients with access to speech and language therapy at any stage in their rehabilitation.

3 To work within a multi-disciplinary approach to rehabilitation; this team may include the ENT consultant, head and neck oncologist, radiotherapist, plastic surgeon, oral surgeon, nursing staff, paramedical staff and counsellors.

Referral:

1 **A clear referral procedure will be available to potential referring agents for in-/out-patients.**

2 **All referrals will be discussed and acknowledged with other team members where appropriate.**

3 The speech and language therapist should have open access to the medical notes.

Assessment:

The client's abilities and deficits change as healing and recovery processes occur. Assessment, therefore, is ongoing and may not be a formalised procedure in terms of content and timing. Ongoing monitoring of the mechanisms of articulation, swallowing and phonation is likely to be appropriate.

Assessment procedures will depend upon whether or not surgery is indicated.

Procedures for clients undergoing surgery:

Pre-operative Stage

1 Prior to seeing the client/carer, the speech and language therapist should examine the medical notes and planned surgical procedure. The therapist should also ascertain from the ward staff the information that the client has been given.

2 Assessment pre-operatively is always recommended and may include:

- taking a full case history, including social history and medical history which may be obtained from the client's medical notes;

- an evaluation of the oral/physical mechanism, including areas such as lips, tongue, dentition, palate, etc.;

- an assessment of the client's communication and swallowing abilities;

- an assessment of the client's literacy skills;

- an assessment of the interaction between the client and his/her carer in order that the carer's role in therapy may be established;

- an explanation of the normal process of speech and swallowing and a discussion of potential difficulties post-surgery.

- an explanation of communication aids and their application.

Immediate post-operative stage

1 The speech and language therapist should continue to consolidate contact with the client and carer during the early post-operative stage.

2 The speech and language therapist will discuss and agree on the exact timing of the commencement of voice/articulation/swallowing therapy with the multi-disciplinary team and, in particular, with the consultant in charge. This will not usually be until adequate healing has occurred.

3 In addition to bedside assessment the need for objective assessment of the client's voice/articulation/swallowing mechanisms (e.g. nasendoscopy/videofluoroscopy) may be indicated and should be initiated as appropriate.

4 The speech and language therapist must be acquainted with the different types of tracheostomy tube, and the implications for therapy, when dealing with clients who require such appliances.

Procedures for clients not undergoing surgery:

If the client is to receive a course of radiotherapy, the speech and language therapist should be familiar with the potential effects of this treatment on the voice/articulation/swallowing mechanisms and advise the client accordingly.

Intervention:

1 Assessment and monitoring should identify clients who will benefit from a course of therapy.

2 The therapist should use her/his experience and knowledge of the course and management of the disease, as well as the apparent recovery processes taking place, in order to make this decision.

3 Therapy for articulation, voice and swallowing is aimed at:

- facilitating neuro-muscular recovery;

- facilitating compensating strategies where structural/functional recovery is not achievable;

- introducing and teaching other means of communication, e.g. oesophageal speech, artificial larynges or tracheo-oesophageal voice prosthesis;

- teaching clients and carers how to manage swallowing difficulties.

4 Therapy may be offered on an in- and/or out-patient basis, either individually or in a group.

5 Therapy may be short-term, long-term, intensive or occasional, depending on the nature and extent of the problems.

6 Clients' surgical and radiotherapy management differs, as does the recovery process. Specifying a timescale for intervention from the outset is, therefore, not appropriate.

7 Intervention, including counselling, may be appropriate in cases where the client is in the terminal stage of a disease.

Discharge:

1 Clients should be given clear information on when a period of speech and language therapy intervention is to end.

2 **Clear information will be given on whether or not any further intervention is an option and how the service can be accessed.**

3 Clients should be given information on how to access appropriate support groups.

Interface/Liaison with Other Professionals:

1 Head and neck oncology clinics usually provide an open access facility for clients, even after medical intervention and follow-up has finished. Likewise, the speech and language therapy service will provide open access for clients, even when a period of active therapy is over.

2 Regular monitoring of clients during the follow-up period in the head and neck oncology clinic is appropriate, even though active therapy is not being undertaken, for the following reasons:

- change in function may indicate recurrence of the disease. A minimal change in function may be a first sign of recurrence, without visible disease;

- communication aid use should be monitored and any required changes should be made;

- if any further medical intervention is indicated, the speech and language therapist should be involved in decisions which make demands on the speech and language therapy service. This has obvious advantages for the client in terms of speed and effectiveness of service.

Skill Mix:

There are currently few speech and language therapists with specific responsibilities working with this client group and there is a need for further training courses and research in this area. Services to these clients are usually available at centres of excellence with large caseloads. Some clients may be managed within general hospitals. Little has been written about speech and language therapy involvement with this client group and it seems that training at undergraduate level is sparse. Therapists therefore tend to learn by experience.

Resource Requirements:

1 Access to case supervision.

2 Artificial larynges.

3 Other augmentative/alternative systems of communication.

4 Access to oral prosthesis service.

See general guidelines for accommodation and equipment (Chapter 8).

Laryngectomy

Definition/Description of Client Group:

Laryngectomy refers to partial or total surgical removal of the larynx. For some clients more extensive surgery may be needed, with radical neck dissection and/or excision and resection of a whole section of the laryngopharynx and cervical oesophagus.

Aims/Principles of Service Delivery:

1 To provide ongoing therapy and counselling to clients and carers in the pre-operative and post-operative stages.

2 To give advice and support to nursing staff/carers regarding the most appropriate management of the client's communicative difficulties in the early post-operative stages.

3 To ensure an adequate means of communication for the client in the early post-operative stage by encouraging the use of communication aids/gesture/writing etc.

4 To plan the most appropriate action for vocal rehabilitation, and to establish and develop whatever communication method the client chooses to use, whether this be oesophageal voice, the use of a tracheo-oesophageal voice prosthesis, an artificial larynx or a combination of the above.

Referral:

1 **A clear referral procedure will be available to medical staff for clients requiring pre- and post-operative assessment/intervention.**

2 All referrals should be discussed with the appropriate medical staff.

Medical and ward notes to be available to the speech and language therapist.

3 Pre-operative referrals should be treated as a priority in order that:

- the speech and language therapist is able to establish the date of the surgical procedure;

- the client/carer and ward staff receive appropriate advice;

- the speech and language therapist begins to establish a relationship with the client;

- the speech and language therapist is able to carry out a pre-operative assessment.

Assessment:

Pre-operative Stage

1 Prior to seeing the client and carer, the speech and language therapist should examine the medical notes and ascertain from the ward staff what information the client has been given.

2 Assessment pre-operatively is always recommended, and may include:

- taking a full case history, including social history and medical history, which may be obtained from the client's medical notes;

- an evaluation of the oral/physical mechanism - including areas such as lips, tongue, dentition, palate etc.;

- an assessment of the client's communication, e.g. rate of speech, articulation, dialect, literacy skills;

- an assessment of the interaction between the client and carers, in order that the carer's role in therapy may be established and that their response to the post-operative communicative state of the client can be assessed.

3 In the pre-operative interview, the client's carer should be present wherever possible. The speech and language therapist should be prepared to answer questions relevant to post-operative communication, which may involve an explanation of the normal process of speaking in comparison to the process after the laryngectomy.

4 The speech and language therapist must be sensitive to the client's/carer's needs and emotional state, and should recognise that some people will want to be given more information than others. The speech and language therapist should respond to this accordingly. However, the speech and language therapist should explain that there will be a loss of voice immediately post-operatively and that while healing is occurring the client will need to communicate through writing/gesture.

5 It may be appropriate at the pre-operative stage to introduce a client who has already undergone a laryngectomy to the client. The appropriateness and timing of this must be fully discussed with the multi-disciplinary team. The individual should be carefully chosen for each client.

Immediate Post-Operative Stage

1 The speech and language therapist should continue to consolidate contact with the client and carers in the early post-operative stage:

- to ensure that the client is encouraged to continue in non-oral communication and, where appropriate, has pen and paper available;

- to continue to answer any questions and deal with any concerns from the client or carer, and to reiterate the speech and language therapist's continuing involvement.

2 The speech and language therapist will discuss and agree on the exact timing of the commencement of voice therapy with the multi-disciplinary team and in particular the consultant in charge.

This will not usually be until:

- the naso-gastric tube has been removed;

- sufficient healing has occurred.

3   The decision on the particular method of voice restoration to be used, will be based on:

- medical information;

- the particular circumstances of the client;

- clinical judgement;

- client choice.

Ongoing Intervention:

1 Management is very much dependent on the client's method of communication, i.e. whether via oesophageal speech, tracheo-oesophageal voice prosthesis, artificial larynx, etc. Some clients may choose to use a combination of methods.

2 Liaison with the ENT team should be maintained as appropriate.

Oesophageal Speech

1 May begin as soon as sufficient healing has taken place and in full consultation with medical staff.

2 Methods of air intake may be either inhalation or injection technique, as appropriate for the client.

3 Clients may be given an artificial larynx in the early stages in order to help establish functional communication.

4 Following intervention some clients may fail to acquire oesophageal speech and it may be appropriate for further investigations to be carried out.

Surgical and Prosthetic Approaches to Speech Rehabilitation

1 This may be done as a primary procedure, i.e. at the time of the initial surgery, or as a secondary procedure some time after the initial surgery.

2 In the case where surgical voce restoration is performed as a secondary procedure, the speech and language therapist should have knowledge and skills in the use and interpretation of the air insufflation technique to determine pharyngo-oesophageal segment function. This technique should be performed and interpreted in conjunction with radiology and ENT colleagues.

3 A variety of modified tracheal cannulae and tracheo-oesophageal voice prostheses may be used. It is important that the speech and language therapist is familiar with the nature of the reconstruction for each client, since it will have implications for their therapeutic intervention.

4 Close liaison with the ENT team should be maintained, particularly in the light of any complications arising.

5 The sizing, fitting and changing of tracheo-oesophageal voice prosthesis should not be undertaken by any speech and language therapist who has not received appropriate post-graduate training.

6 The speech and language therapy department should have a clear protocol of practice for dealing with prosthesis-related problems.

Artificial Larynx

1 An artificial larynx may be used exclusively for voice production or may be used in combination with oesophageal speech. The client then decides when to use either method.

2 A range of artificial larynges should be available, and whenever possible demonstrated to the client in order that the client and the speech and language therapist jointly select the most suitable artificial larynx.

3 The effective use of an artificial larynx will need to be learned. The speech and language therapist will have the required expertise, and will be equipped to enhance the client's intelligibility and communication performance through the use of the aid.

This process will include issues such as:

- placement;

- on-off timing;

- articulation;

- rate and pausing;

- pitch and loudness.

4 The loan of any communication aid to a client should follow a standard procedure with a clearly defined agreement regarding the length of the loan and the procedure for maintenance.

Discharge:

1 The decision to discharge should be taken in full consultation with the client.

2 **The speech and language therapist will inform the ENT staff and team members as appropriate.**

3 The client, carer and other team members should be informed of the process for re-referral.

4 The speech and language therapist should ensure that the client and carer are informed of local support groups.

Interface/Liaison with Other Professionals:

1 **It is imperative that the speech and language therapist works in close liaison with the ENT team throughout the therapeutic process, as organic changes in the client's condition may occur and therefore require monitoring.**

2 The client's general practitioner should be kept informed of the client's response to therapy and the process of therapy.

3 On occasions a client will receive his/her acute care from one therapist and subsequently be referred to a locally-based therapist for ongoing rehabilitation. In these circumstances it is vital that the speech and

language therapists liaise closely and exchange all relevant information.

Skill Mix:

It is recommended that speech and language therapists engaged in laryngectomy therapy should, where possible, work as part of a department with professional accountability to a speech and language therapist.

It is recommended that, where possible, speech and language therapists with specific responsibilities in laryngectomy should be the main channel of service delivery. It is recommended that clients with laryngectomy disorder are not seen as part of a generic caseload without the support of a speech and language therapist with specific responsibilities.

Speech and language therapists with specific responsibilities must have undertaken:

- a period of work experience fully supervised by a more senior therapist;

- post-graduate education and training in the following skills:

  - the use of instrumentation in vocal examination;

  - the use of objective measures in the assessment of laryngectomy;

  - surgical voice restoration;

  - counselling skills.

A speech and language therapist with specific responsibilities will be a member of the appropriate College Specific Interest Group.

Speech and language therapists with specific duties, i.e. those clinicians holding a generic caseload or a dedicated caseload with the support of speech and language therapists with specific responsibilities are recognised as being able to treat clients presenting with laryngectomy disorders.

However, these clinicians must be able to refer to colleagues with specific responsibilities or to the College advisers in voice disorders. Staff with specific duties working independently will be required to give evidence to College of their ability to obtain peer and case supervisory support. Such staff are encouraged to join College Specific Interest Groups and relevant organisations in order to ensure the delivery of the highest quality standards of care for clients.

Resource Requirements:
See general guidelines for accommodation and equipment (Chapter 8).

See voice guidelines.

Speech and language therapists should have access to the following:

1 Artificial Larynges, e.g.
- pneumatic artificial larynges;

- electronic mouth type artificial larynges;

- electronic neck type artificial larynges ;

NB: Tracheo-oesophageal voice prosthesis should only be changed within a clinically sterile environment with access to:

  - suction machines;

- medical and/or nursing assistance;

- suitable equipment.

2 Voice amplifiers

3 Pressure Bands

4 Stoma Care Items, e.g.

■ Stoma protectors;

■ Stoma sprays.

Voice

Definition/Description of Client Group:

This client group includes clients whose voice quality, pitch, volume or flexibility differs significantly from the voices of those of similar age, sex and cultural group.

Aims/Principles of Service Delivery:

1 To be sensitive to the needs of the client presenting with voice disorder, whether arising from an actual or potential laryngeal pathology.

2 To recognise the effects upon the lifestyle, interpersonal relationships and emotional state of the client.

3 To facilitate the receipt of early referral in situations where a pro-active approach may lead to the prevention of a severe and/or chronic disorder.

4 To assess, diagnose and treat the client referred in the light of medical, social, psychological factors and the information gained from the ENT examination.

5 To enable a client to identify those aspects of his/her lifestyle and environment which may be contributory factors to the voice disorder and to enable the client to make any necessary changes.

6 To provide the client with a co-ordinated team approach involving close liaison between medical staff and the speech and language therapist.

7 To plan and develop services with reference to current knowledge and research findings.

Referral:

1 **A clear referral procedure will be available to potential referring agents for both out-patients and ward-based clients requiring pre- and post-operative assessment/intervention.**

2 **An open referral system will operate, with the proviso that all clients must be seen by a consultant ENT surgeon prior to admission to the speech and language therapy service.**

3 Wherever possible, a joint consultation between the ENT staff and the speech and language therapist should take place at the time of examination and following subsequent intervention.

4 Where appropriate, on receipt and acceptance of the referral, an acknowledgement will be sent to the client and referring agent.

5 Where appropriate, pre-appointment literature may be sent to the client.

6 The speech and language therapist will have open access to a client's notes.

7 The speech and language therapist will be able to request audiological testing as necessary.

Assessment:

1 At first contact with the client, screening takes place as to their suitability for full assessment and intervention.

2 The client, at that time or subsequently, will receive a full assessment which would normally include:

- full case history;

- acoustic and perceptual evaluation, including objective measurement of, for example, breathing and frequency range;

- clinical observation.

3 It may be appropriate for the client to be assessed jointly by the ENT consultant and the speech and language therapist at a joint voice clinic, using stroboscopic techniques.

4 Clients should be informed of the assessment results and encouraged to participate in the decisions regarding their future management.

5 **A management plan detailing aims and objectives of therapy, expected duration and appointment procedures will be drawn up in conjunction with the client and recorded in the case notes.**

6 On the basis of the assessment, referral to other agencies may be appropriate after consultation with the consultant in charge and should be made with the client's consent.

7 **Following assessment, therapists will report back to the referring agent, the ENT consultant and the client's general practitioner.**

Intervention:

1 **The client and the speech and language therapist will establish an agreement with**

regard to shared aims, expectations and responsibilities.

2   The agreement will include arrangements on the number of sessions therapy will initially involve. Reassessment and further decisions will be made at the end of this period.

3   In order to implement a programme effectively, the speech and language therapist will liaise with others in the client's environment, e.g. carers, teachers, medical staff, social services etc. as appropriate.

4   Therapy on an individual or group basis may include:

▪   An explanation of normal voice production and the client's presenting disorder;

▪   vocal rehabilitation including specific techniques for:
posture
relaxation
breathing
pitch
resonance
lifestyle application;

▪   counselling skills - directed at issues pertaining to the aetiology and/or the recovery process. Clients who require a full counselling course may require referral to another agency;

▪   advice on the establishment of good vocal hygiene, including advice on the medical and environmental aspects of voice disorder.

5   The progress of clients will be assessed and recorded at the end of an agreed course of therapy and further action agreed accordingly.

6   **Prior to discharge, the actual outcome of therapy will be evaluated against the recorded expected outcome.**

7   Speech and language therapists are advised to consult the College guidelines on the use of endoscopic procedures (RCSLT, 1996).

Discharge:

1   The client will be adequately prepared for the cessation of intervention.

2   In the absence of a known organic pathology, discharge will be at the discretion of the therapist responsible for the client's care.

3   In the event of organic pathology, discharge will be at the discretion of the therapist in consultation with the ENT medical staff.

4   The discharge decision and the process for re-referral will be explained to the client/carer.

5   If a re-referral occurs, all clients will be re-referred to the ENT medical department.

6   **A discharge summary will be sent to the referring agent, the ENT consultant and the client's general practitioner.**

Interface/Liaison with Other Professionals:

1   Liaison is most successful where joint clinics between ENT medical staff and speech and language therapists are in operation. Where appropriate, this is

recommended as the preferred option for joint working.

2   It is imperative that the speech and language therapist works in close liaison with ENT medical staff throughout the therapeutic process as organic changes in the client's condition may occur and need careful monitoring.

3   The speech and language therapist is advised to be aware of the range of professionals who may potentially play a part in voice therapy. They may include, for example, colleagues in the fields of psychological medicine, counselling and social work, osteopathy and physiotherapy.

Skill Mix:

It is recommended that speech and language therapists engaged in voice therapy should where possible work as part of a department with professional accountability to a senior speech and language therapist. This is due to the nature of voice therapy and the need for positive supervision.

The speech and language therapist is also required to work in close liaison with the ENT department.

It is recommended that, where possible, speech and language therapists with specific responsibilities in voice should be the main channel of service delivery. It is recommended that clients with voice disorder are not seen as part of a generic caseload without the support of a speech and language therapist experienced in voice.

A speech and language therapist with specific responsibilities in voice must have undertaken:

- a period of work experience fully supervised by an experienced therapist;

- post-graduate education and training in the following skills:

    - the use of instrumentation in vocal examination;

    - the use of objective measures in the assessment of voice;

    - counselling skills.

Therapists engaged in active counselling as a key therapy approach will have access to case supervision outside the line management structure.

A speech and language therapist with specific responsibilities in voice will be a member of the College Specific Interest Group for voice and/or the British Voice Association or equivalent.

Speech and language therapists with specific duties, i.e. those clinicians holding a generic caseload or a dedicated caseload with the support of speech and language therapists with specific responsibilities are recognised as being able to treat clients presenting with voice disorders.

However, these clinicians must be able to refer to more experienced colleagues or to the College advisers in voice disorders. Speech and language therapists with specific duties working independently will be required to give evidence to College of their ability to obtain peer and case supervisory support. Such staff are encouraged to join College Specific Interest Groups and relevant organisations in order to ensure the delivery of the highest standards of care for clients.

Assistants:

There may be a limited role for assistants working with this client group, as much of the work of the speech and language therapists involves the delivery of ongoing assessment as well as intervention. In addition, the medical status of the client requires careful monitoring in view of the potential for laryngeal disease. Taken together, these factors restrict the use of assistants in direct intervention with clients with voice disorders. If assistants are used, their work should be confined to non-client related activity.

See guidelines on skill mix (Chapter 9).

Resource Requirements:

1   Quiet room with comfortable furnishings.

2   Equipment for the objective analysis of voice production.

3   Access to equipment necessary for augmentative/alternative systems of communication.

4   Access to case supervisors.

See general guidelines for accommodation and equipment (Chapter 8).

See personal safety guidelines (Chapter 8).

HUMAN IMMUNODEFICIENCY VIRUS (HIV) DISEASE

Definition/Description of Client Group:

HIV (Human Immunodeficiency Virus) refers to a disease of the immune system. The term is used to describe a range of consequences arising from damage to the immune system caused by the virus. This range extends from no observed symptoms to AIDS (Acquired Immune Deficiency Syndrome). HIV may give rise to disorders of communication and/or swallowing and eating difficulties.

Clients requiring the services of the HIV team will have a diagnosis of being anti-body positive, or seropositive.

This section describes the management of clients with HIV disease. However, it is recognised that intervention may follow the general model of care for a defined client group, e.g. stroke, dementia, dysphagia etc.

Aims/Principles of Service Delivery:

1   To work within the framework of the multi-disciplinary team and thereby provide a co-ordinated approach to all phases of the management of clients with HIV disease.

2   To provide assessment, advice and management of speech and language skills which may be compromised as a consequence of opportunistic infection incurred as a result of infection by HIV.

3   To provide ongoing assessment, advice and management programmes to clients with a progressive neurological disorder arising

as a consequence of infection by HIV.

4   To provide assessment, advice and management of speech and language skills which may be compromised as a consequence of adjustment/reaction difficulties attributed to HIV disease.

5   To provide a comprehensive and responsive service to clients presenting with eating and swallowing disorders attributed to infection by HIV.

6   To offer ongoing support, advice, and training to carers, staff and students as required.

7   To offer information and advice regarding communication and swallowing/eating difficulties attributed to HIV disease to other statutory and non statutory agencies.

Referral:

1   Written information regarding the service will be available to health service staff, other professionals, relevant agencies and the general public.

2   **Open referral will exist except in instances where the client presents with a swallowing\eating disorder, where a medical referral will be required.**

3   Early referrals of clients with progressive neurological disorders is advocated.

4   Prior to assessment, accurate information will be gathered on the client's medical and social history. In addition, close liaison between the relevant medical paramedical and social care team will be established in order to gain the maximum information regarding the client and the presenting difficulties.

5   Clients presenting with dysphagia should gain access to the service via a written referral from the medical practitioner responsible for their management.

6   **The service will respond promptly to new referrals:**

- **in-patient referrals will be seen within two working days of receipt of referrals;**

- **out-patients/community referrals will be seen within one week.**

Assessment:
Disorders of Communication

1   Assessment may take place over several sessions and will seek to establish the presence and specific diagnosis of speech, language or communication disorder.

2   Assessment may involve using a range of standardised and non-standardised materials appropriate to the initial diagnoses.

3   Qualitative and quantitative results from the assessment will enable the speech and language therapist to establish:

- type of disorder, by name, with description and examples,

- severity of disorder and level of skill;

- other factors which may influence communication.

4   **The outcome of the assessment will be made known to the lead clinician, client,**

carer and other relevant professionals, and will be included in the client's case notes.

Dysphagia

1 Effective assessment, treatment and management of clients with dysphagia require expertise from a number of different professionals. It is recommended that the speech and language therapist working with dysphagic clients should function as a member of a multi-disciplinary team.

2 In instances where a client is already taking some food/liquid orally, it is recommended that the speech and language therapist should observe the client drinking and/or eating, provided that it is not contra-indicated by clinical examination.

3 Where the client is being fed non-orally, the lead clinician responsible for the client's care should be consulted before trial swallows are attempted.

4 If the speech and language therapist considers further investigation using radiographic techniques is required, results and interpretations will be discussed with the lead clinician or the multi-disciplinary team.

5 **Results of investigations, assessment findings and proposed management will be discussed with the lead clinician, the client and carers and reported in writing to the team.**

Intervention:

1 The appropriateness and timing of speech and language therapy interventions will need to take into consideration features such as:

- the client's health status and level of awareness;

- the medical team's opinion regarding the client's overall prognosis;

- the information shared by the multi-disciplinary team.

2 The lead clinician responsible for the client's care may require information from the speech and language therapist regarding the client's ability to understand what is happening to him/her.

3 **The aims of a therapy programme will be clearly explained to the client and carers, particularly regarding the long-term maintenance role of intervention.**

4 **Speech and language therapy assessments and recommendations will be reported to the team and discussed with the client and carers, as appropriate.**

5 The progressive nature of the acquired neurological disorders which present in people with HIV disease means that for many clients with communication and/or swallowing difficulties their needs will change over time. Therapy aims will need to be re-defined accordingly.

For this reason, a structured management program is required to ensure that clients are able to receive long-term help. A programme may include:

- regular therapy;

- intensive therapy either individually or in groups run on a periodic basis, with review appointments in the interim;

- the use of appointments for ongoing advice;

- support and advice to client/carer and staff.

6 Therapy may involve the teaching of compensatory strategies to improve verbal communications. The use of audio visual aids may be useful to encourage self-monitoring of communicative competence.

7 The speech and language therapist may be the first point of contact to identify persisting cognitive problems, and/or make a differential diagnosis between communication difficulties and specific cognitive, sensory or perceptional deficits.

8 Therapy will be offered at different locations to help facilitate easy access.

Interface/Liaison with Other Professionals:

1 Medical staff responsible for the client must be kept informed of the aims and methods of dysphagia therapy intervention, together with the possible risks of intervention and expected outcome. Medical staff will need to give consent before proposed intervention is initiated.

2 The client with a progressive neurological disorder resulting from HIV disease may experience a range of difficulties and it is understood that a range of professionals may be involved with the client. The importance and advantages of multi-disciplinary practice and establishing clear role definition amongst professionals is recognised.

3 In some circumstances it may be appropriate for the multi-disciplinary team to work in an inter-disciplinary manner and adopt selective roles for each other. It is also recognised that the speech and language therapist may work in close conjunction with a range of agencies including social services, educational services and non-statutory groups.

Skill Mix:

A speech and language therapist with specific responsibilties for working with people affected by HIV disease should have post-graduate training to develop specific skills and expertise in dysphagia, dysarthria and dysphasia therapy. Post-graduate training in specific communication and swallowing/eating difficulties associated with HIV disease is an essential requirement.

Further opportunities should also be taken to attend multi-disciplinary courses/conferences to develop knowledge and expertise in associate areas that are not generally covered in sufficient depth in undergraduate training. These areas include: epidemiology of HIV disease, HIV disease and women, HIV disease and children, medico-legal affairs, nutrition and HIV disease, drug effects, infection control, mental health, health promotion and safer sex.

Speech and language therapists with specific duties working with people affected by HIV disease should work with the support and guidance of a colleague with specific responsibilities, or have the ability to refer to specialist colleagues in related fields. Membership of appropriate Specific Interest Groups is advised for all therapists working with people affected by HIV disease.

Resource Requirements:

The speech and language therapist needs to work within a multi-disciplinary team and, therefore, requires time for liaison and appropriate clinical and office accommodation in close proximity to the other team members.

Access to a range of assessment and intervention materials will also be required.

LEARNING DISABILITIES

Definition/Description of Client Group:

This client group includes those children and adults who have an identified intellectual or cognitive disability present from birth onwards. This learning disability may or may not have an identified genetic basis such as Down's syndrome, or Fragile X syndrome. Learning disabilities vary in severity and characteristics as well as cause. This section reflects general principles and practice with adults and children with learning disabilities.

Aims /Principles of Service Delivery:

The speech and language therapy profession recognises the importance of good functional communication and eating and drinking skills in the pursuit of independence in ordinary life.

1 All people with learning disabilities should have equal access to a specialist speech and language therapy service provided in the most suitable location e.g. home, school, day centre, community (shops, library, sports centre) etc.

2 It should be noted that carryover of intervention is frequently difficult for this client group and therefore the actual locations and situations themselves should be used wherever possible.

3 Contracts of care should be available to any age group, reflecting the varying and changing needs of the clients throughout their lives.

4 While the goals and the nature of intervention may change throughout a client's life, therapists should provide continuity and smooth transfer of care.

5 Access to generic services should be sought wherever possible. In cases where communication disorders are not a direct result of learning disability the appropriate therapist with specific responsibilities should provide advice or intervention.

6 A client-centred approach must be adopted, respecting the individual's needs and opinions and promoting his/her active participation in any intervention and the decision-making processes associated with it.

7 The active role of carers is seen as essential, with therapists positively supporting their involvement.

8 Therapy should always aim to enable the client to function more independently in the activities of daily life and to discourage dependence on the therapist.

9 Building an environment that is conducive to good communication is particularly significant to this client group. It must be recognised that developing improved physical surroundings, personal circumstances and appropriate communication used by carers will significantly benefit the client's

communicative success. These should always be regarded as a primary focus for intervention.

10 At all times therapy aims to promote maximum independence and functional communication by building on the client's strengths.

11 Each service to people with learning disabilities should have a clearly stated philosophy and operational policy, and all those working within the team concerned should have a working knowledge of them.

12 The College recognises the duty of any speech and language therapy service to this client group:

- to provide a specialist service equally accessible to any person with a learning disability, who has need of help with any aspect of their communication, or eating/drinking;

- to identify this population via screening assessment where required;

- to carry out a full assessment of those clients identified, including a full analysis of their environment and circumstances;

- to identify the correct course of action following assessment, whether this be no further action, re-referral to another agency, direct intervention or indirect intervention;

- to provide specific training to carers and other professionals;

- to provide advice and support to carers;

- to work as part of a multi-disciplinary team providing a well co-ordinated package of care to this client group.

13 All aspects of service delivery must adhere to O'Brien and Tyne's five principles of service delivery for people with learning disabilities (O'Brien and Tyne, 1981). People with learning disabilities have the right to dignity and respect, choice, community presence and participation, as well as the right to achieve their maximum potential. These principles are based upon normalisation/social role valorisation theory outlined by Wolfensberger (1974).

14 In the current purchaser/ provider culture, the speech and language therapist will play a diverse role in assisting the person with a learning disability to take his/her place in society in accordance with the principles outlined by O'Brien and Tyne. This role will include raising awareness of the communicative needs of the individual and, by so doing, to contribute a more informed allocation of resources. The speech and language therapist is in a position to advise service purchasers on policy issues as they relate to the communicative needs of the individual with a learning disability. She/he will therefore play a key role in educating these groups, who may include:

- locality commission team;

- general practitioners;

- local social services;

- further education funding bodies;

- care managers.

15 **The speech and language therapist will be involved in the development of local standards and local service level agreements, working in a multi-agency team.**

16 **The speech and language therapist will liaise with local service providers, to ensure that they are aware of the communicative needs of their client and to advise as to how these might be provided. Local service providers might include:**

- colleges of further education;

- private and voluntary day provision;

- private and voluntary residential provision.

Referral:

1 **Referrals to speech and language therapy for this group are open, allowing an individual the right to request an assessment directly.**

2 All referrals should be acknowledged in writing.

3 A published referral procedure should be available to all potential referring agents including the clients themselves.

Assessment:

1 If the client is under sixteen, carer consent should normally be received prior to proceeding.

2 Wherever possible consent should be gained from the client prior to proceeding. Where a client is unable to give consent the speech and language therapist should consider the need for "substituted judgement".

3 Assessment may consist of a screening procedure where the referring agent requires a large number of clients to receive an assessment in order to establish priorities for intervention.

4 Liaison between those involved with the client should be undertaken during the initial stages of assessment, and relevant information shared.

5 All direct client assessment will be carried out in conjunction with at least one other person who knows the client well.

6 Assessment should involve both formal and informal techniques.

7 The assessment procedure should enable a differential diagnosis to be made.

8 Assessment will include information on:

- the client's communication skills and needs;

- the client's eating and drinking skills, where appropriate;

- the nature of the physical environments surrounding the client with particular reference to the ways in which they influence the individual's communicative competence.

- the nature of the communication used by carers in the client's life;

- additional factors which may influence communication, such as general health, eyesight, hearing etc.;

- the client's communicative competence across all his/her primary locations e.g. school, day centre, group home, at home with parents etc.

9 Assessment of the client's communicative skills and needs will include information on:

- basic interactional skills, i.e. eye contact, attention, turn-taking etc.;

- personal/social skills;

- comprehension - strategies and components of understanding;

- expression   - form of expression

                        - content of expression;

- discourse skills;

- non-verbal communication skills - natural gesture, body language;

- use of augmentative and alternative communication systems;

- fluency;

- voice.

10 **Assessments must be fully written up in a clear statement of communication skills and needs in the form of an initial report and circulated to the source of referral and all relevant parties.**

Intervention:

1 The options for intervention must be fully discussed with the client and others involved.

2 If a decision of "no intervention" is reached, the situation may be reviewed again within six months. Should the same be decided at this stage, the case should be formally discharged and further action will require a further referral.

3 If intervention is appropriate, a key worker should be appointed, by consensus, to co-ordinate the programme. This person should be someone in frequent contact with the client. Joint planning between the client, therapist and carers is essential to the success of the programme.

4 **A clear plan for intervention will be drawn up, with clear aims and objectives agreed and understood by the therapist, key-worker and, where possible, the client.**

5 **A contract for intervention will be established between all concerned. The contract will have a clearly defined timescale agreed by all parties.**

6 The key-worker will work closely with clients, involving them as much as possible and helping them to assume increasing amounts of responsibility for their own programme.

7 The style of intervention should be one of the following:

- direct: therapy which concentrates on developing the client's communication abilities;

- indirect: therapy which concentrates on developing opportunities for communication.

- combination of the above.

8 Clear goal planning techniques with recognised teaching strategies should be used

for most direct intervention.

9 Intervention should always be designed with a realistic understanding of the resource levels required. It should always be established to succeed.

10 Skill 'use' is frequently significantly lower than a client's actual skill level; as a result much of therapy will be aimed at improving 'use'.

11 All therapy should be aimed at improving communication in real and functional situations relevant to the client concerned.

13 It is important to establish the strategies by which an individual learns most effectively, and to exploit these when designing intervention.

14 The physical and communication environments, as well as a person's personal circumstances, significantly influence the degree to which an individual reaches his/her potential.

15 Direct intervention will involve one or more of the following:

- individual goal planning integrated into daily one-to-one situations;

- individual goal planning integrated into already existing group situations;

- the use of specifically planned groups to develop targeted skills.

16 Indirect intervention will involve one or more of the following:

- training for carers in any aspect of communication pertinent to the client;

- a programme to make the physical environment more conducive to good communication for the client;

- a programme to amend carer communication to any appropriate style thus enhancing the client's communication skills;

- advice and support to the carers;

- referral on to another agency, e.g. occupational therapist, physiotherapist etc.

17 All intervention must be clearly monitored.

18 **A review of progress will be agreed.**

Discharge:

1 An adult client retains the right of self-discharge at any time during the term of the contract.

2 The therapist has the right of discharge once a contract has been completed.

3 The therapist adheres to the original contract in all but exceptional circumstances, unless the aims and objectives laid out are met earlier than anticipated.

4 **Discharge may occur earlier than anticipated in one or more of the following situations:**

- **the intervention contract is broken due to inadequate resources or poor management;**

- **the carers are unable to adopt and effect the necessary change for goals to be achieved.**

- the carers do not attend the training required to effect change.

5 A full report is to be written and circulated prior to discharge detailing:

- summary of client's initial assessment and current communication status;

- summary of initial aims and objectives;

- principles of communication maintenance;

- essential review items such as hearing aid, AAC system;

- progress since assessment;

- reason for discharge;

- **clear guidance on re-referral procedure.**

6 Upon completion of the contract, the client will be discharged.

7 A referral may be re-initiated at any time after the initial discharge.

Interface/Liaison with Other Professionals:

The College recognises the following to be essential for good practice:

1 Therapists are responsible for disseminating information concerning every client's assessment and intervention programme to all those for whom it may have management implications.

2 The appropriateness of joint management with any relevant professionals should be considered with each client.

3 Speech and language therapy objectives for adults must be integrated into any "care plans" that are in operation for the client.

4 Speech and language therapy objectives for children will be included in their statement of educational need/record.

5 As part of a multi-disciplinary team, the therapist will be involved in working in groups with other professionals.

6 Speech and language therapists must aim to provide intervention in a fully integrated way, with their contribution as one part of a much larger whole. As such, they should view themselves as part of a multi-disciplinary team, even when this has not been formally established.

7 The speech and language therapist has skills which can be shared to facilitate effective delivery of other services such as dietetics, psychology, care management etc.

Skill Mix:

Speech and language therapists with specific responsibilities working with this client group should have had a period of work experience working closely with specialist colleagues in a range of settings. This may include working in an educational setting, a community team, a day centre and/or within a domiciliary service.

Speech and language therapists working with learning disabled adults and children will have undertaken uni-/multi-disciplinary post-graduate education and training in a variety of relevant subjects, e.g.:

- principles of normalisation/social role valorisation;

- goal planning techniques ;

- teaching strategies for use with clients;

- teaching strategies for transferring skills to carers and staff;

- augmentative and alternative communication;

- the management of challenging behaviour;

- multiple sensory impairment and its effects on communication;

- hearing rehabilitation;

- lifting and handling techniques;

- the development of eating and drinking skills;

- dysphagia.

Speech and language therapists with specific duties working with this client group should do so with active support of colleagues with specific responsibilities. Where possible, speech and language therapists should work as members of a team both in the multi-disciplinary setting and within the professional context. Joint working through 'team intervention' is vital in order to ensure the appropriate level of skill sharing and the provision of quality services. In order to encourage entrants into the profession to develop an interest and expertise with this client group, they must be offered opportunities to work alongside more experienced colleagues.

Assistants:

The model of care for clients with a learning disability stresses the importance of utilising the skills and involvement of significant people in the client's life including teachers,

instructors and carers. This is the appropriate manner in which to deliver therapy and if these people are not involved, the programme of intervention will be unsuccessful. However, assistants may have a role to play in supporting the speech and language therapist in her work with people with learning disabilities.

See guidelines on skill mix (Chapter 9).

Resource Requirements:

See general guidelines for accommodation and equipment (Chapter 8).

LEARNING DISABILITIES AND CHALLENGING BEHAVIOUR

Definition/Description of Client Group:

"Severely challenging behaviour refers to behaviour of such an intensity, frequency or duration that the physical safety of the person or others is likely to be placed in serious jeopardy, or behaviour which is likely to seriously limit or delay access to and use of ordinary community facilities."

Behaviour which challenges services occurs along a continuum, with active behaviour (often referred to as aggression) at one end and passive behaviour (often referred to as withdrawal) at the other. Clients may have additional mental health needs (see section Mental Health).

Aims/Principles of Service Delivery:

The speech and language therapy profession

recognises that challenging behaviour often has or can be interpreted as having a communicative function. Any attempt to improve the quality of life of individuals with learning disabilities and challenging behaviour and their carers should therefore take into account the following:

1 All individuals with challenging behaviour have the same rights and needs as other members of society and should not be discriminated against because of their behaviour.

2 Communication is a two-way process. Carers, therefore, have an essential role in developing and influencing appropriate responses.

3 Communication does not occur in isolation and cannot be construed separately from an individual's other activities, general lifestyle and the services they use.

4 Speech and language therapists should not work with clients who challenge services unless they are working as part of a co-ordinated multi-disciplinary team, with agreed roles for each team member.

5 A person's challenging behaviour reflects their emotional and physical wellbeing. Therefore, health promotion projects, e.g. individual planning, self advocacy and health screening should be seen as part of the therapist's intervention to the service.

6 Local service guidelines for working with clients, e.g. the management of challenging behaviour, reporting of incidents, should be adhered to.

7 Debriefing is essential. This should be accessible on the day the incident occured.

Incidents that will require debriefing include:

- violent or aggressive behaviour;

- inappropriate behaviour of a sexual nature;

- any other behaviour that causes distress to the therapist.

8 Speech and language therapists should not work alone with clients who are known to react to certain situations in a violent or aggressive way unless there is an alarm system or immediate access to staff.

9 Approaches based on punishment and aversive techniques are not considered ethical.

Referral: (as defined in the Learning Disabilities section above)

1. Where speech and language therapists work as part of a challenging behaviour team, a joint team referral may be accepted.

Assessment: (as defined in the Learning Disabilities section above)

As part of a team assessment, a speech and language therapy assessment would include assessment of:

1 The individual's mode of communication, including those behaviours which may have a communicative function.

2 The impact of the client's previous history and communication experiences.

3 The impact of the attitudes of carers and the service values on the client and his/her communication.

4   The communicative strengths and needs of carers in their interaction with the client.

Intervention: (as defined in the Learning Disabilities section above)

As part of a team intervention, speech and language therapists have a role in the following:

1   facilitating carers in their understanding of the nature and causes of challenging behaviour, particularly in relation to communication;

2   facilitating carers in understanding the role of the environment and their own communication in relation to clients' challenging behaviour;

3   facilitating carers in developing more appropriate and consistent ways of communicating with clients with challenging behaviour, e.g. use of modelling, reinforcement, feedback, etc.;

4   supporting carers in developing appropriate activities for the client;

5   challenging the negative concepts associated with the label 'challenging behaviour' and advocating on behalf of clients where necessary;

6   enabling access to other specialisms and/or generic services where appropriate e.g. audiology;

7   involvement in the development and provision of appropriate support mechanisms (e.g. supervision, debriefing) for others working with people with learning

disabilities and challenging behaviour.

Discharge: (as defined in the Learning Disabilities section above)

1   **Where speech and language therapists work as part of a challenging behaviour team, a joint decision to discharge may be made.**

Interface/Liaison with other Professionals:

Within a team approach, speech and language therapists may also be expected to take on more general roles:

1   as case manager/co-ordinator for a particular client;

2   in identifying needs for this client group as a whole and developing protocols or procedures to meet these;

3   in establishing systems to record incidents;

4   involvement in developing guidelines for working with clients, e.g. management of a particular behaviour.

5   providing supervision/support to colleagues and other members of the team.;

6   providing information and advice to managers on service evaluation and areas for service development;

7   promoting physical and emotional well-being of clients in order to prevent challenging behaviour;

8   providing training on challenging

behaviour to other services;

9 initiating and taking part in research.

10 evaluating the effectiveness of the team as a whole;

11 working with other members of the team to develop and meet overall team objectives.

Skill Mix:

Speech and language therapists working with learning dsabled adults and children will have undertaken uni/multi-disciplinary post graduate education and training in a variety of relevant subjects (see section on Learning Disabilites above). In addition , they will have undertaken post graduate training in the following;

- current theories and approaches to working with people with challenging behaviour;

- training in de-escalation and control procedures.

MENTAL HEALTH

Adults

Definition/Description of Client Group:

This client group refers to adults experiencing communication difficulties associated with any of the major mental disorders. The mental disorders may be of acute onset, or may be a long-term illness involving residency in an institutional setting. Some of these clients may be undergoing resettlement in the community.

Elderly clients with functional and organic problems are also included in this client group.

This client group also includes clients using forensic services. Forensic psychiatry deals with assessment and treatment of offenders with mental health problems.

Aims/Principles of Service Delivery:

1 The aim of speech and language therapy is to facilitate optimum communication skills amongst all clients receiving psychiatric care who have an identified communication difficulty.

2 The primary concern of a speech and language therapy service in psychiatry is the communication skills and welfare of the individual client. Speech and language therapy operates within the context of a multi-disciplinary approach. The service offered must be available and sufficiently flexible to meet individual needs in accordance with local management policies.

3 Communication difficulties are highly correlated with mental illness. The content of verbal communication is an important diagnostic criteria, and observations of non-verbal communication, e.g. gestures, facial expressions, quality of voice etc., provide significant information which may contribute to diagnosis. Speech and language therapists' expertise means that they are uniquely placed to contribute to the diagnostic process and the subsequent management of communication difficulties/disorders.

4 Enabling transition into the community and effective maintenance in the community

will depend to a large extent on maximising the client's communication skills.

5   The speech and language therapist has a role in assessing communication strengths and needs of clients with mental health disorders. This includes the provision of specialist evaluation of the client's communication, speech, language function and communicative environment.

6   The speech and language therapist has a role in maximising communication skills where these may be compromised by:

■   environmental factors;

■   mental and physical state;

■   medication.

7   To offer support and guidance to all those associated with the client's care.

8   To provide education and training in the field of communication in mental health.

9   To promote good practices which help to prevent breakdown in communication.

Referral:

1   Within mental health services, speech and language therapy may be provided in the following locations:

■   closed institutions;

■   psychiatric hospitals;

■   mental health units;

■   residential units;

■   day care facilities (including health service, social services and voluntary);

■   out-patient clinics;

■   educational establishments;

■   domiciliary settings;

and to people with additional specific disabilities:

■   other physical disability or self-injury;

■   visual handicap;

■   neurological disorder;

■   hearing impairment;

■   learning disability.

The referral system will need to ensure that these locations and client groups have access to the speech and language therapy service where it is available.

2   **An open referral will operate. (Medical referral will be sought for clients with dysphagia).**

3   The speech and language therapist should ensure that staff/clients/carers are kept fully informed about the scope of the service.

4   Priorities for case management will be set according to the needs of individual clients and available resources.

5   If a referral is deemed inappropriate, then the referring agent will be informed and the client may be referred elsewhere with an explanation and possible suggestions for alternative management if appropriate.

6   Response to referrals and procedures thereafter will be in line with locally devised

quality standards, which should be measurable.

Assessment:

1 The client and keyworker should be informed of the purpose of the assessment. The assessment will include an appropriate range of formal and/or informal assessments and observations as well as a complete and relevant case history. Ideally the assessment would form part of the multi-disciplinary team assesment.

2 The initial assessment should be repeatable to allow for a re-assessment at a later date.

3 Full assessment should take account of all areas relevant to the client's communication, including personal, social and environmental factors. Therapists will have access to a range of assessment materials.

4 The assessment period may extend over several sessions.

5 **The findings and implications for future management will be discussed with the client/carers/keyworker and the team.**

Intervention:

1 Therapy will of necessity be flexible. Various forms of intervention may be appropriate, often delivered in collaboration with other members of the team. The most appropriate programme of care will be offered at the earliest opportunity.

2 **Care planning should take place in consultation with the client/carer/keyworker and other members of the multi-disciplinary team as appropriate. All episodes of care will be explained by the therapist and agreed with the client/carer/keyworker.**

3 Ongoing evaluation of the effectiveness of the programme by both the speech and language therapist and the client/carer/keyworker, will take place with modifications and a second opinion as necessary.

4 Any significant changes in the client's mental or physical state should be documented and reported to the appropriate agencies.

5 The speech and language therapist may be required to act with a second medical opinion in certain cases involving implementation of sections of the Mental Health Act and changes to treatment orders.

6 Throughout the period of contact, the speech and language therapist will ensure that any other professional agency involved with the client is kept informed of progress as appropriate. There will be regular written and verbal reports and discussion at case conferences, Section 117 meetings and care management meetings.

7 Advice and training on aspects of the programme of care as well as on language and communication generally, should be considered part of the role of the speech and language therapist in mental health. Written and verbal packages for training, support and advice to staff and carers will be made available to enable them to increase their insight and skills in relation to communication.

8 Repeatable assessments should be used to evaluate progress during the episode of

care and results provide the baseline for a case review and possible changes.

Discharge:

1 **The outcome of therapy will be recorded and reported to the referring agent and other relevant professionals.** Speech and language therapists working in a multi-disciplinary team will follow the discharge procedures which are part of the team policy.

2 Discharge under a Supervision Order will demand that the therapist is conversant with the terms and local implementation standards of that order.

Interface/Liaison with Other Professionals:

1 The speech and language therapist will attend any relevant case conferences, multi-disciplinary team meetings, care programme approach and Section 117 meetings called to review the client's progress/needs.

2 Where attendance is not possible, a report will be provided which details the progress/evaluation of communication skills and implications for future management.

3 There should be regular dissemination of information between multi-disciplinary team members. This is crucial when the programme of care using a multi-disciplinary approach may include joint aims and intervention procedures.

4 Speech and language therapists working in Mental Health Units will be required to give specialist evaluations and recommendations of communication needs of clients who become the responsibility of social services departments.

Skill Mix:

Adult Mental Health Services should be viewed as a specialist service requiring the skills of a speech and language therapist with specific responsibilities who has had a period of supervised work experience with this client group and undertaken relevant post-graduate courses.

The speech and language therapist with specific responsibilities working in adult mental health will ensure that advice and/or training is available and provided for carers, other professionals and voluntary agencies relevant to an individual client or group of clients.

Speech and language therapists with specific duties working with this population must do so with the ability to refer to specialist colleagues. This may be on a regional or national basis.

Speech and language therapists working in this area should undertake specialist post-graduate courses to promote the development of academic and clinical expertise. They should be members of relevant professional groups i.e. College Specific Interest Groups in psychiatry, counselling etc.

Speech and language therapists should be aware of relevant legislation, litigation issues, diagnostic critiera (APA, WHO 1994), health and safety issues and receive training in the management of violent incidents.

Speech and language therapists working in mental health may need to have some familiarity with conditions associated with this client group such as drug and alcohol abusers, self-injury and eating disorders.

The speech and language therapist will need to consider such factors as insurance (person or property) as this could be a high risk area in which to work.

Assistants:

The model of care for clients with a mental health disorder stresses the importance of utilising the skills and involvement of significant people in the client's life; nursing staff, mental health workers, teachers, instructors and carers. This is the appropriate manner in which to deliver therapy and may reduce the need for speech and language therapists' assistants, as the 'regular intervention' will be carried out by carers and other professionals. If these individuals are not involved, the programme of intervention will be unsuccessful.

Assistants may have a role to play by assisting the speech and language therapist in carrying out specific group programmes and in building and maintaining the dialogue between the non-qualified staff of both parties, i.e. nursing assistants and mental health workers, which can lead to positive outcomes for intervention.

Assistants are also considered to have a role in the preparation of equipment, the transportation of clients and in administrative duties.

See guidelines on skill mix (Chapter 9).

Resource Requirements:

Access to a range of assessment materials appropriate to the client's diagnosis and presenting disorder.

See general guidelines for accommodation and equipment and personal safety (Chapter 8).

MENTAL HEALTH

Children

Definition/Description of Client Group:

This client group refers to children and adolescents experiencing communication difficulties associated with an emotional, behavioural or psychiatric problem.

Aims/Principles of Service Delivery:

1 Emotional/behavioural problems and communication breakdown are frequently closely related. The speech and language therapist is, therefore, an essential member of the team working with this population.

2 The speech and language therapist should work closely with, or as a member of, the multi-disciplinary team, contributing to the differential diagnosis procedure and full assessment of the child's/adolescent's needs and the provision of a full management service as appropriate.

3 The speech and language therapist should at all times respect the rights and dignities of both the child/adolescent and his/her carers.

4 The child/adolescent should at all times be viewed within the context of his/her family, social and educational experience.

Referral:

1 **An open referral system will operate.**

2 Close liaison with all members of the multi-disciplinary team will occur upon receipt of the referral.

3 **Referrals for in-patients will be acknowledged within 24 hours, and for day-care patients, within one week of receipt. Referral of clients in the community and out-patients will be acknowledged within two weeks.**

4 **An appointment for an initial assessment will be offered within four weeks of receipt of referral.**

Assessment:

1 Assessment may take place over a number of appointments and it may be necessary to observe the child/adolescent in a range of situations including home, school, nursery, as appropriate.

2 Assessment may include one or more of the following:

■ parental interview - including a full case history;

■ observation in a range of locations appropriate to the child/adolescent;

■ informal assessment;

■ formal assessment;

■ gathering perceptions, possibly using questionnaires, of other professionals involved.

3 The assessment process will aim to identify factors in the client's life which influence his/her ability to communicate effectively.

4 The aim of the assessment is to form a comprehensive picture of the child's/adolescent's communicative functioning, in order that a management plan may be formulated and implemented.

5 **The assessment results and recommendations for management will be fully discussed with the carers and may be followed up by a written report.**

6 **The outcome of the assessment will be reported in a written and verbal form to all key professionals responsible for the overall management of the child/adolescent.**

Intervention:

1 Intervention may take the form of one or more of the following approaches:

■ programme planning for other professional and/or carer-facilitated intervention;

■ direct therapy on an individual basis;

■ direct therapy on a group basis;

■ advice to carers and relevant professionals;

■ follow-up review.

2 Factors within the client's environment, which may have been identified as influencing his/her communicative functioning, may be targeted as part of an intervention plan.

3 **A management plan detailing the aims and objectives of therapy will be formulated**

in conjunction with the carers and other team members involved with the client. This plan will be shared with all relevant people and recorded in the client's casenotes. The timescale for review will also be noted.

4 Intervention may take place in a range of locations including child psychiatry out-patient departments, child guidance units, child development centres, community clinics or the client's own home. In the case of the school-aged child, therapy may take place within an educational setting.

Discharge:

1 Discharge will be at the discretion of the therapist after full consultation with the carer and other professionals involved with the client.

2 Discharge will take place at the request of the carer or on the achievement of the aims of therapy.

3 A full discharge report will be completed and sent to other team members as appropriate.

4 The process for re-referral should be made clear to the client and carers.

Interface/Liaison with Other Professionals:

1 In order to ensure a holistic approach to the client's management, it is imperative that close liaison with other professionals involved in the care of the client is established and maintained.

2 Collaboration with social services is essential where there are issues of child protection.

3 On occasions it will be appropriate for joint assessments and intervention to be carried out.

4 The speech and language therapist is responsible for ensuring that colleagues are fully informed regarding communication difficulties and for offering appropriate training and education for other professionals.

5 Due to the range of speech and language difficulties with which the child/adolescent may present, close contact and liaison with speech and language therapy colleagues in general and specialist paediatrics will be essential.

6 The preparation of reports, case notes and letters should follow general guidelines, although particular care should be taken to consider the potentially sensitive nature of some of the information included in such written material.

Skill Mix:

Speech and language therapists with specific responsibilities working within this client group must have had a period of clinical practice at a post-graduate level, working with a general paediatric population.

Speech and language therapists with specific responsibilities are required to have undertaken post-graduate education in related subjects such as: emotional, behavioural and psychiatric conditions of childhood, psychotherapeutic techniques, counselling, child protection and the management of challenging behaviour.

Speech and language therapists with specific responsibilities are advised to belong to the

College Specific Interest Groups for emotional and behavioural problems in children and adolescents.

Regular supervision is essential.

Speech and language therapists not fulfilling the criteria detailed above must work with the support of specialist colleagues. Their advice and support should be sought on appropriate assessment procedures and programme planning.

Assistants:

Their role is likely to be confined to the preparation of rooms and equipment for therapy, supervised group therapy and general administrative duties.

See guidelines on skill mix (Chapter 9).

Resource Requirements:

See general guidelines for accommodation and equipment (Chapter 8).

Personal Safety:

See general guidelines for personal safety (Chapter 8).

SPEECH AND LANGUAGE THERAPY IN A MULTI-CULTURAL MULTI-RACIAL SOCIETY

Definition/Description of Client Group:

The College acknowledges the right of every individual to have access to an appropriate speech and language therapy service for his/her identified needs. The presence of a second language, or a first language other than English, does not alter this philosophy.

Aims/Principles of Service Delivery:

1 The profession recognises that bilingualism in a child or adult is an advantage.

2 The speech and language therapist will make every effort to assess in both (all) languages to facilitate differential diagnosis.

3 Therapy will be offered in the language of choice after full discussion with client and carer.

4 Clients and carers should never be advised to give up speaking in their home language as a means of supporting language progress in English.

5 Children with difficulty learning English will be supported through education services.

6 Children with language learning difficulties in both (all) languages will be supported by the speech and language therapy service.

Referral:

1 **An open referral system will operate.**

2 Information on referral and assessment will be available in the language of choice.

Assessment:

1 Every effort will be made to clarify whether language learning difficulties are influencing English only or both (all) languages.

2 Appropriate language assessment material should be available in the required languages. This will encompass phonology, vocabulary, syntax and fluency.

3 As language assessments do not readily translate from one language to another due to cultural bias, they should be used as part of a qualitative assessment.

4 Every effort will be made to obtain appropriate information on the patterns of language used by the client and carers.

Intervention:

1 The speech and language therapy team must aim to offer clients from ethnic and linguistic minorities equal access and an equal quality service.

2 The team needs to be aware of the implications for assessment and intervention in situations where there is no bilingual worker available in the client's home language.

3 The speech and language therapist must ensure that intervention programmes are carried over into all contexts.

Discharge:

1 **The decision to discharge will be made in full consultation with the client and carers.**

2 The procedure for re-referral will be explained.

Interface/liaison with Other Professionals:

1 It is essential that a bilingual professional, para-professional, co-worker or translator in the client's home language is involved.

2 **All the relevant professionals will be kept informed, e.g. general practitioner, nursery, school staff, and will be involved in the intervention where appropriate.**

Skill Mix:

The College recognises the need for appropriately skilled speech and language therapists to assess and manage the client's disorder, taking into account the sociolinguistic influence on language and communication.

Appropriately trained co-workers, bilingual speech and language therapists, interpreters or translators need to be involved.

Speech and language therapists with specific responsibilities for working with ethnic minority groups need to have undertaken courses related to cultural and linguistic diversity.

Speech and language therapists with specific responsibilities for working with ethnic minority groups should be members of the College Specific Interest Group(s) in Bilingualism.

See guidelines on skill mix (Chapter 9).

Resource requirements:

The College recognises that providing professionals, para-professionals or co-workers in every language may not be possible. However, speech and language therapy departments need to be working towards equal opportunities for all clients.

Further investigation of the range of cultural and linguistic features present in the population served by speech and language therapists would contribute to the development of more appropriate services on a national basis.

See general guidelines for accommodation and equipment (Chapter 8).

4

PRESENTING
DISORDERS

*T*his chapter describes the model of care offered by speech and language therapists for a range of communication and swallowing disorders.

The contents serve to provide 'guidelines' to good practice with any one disorder. A number of points have been highlighted and form 'standards' of good practice. These standards may be taken as indicators of good practice on a wider basis. They may be of particular interest to purchasing authorities and speech and language therapists engaged in drawing up quality indicators for service specifications.

ACQUIRED CHILDHOOD APHASIA

Definition/Description of Client Group:

Acquired childhood aphasia is a language disorder secondary to cerebral dysfunction in childhood appearing after a period of normal language development. The cerebral dysfunction may be:

1   the result of a focal lesion of one of the cerebral hemispheres or other area primary for language processing;

2   the result of a diffuse lesion of the central nervous system above the level of the brain stem secondary to closed or open head injury or cerebral infection (viral or bacterial);

3   of unknown aetiology, as in the Landau Kleffner syndrome.

4   The cerebral dysfunction may also be a temporary phenomenon following a seizure.

For this definition, a language disorder is defined as a language profile which deviates from the normally expected profile of the child's peers in one or more areas, i.e. phonology, grammar, semantics, pragmatics, such that the child is disadvantaged in relation to their communication potential.

Aims/Principles of Service Delivery:

1   The speech and language therapist recognises that the child with acquired childhood aphasia is entering the social and educational context at a disadvantage due to the loss of previously held skills and abilities.

2   The speech and language therapist should recognise that whilst the usually held model of ongoing development throughout childhood is still pertinent to this group, it must be viewed against a background of specific neural damage leading to significant deficits, which may make a long-term contribution to a lack of progress in specific areas.

3   The speech and language therapist recognises that the complex nature of neural damage in childhood means that these children's needs are best served in a multi-disciplinary setting.

4   The speech and language therapist recognises that the rate of recovery of a child with acquired childhood aphasia will vary depending on both the severity of the initial damage and the stage of recovery the child has reached. Aims and objectives will require constant review, and ongoing

longitudinal assessment will be vital for appropriate placement.

5 The speech and language therapist recognises that whilst the child may make a remarkable amount of recovery, present knowledge does not allow us to believe that complete long-term recovery to previously held levels is likely to be available for the majority.

6 The speech and language therapist must continue to be aware of current research developments in this field and seek to relate these to her/his practice.

7 The speech and language therapist recognises that the child with acquired childhood aphasia is a potentially different child to the one the carer has always known and should seek to support and encourage appropriate communication within the carer setting.

Referral:

1 **Medical information relating to the child will be ascertained prior to intervention.**

2 **The previous developmental history and educational attainment will be ascertained prior to intervention.**

3 The change in situation since the onset of the disorder should be known.

4 If the referral is taken from another speech and language therapist the previous speech and language therapy history should be ascertained prior to intervention.

5 **When replying to a referral the speech and language therapist will communicate with all members of the multi-disciplinary team: educational, social, medical, therapeutic, psychological, etc.**

6 The speech and language therapist should aim towards developing a comprehensive referral system for all children with complex brain injury.

Assessment:

1 Few specific assessment techniques are available for this client group and the speech and language therapist should seek to inform herself/himself about the use of the most appropriate assessments for the child's age, background and needs.

2 The speech and language therapist should be aware of the complex association of motor, cognitive, perceptual, emotional and communication problems which can arise from brain injury in childhood.

3 The speech and language therapist should be aware of the changing nature of these deficits both during the initial stages of recovery, where improvements may be rapid, and in the longer term, when the child's progress may have reached a plateau.

4 The uncommon nature and complex range of these children's problems may mean that the speech and language therapist may need to refer to a more specialist speech and language therapist for advice during any stage of the management of the child.

5 The speech and language therapist should remember the importance of an appropriate longitudinal re-assessment protocol to map change either as a result of spontaneous recovery or as a response to intervention, such that the procedure may be repeatable as necessary and ensure that assessments relevant to this are utilised.

6 The speech and language therapist should seek to establish a comprehensive profile of the child's language skills in a wide range of situations both formal and informal, including observations of the child in his/her environment and carer setting.

7 Areas for assessment may include:

■ auditory-verbal comprehension;

■ word-finding problems;

■ the presence of jargon aphasia, the presence of phonemic and semantic paraphasias, and the presence of errors including perseveration and non-verbal communication.

8 Timing of assessment:
During the first three months of recovery, assessment should be continuous. During the remainder of the first year of recovery, assessments should be carried out regularly and at least every three months. After the first year of recovery, long-term assessment plans should be carried out between six months and annually until the child leaves school or when recovery is thought to have maximised. Research suggests that a few severely impaired children can show marked change in the long-term, therefore a speech and language therapist needs to be available to identify and document this change as appropriate.

Intervention:

1 **At all stages the speech and language therapist should function as a member of a multi-disciplinary team.**

2 At all stages the speech and language therapist, whilst being aware of the child's deficits, should seek to maximise the child's communication skills by working through the child's strengths in an atmosphere of success.

3 The speech and language therapist should avoid unnecessary, prolonged and ineffective strategies which concentrate on the child's deficits such that the child's experience of failure is reinforced.

4 During the acute stage the therapist should concentrate on assessing the direction of change in communication skills and where possible, build on residual skills, encouraging the child to widen his/her range of communicative acts.

5 During the period of rehabilitation the speech and language therapist should be aware of the range of contexts in which therapy needs to be presented in order to achieve a well-balanced, diverse and relevant programme.

6 The speech and language therapist should take account of the long-term residual problems, which may be at a high level and which require practical and functionally based therapy.

7 These children usually have complex educational needs which change during the course of recovery. The speech and language therapist should seek to represent the child's changing communication needs

in the educational context and work within this team.

8 The speech and language therapist should be aware that the child's communication needs are best served by a broadly functional approach which extends through all the child's learning contexts.

Discharge:

1 The speech and language therapist should remember that the changing nature of this disorder warrants continued long-term review rather than premature discharge.

2 There will be an open re-referral system for those discharged.

Interface/Liaison with Other Professionals:

Due to the range of difficulties faced by children with acquired childhood aphasia, it is imperative that the speech and language therapist liaises closely both at the assessment and intervention stage with all appropriate individuals in the child's life. Any intervention taking place within the acute phase will be fully agreed with the medical team.

Skill Mix:

Speech and language therapists with specific responsibilities in childhood aphasia should:

- have had a period of experience working with both language disorder and physical disability (children);

- be aware of current research in this area;

- be a member of the relevant College Specific Interest Group;

- be prepared to liaise with speech and language therapists and others working in relevant areas including adult aphasia, augmentative communication, special education (language disorder) and physical handicap, as required.

Traditionally, speech and language therapy services to children have concentrated on a developmental model and, where neural damage was evident, have expected to see only one type of deficit. However, neither of these approaches is very relevant for this group and staff may find themselves poorly prepared to deal with these children's needs. A speech and language therapist with specific responsibilities must therefore be available to prepare the necessary programmes for children in this group, although these may be carried out by another member of staff under supervision.

Owing to the rare nature of these problems, a speech and language therapist with specific responsibilities should undertake, at the very least, to document all cases of acquired childhood aphasia which they see and share this information as widely as possible with the College research data base.

The speech and language therapist with specific duties should refer to a speech and language therapist with specific responsibilities in all cases, at least for advice. The speech and language therapist with specific duties should not attempt to undertake the assessment and case planning of these children without such advice.

See guidelines on skill mix (Chapter 9).

Resource Requirements:
See general guidelines for accommodation and equipment (Chapter 8).

ACQUIRED DYSARTHRIA/ ARTICULATION PROBLEMS

Definition/Description of Client Group:

Dysarthria is a speech disorder resulting from the disturbance of neuromuscular control. This is caused by damage to the central or peripheral nervous system, which may result in weakness, slowing, inco-ordination or altered muscle tone, and changes the characteristics of speech produced.

In addition, an acquired articulation disorder may result from maxillo-facial or oral surgery.

Aims/Principles of Service Delivery:

1 To provide a specialist service to clients referred to speech and language therapy at any stage in their medical condition.

2 To facilitate intervention within a multi-disciplinary approach to rehabilitation. This team may include the neurologist, neurosurgeon, ENT/head and neck consultant, radiotherapist, plastic surgeon, oral surgeon, nursing staff, paramedical staff and counsellors.

3 To maximise communication effectiveness, and to advise on the use of augmentative/alternative communication where appropriate.

4 To inform carers and other professionals of the specific difficulties and requirements of this client group.

5 To provide a structured management programme.

Referral:

1 An 'open referral' system operates so that the client may be referred from any source. The therapist will notify the general practitioner (and/or the consultant if appropriate) of the therapist's intentions.

2 In the case of an in-patient, the therapist will always acknowledge the referral in the medical notes and liaise with the medical team prior to carrying out an assessment.

3 In-patients: initial contact will be made with the client within two working days of receipt of referral.

Out-patients: initial appointment will be offered within two weeks of receipt of referral.

Assessment:

1 The speech and language therapist may need to obtain further medical information regarding the disorder, including the prognosis of any medical condition that may be present. The abilities of clients undergoing maxillo-facial or oral surgery may change as healing and recovery processes occur. Assessment is therefore ongoing, and may not be a formalised procedure in terms of content and timing.

2 Assessment may include a formal/informal measurement of :

■ posture;

■ breathing;

■ phonation;

■ rate of speech;

■ resonance;

■ intelligibility;

■ prosody.

A tape/video recording may be made.

3 Assessments should be recorded so that monitoring of progress at re-assessment can be achieved.

4 Assessment/monitoring may continue throughout the client's life, to ensure early identification of potential difficulties.

Intervention:

1 **The assessment results will be communicated to the client, carer, referring agent and other relevant professionals and should be placed in the casenotes.**

Following assessment and, where appropriate, in consultation with the multi-disciplinary team, a management decision will be made. This may include:

- a period of active therapy to improve deficits identified at the assessment stage, or maintain identified skills;

- discussion of the communication deficit and rationale for intervention in relation to the underlying medical condition/diagnosis;

- review appointments for monitoring progress.

2 At the end of a course of active therapy, the speech and language therapist will decide whether to:

- offer a second course of therapy;

- review the client;

- discharge.

Further courses of therapy may be offered,

depending upon the client's demonstration of progress and need for therapy.

Discharge:

1 **The decision to discharge will be made in full consultation with the client and his/her carer.**

2 The procedure for re-referral will be explained to the client.

Interface/Liaison with Other Professionals:

Depending on the medical status of the client with acquired dysarthria/articulation disorders, a range of professionals may be involved. It is important that the speech and language therapist works in close conjunction with all team members and shares her/his skills with these team members.

Skill Mix:

Speech and language therapists with specific responsibilities working in the field of acquired dysarthria/articulation disorders should:

- have undertaken post-graduate education and training in subjects related to acquired dysarthria/articulation disorders;

- have experience of working as an integral team member with colleagues in the medical/educational fields;

- be a member of an appropriate College Specific Interest Group.

Therapists who are developing clinical skills in this area are advised to seek advice, support and supervision from more experienced colleagues, to ensure that an appropriate therapeutic management plan is in place.

See guidelines on skill mix (Chapter 9).

Resource Requirements:

See general guidelines for accommodation and equipment (Chapter 8).

The speech and language therapist should have access to the following:

- nasal anemometry;

- x-ray facilities;

- voice analysis equipment;

- oral prosthetics service.

ACQUIRED LANGUAGE DISORDER/ADULT APHASIA

Definition/Description of Client Group:

Acquired aphasia is a language disorder resulting from localised neurological damage. It may present the client with difficulties in the perception, recognition, comprehension and expression of language through both the verbal and/or written modalities.

While most individuals with aphasia are adults, childhood aphasias do occur.

In such instances there is a complex interaction between the acquired problem and the processes of the developing language system (see section on Acquired Childhood Aphasia).

'Aphasia' indicates a total loss of language. 'Dysphasia' refers to a partial loss of language. The terms are often used interchangeably and will be used as such in this chapter.

Aims/Principles of Service Delivery:

1 Aphasia affects interpersonal relationships, social and economic status as well as more intrinsic characteristics such as confidence and self-esteem. In the personal cost of aphasia, one client cannot be rated against another.

2 All people with aphasia should have an equal access to the service, regardless of age, the time post-onset, severity of disorder, geographical location, economic status, linguistic and cultural background.

3 The speech and language therapist should aim to provide a service which meets the communicative and interpersonal needs arising from aphasia.

4 The speech and language therapist should aim to provide rehabilitation which, as far as possible, enables people with aphasia to regain communicative autonomy and self-determination, and achieve a fulfilling lifestyle.

5 The speech and language therapist should aim to respond rapidly to the referral of people with aphasia and to ensure that all people with aphasia and their carers are aware of the service and have access to it.

6 The speech and language therapist should aim to offer a variety of therapy approaches and regimes. These might include:

- remediation aimed at reducing the linguistic impairment;

- remediation aimed at reducing the communicative disability;

- remediation aimed at alleviating the emotional and psychological problems associated with aphasia;

- facilitation of retained communicative abilities.

7 The speech and language therapist should aim to educate professionals, employers and others in positions of social significance in order to increase their understanding of aphasia.

8 The speech and language therapist should aim to be aware of the global needs of the aphasic person (i.e. arising from physical disability, economic hardship, psychological trauma), to conduct appropriate liaison and, where necessary, to refer the client to other professionals and agencies.

9 The speech and language therapist should aim to increase society's understanding of aphasia by promoting awareness of the nature of the impairment and its disabling effects.

Referral:

1 **The service will operate a policy of open referral.**

2 **All locations will have a policy regarding referrals which will specify response times,** **acknowledgement procedures and which will set down the decision-making process following referral.** The policy should be freely available to all those interested in the service, including referrers, clients and their carers. This information should include an indication of whether or not a limit is set by individual departments on the maximum number of sessions per client.

3 **In-patient referrals will be seen within two working days of receipt of referral. Out-patients will be seen within two weeks of receipt of referral.**

4 The service as a whole should collate referral data to provide epidemiological information to assist in service planning.

5 The service manager should regularly evaluate the impact of providing services for other care groups (for example people with dysphagia) on the aphasia service, in order to ensure the needs of aphasic people are met and to undertake appropriate planning of resources.

Assessment:

1 In order to take the most appropriate course of action for each new aphasic client, the speech and language therapist approaches intervention as a series of stages.

2 At the first stage the speech and language therapist acknowledges that appropriate therapy cannot be instituted until the nature of the language impairment is understood. However, the speech and language therapist need not demonstrate beyond all doubt where the language system has broken down and why. What is required is a hypothesis about the nature of the client's problem. This must be sufficiently detailed

to guide therapy. Therapy becomes the means for testing the hypothesis.

3 Formulation of the hypothesis should be driven by careful observation of the client and include attention to the client's own insights regarding his/her language difficulties.

4 The approach/materials used in assessment must allow for re-assessment in order to monitor progress.

5 Speech and language therapists should be familiar with appropriate standardised assessment procedures. However, assessment procedures should be designed to test the hypothesis made through observation. Selection should not be based simply on availability of or familiarity with particular standardised tests. Speech and language therapists should be aware that:

■ no battery of tests can be exhaustive in determining the nature of deficits;

■ there may as yet be no suitable standardised assessments for testing each new hypothesis.

6 Speech and language therapists should remember that investigation of the communication breakdown is an integral part of therapy. Consideration of this question should therefore involve a similar process of observation, enquiry and hypothesis testing.

7 Observation of how clients communicate despite their disorder is essential. This information should be enhanced by discussing this aspect with carers.

Such observation and enquiry should lead to information regarding:

■ the limits placed on communication for individuals by their language impairment;

■ communication strategies used to overcome these limits which might be enhanced and extended in therapy;

■ ways in which the communicative environment may be usefully adapted to meet the needs of the person with aphasia.

8 Speech and language therapists should be familiar with appropriate methods of examining functional communication, e.g. the use of formalised procedures and the analysis of natural conversation.

9 It is important that the speech and language therapist recognises the potential effects of the language deficit on clients' thinking. In view of the lack of information in this area, therapists are advised not to make assumptions about the integrity of clients' underlying thought processes but to consider whether there are any implications for management.

10 Speech and language therapists must consider the effects of the communication disability on the lives of clients and their carers. This issue can only be addressed with the full involvement of the client and those around him/her. However, it must be recognised that assessment of and provision of therapy for problems in relationships demands the highest level of skilled and carefully trained handling. It is therefore vital that speech and language therapists who are not trained in counselling recognise their

limitations and make appropriate onward referrals. Speech and language therapists should inform those to whom referral is made about the nature of aphasia, and the particular communicative needs and abilities of the person referred.

11 All of the issues discussed separately above have to be considered together when planning intervention. Whilst it could be argued that the language impairment is of paramount importance, and the area in which the speech and language therapist's greatest skills should lie, intervention at that level cannot be instituted at the expense of other parameters if it is to be successful.

Summary of Assessment:

1 Assessment should be undertaken in order to:

- direct the focus of therapy;

- provide information which will enable the speech and language therapist to advise the clients and carers about the nature of the communicative impairment and disability and ways of coping with these;

- provide a baseline of skills against which the effects of therapy can be measured.

2 Assessment takes place throughout a speech and language therapist's contact with a client. Observations during therapy provide continuing information about the nature of the linguistic disability.

3 Decisions about which 'formal assessments' to administer should be based on the hypotheses made in observation.

Assessments should only be administered if the speech and language therapist believes they may aid therapeutic decisions.

4 Speech and language therapists should not depend on indiscriminate use of familiar standardised test batteries. The rationale for the use of the test will be recorded in the notes.

5 **A time limit will be set on any 'assessment period'.** Clients should not be subjected to long periods of assessment without good reason before active therapy begins.

6 **Assessment rationale will be explained to the client and carer before assessment begins.**

The results of assessments will be fully discussed with the client and carer.

7 Assessment must include consideration of 'functional' skills and attention to the aphasic person's communicative environment, including factors which may be perceived as barriers to the individual's autonomy.

8 Assessment should also assist the speech and language therapist in deciding whether referral to other agencies is necessary and appropriate.

Intervention:

1 When planning intervention, it is important that the speech and language therapist consults the client, carer and other disciplines about the specific impairments to be addressed, the type of approach to be taken and the measures of change to be used.

2 **The aims of therapy at any particular time must be clear and will be recorded in the client's notes.**

3 A distinction needs to be drawn between the type of approach and the type of task being used. If the therapist has a clear rationale for implementation of a particular approach and views the therapy as a test of that rationale, then the particular tasks chosen should closely relate to the aims of the approach.

4 Speech and language therapists must have available a wide variety of potential approaches to therapy, including awareness of the latest techniques.

Whatever a therapist's particular professional interest or skills, the client's needs demand an eclectic approach in therapy. Speech and language therapists should, therefore, strive to keep informed of developments in the theory and practice of aphasia therapy, and should have access to appropriate training.

5 Therapy should be made available to meet the needs of clients in the acute phase, during prolonged periods of rehabilitation and clients with chronic aphasia as appropriate. This may mean that the focus of the therapy shifts from the linguistic impairment (including functional impairment) to the disabling effects of aphasia as time passes and the needs and circumstances of the aphasic person change.

6 In approaching any therapy, the following steps should be specified:

- select and justify a therapeutic strategy;

- design tasks to implement that strategy;

- form a hierarchy of therapy tasks, with criteria for moving from one step to another;

- design a method of measurement of the extent of the initial problem, the function to be treated and a method of measuring the effects of therapy on that impairment and on other impairments which should or should not be affected by the therapy;

- measure the outcome on functions which have and have not received therapy;

- re-evaluate the appropriateness of both the aims and the therapeutic tasks used in the light of the original hypothesis and record in the case notes.

7 Therapy regimes can take a number of forms, and these should be selected to meet the changing needs of the person with aphasia:

- An aphasia service must be able to offer regimes of intensive therapy. These are considered to be three-four times per week of no less than one hour.

- An aphasia service should be able to offer long-term therapy to its clients, that is, therapy which lasts at least six months for selected clients who would benefit from such a regime.

- Aphasia is not a unitary disability. Aphasic people present with very different language needs. To respond to the diversity of problems, the service must be able to offer a variety of regimes, including group and individual therapy.

- Depending on the social and geographical features of an area, the service should be able to offer therapy in a variety of locations, including domiciliary, community and hospital-based settings. Flexibility of therapy location becomes increasingly important as individuals spend less time in hospital following stroke.

- **A therapy regime will be agreed and discussed with the client. The agreement will specify the duration of therapy, key therapy aims and evaluation methods.**

8   Speech and language therapists need to consider their role in managing aphasic caseloads effectively in order to provide an effective therapeutic service.

9   Therapists must consider the client's needs beyond the specific goals of language therapy. This involves discussion with all those concerned with the client. It is incumbent on therapists to ensure that their explanations are expressed clearly. The referring agency must also be kept informed.

10 Speech and language therapists should be aware of other treatments being given to the client and of the aims of these treatments.

11 Speech and language therapists should be aware of the implications for a client's employment and confer with the appropriate agency.

12 An understanding should be reached with the client and carer that time limits have been set for therapy. This, however, entails a responsibility on the speech and language therapist to ensure that management of the caseload is flexible enough to take account of the needs of each client, including the need to be able to give intensive therapy when indicated. Greater flexibility is needed in planning caseloads so that the frequency of therapy can be geared to the client's individual needs at a particular point in time.

Intensive therapy may not be suitable in the initial stage, when some clients are least able to benefit and when counselling and support may be more important. However, at a later date therapy may be more beneficial if intensive.

The frequency of specific therapy and the involvement of volunteer help may vary in relation to which particular aspects of the disorder are receiving attention.

13 Therapists should ensure that clients, their carers and friends are aware of the existence of voluntary and charitable organisations which represent and support people with aphasia. They should facilitate contact with these organisations if required.

14 A variety of support mechanisms should form an intrinsic part of any aphasia service. Resources on offer to clients and their carers might include carer support groups, social groups and counselling groups.

Discharge:

1   **Clients will be made aware of the expected duration of speech and language therapy at the onset of each therapy period.** Discharge planning is therefore an integral part of therapy planning.

2 Termination of therapy should follow an analysis of the effects of therapy and a discussion of those effects with the client and carer, where appropriate.

3 A system for reviewing clients discharged form active therapy should be in existence. It is possible that these clients might benefit from new therapy techniques not previously available.

4 It must be recognised that aphasia is a chronic condition. Good practice therefore will offer people with aphasia long-term support mechanisms. These might include maintenance groups, social support groups and recall periods of maintenance therapy.

Interface/Liaison with Other Professionals:

1 **Information regarding the aphasia service will be made readily available to health service staff, other professionals, local agencies (both voluntary and statutory) and the general public.**

2 There should be appropriate liaison with other members of the health care team, social services and other local agencies, e.g. charities, support groups. The speech and language therapist must be aware of the other treatments being given to the client. Appropriate liaison is essential.

3 Speech and language therapists must be aware of the services available to people with aphasia within both the statutory and voluntary sector.

4 **Procedures will be developed to ensure the immediate and continuing provision of information to clients, carers and staff. This will include information regarding aphasia,** **speech and language therapy and the type and level of service available.**

Skill Mix:

Speech and language therapists with specific responsibilities for aphasia must:

- have at least three years clinical practice working with an aphasia caseload in a range of locations, predominantly with and fully supported by a senior colleague;

- have post-graduate education and training in subjects related to aphasia;

- have experience of working as an integral team member with colleagues in the medical/educational fields;

- act as a resource for colleagues both at a specialist and non-specialist level;

- be a member of the British Aphasiology Society or equivalent;

- be a member of the College Specific Interest Group in Aphasia.

Speech and language therapists with specific duties must have access to supervision from speech and language therapists with specific responsibilities. Supervision should include regular discussion regarding caseload management and therapy plans. The speech and language therapist with specific duties should be able to discuss each client with a colleague with specific responsibilities in order to ensure that an appropriate therapeutic management plan is in place. Assistance in the assessment and intervention planning stages is to be available from a colleague with specific responsibilities. All therapists working in the field of aphasia must have skills in basic counselling and specific skills in counselling those with a communication disability.

Assistants:

Speech and language therapy assistants have a role in the delivery of speech and language therapy services to an aphasic population. This may be in the delivery of therapy tasks under the direct supervision of a qualified therapist; assisting the clinician in the delivery of group therapy for clients; working alone with individuals and small groups carrying out tasks as delegated by the qualified therapist. Assistants may also be used in assisting clients with assignment tasks and community integration.

See guidelines on skill mix (Chapter 9).

Resource Requirements:

See general guidelines for accommodation and equipment (Chapter 8).

DEVELOPMENTAL DYSARTHRIA

Definition/Description of Client Group:

Developmental dysarthria is a disorder manifest from infancy effecting voluntary movement of the oral and pharyngeal structures. It may be associated with a general motor disorder, such as cerebral palsy, or a specific motor disorder, such as muscular dystrophy. It may be associated with other evidence of oral dysfunction, such as dysmorphic features, cranial facial anomalies, disorders of involuntary movements, disorders of motor planning and sensory disorders.

Aims/Principles of Service Delivery:

1 To maximise oral function for eating and drinking.

2 To maximise communicative function of the child presenting with developmental dysarthria.

3 To provide a service from an early age in order to encourage the development of appropriate patterns of eating and speech production in the inter-developmental norms.

4 To encourage and enable carers to participate in the therapeutic process and facilitate communication with the child.

Referral:

1 **Neonates/Premature Infants**
Referrals received regarding infants within this age bracket with a diagnosis of oral motor dysfunction will be seen within twenty four hours of receipt of referral.

2 Infants under one year

In-patients will be seen within forty eight hours of referral. Out-patients: contact will be made within two working days of receipt of referral.

3 All children above the age of one year referred with an oral function disorder associated with an eating difficulty will have an initial contact within five days of receipt of referral.

4 The acknowledgement will be sent/telephoned to the referring agent.

Assessment:

1 The assessment will consist of a group of formal and informal measures and may include the objective analysis of oral function.

2 Where an objective analysis of oral function is indicated, for example, radiographic investigations, the speech and language therapist must liaise closely with the referring agent and the medical team.

3 The assessment procedure will include the observation of the child in a range of situations, including observation of eating and drinking abilities.

4 The speech and language therapist will report the results of the assessment to other professionals involved and to the child's carer, particularly where the assessment results relate to the safety of oral feeding.

5 The speech and language therapist will need to carry out a comprehensive assessment of the other aspects of the child's communication development in relation to the oral function disorder.

6 Onward referral to another agency may be appropriate.

See guidelines for eating and drinking difficulties in children (Chapter 4).

Intervention:

1 The speech and language therapist will be part of a multi-disciplinary team and will communicate all decisions regarding findings and intervention to the team members. This team will include carers.

2 Following the assessment, a management plan will be compiled which will take into account:

■   the assessment findings;

■   the prognosis of the condition;

■   the child's carer circumstances;

■   the child's education or day-care provision.

3 The therapy programme will have the maximum independence of the child as its central aim, especially in relation to eating and drinking abilities.

4 Where daily regular intervention is required, all or part of the therapy programme may be delegated to appropriately trained assistants, family members or carers.

5 Where long-term intervention is required, protocol to evaluate its effectiveness must be

agreed by all those members involved in the implementation of the programme.

6   The speech and language therapist will regularly review the programme goals in conjunction with the multi-disciplinary team.

7   The therapy task will at times take place within a functional framework in order to maximise carryover and facilitate immediate rewards for the child's eating, drinking or communicative attempts.

8   Where appropriate, the speech and language therapist may make arrangements for the assessment and provision of an augmentative/alternative aid to speech, eating or drinking. This may involve an onward referral to a specialist centre for augmentative/alternative communication aids to eating and drinking.

Discharge:

1   Any young child with an oral motor dysfunction should not be discharged until it is clear that the child is not going to benefit from speech and language therapy input.

Where there exists implications for the child's education, the speech and language therapist has an important role to play in assisting the education authorities in their decisions regarding placement and/or support services.

2   The process for re-referral will be made clear to the carers and other professionals concerned.

Interface/Liaison with Other Professionals:

Motor speech disorders and the associated eating/drinking problems are often found in children presenting with complex developmental conditions. The speech and language therapist must therefore be familiar with the associated disorders, and seek to work with the other professionals and carers at each stage of the therapeutic process.

Skill Mix:

Speech and language therapists with specific responsibilities in oral motor dysfunction:

- should have had relevant post-graduate experience of not less than three years and have attended relevant post-graduate courses/training events;

- should attend update courses on a regular basis;

- should act as a resource for non-specialist speech and language therapists treating children with this disorder;

- should be a member of a relevant College Specific Interest Group.

Speech and language therapists with specific duties working with this client group as part of a general caseload must have access to the support and guidance of colleagues with specific responsibilities to aid them in planning an assessment and translating the assessment findings into a management plan.

Assistants:

Speech and language therapy assistants have a role to play in the delivery of therapy to this client group.

The assistant may be involved in the delivery of programmes directed at improving oral motor skills for speech, feeding/eating programmes and developing the child's use of augmentative/alternative communication aids. In all cases the assistant should receive adequate training and supervision on a regular basis.

The assistant should not be left alone to feed a child until the speech and language therapist is completely satisfied that an appropriate level of skill has been achieved. The child's safety is at all times paramount.

Supervision must take place on a regular basis, not less than weekly for an oral skills programme and more regularly in the case of an eating programme. A member of staff who is able to take the appropriate action should a medical emergency occur must be present at all times.

Assistants working with this client group have a valuable role to play in the preparation of equipment, assisting in group therapy and in general administrative tasks.

See guidelines on skill mix. (Chapter 9)

Resource Requirements:

A range of formal and informal test materials should be available.

Access to a range of augmentative/alternative communication aids either locally or through a specialist centre is necessary in addition to a local stock of eating and drinking aids.

See general guidelines for accommodation and equipment. (Chapter 8)

DEVELOPMENTAL SPEECH AND LANGUAGE DISORDERS

Definition/Description of Client Group:

Developmental speech and language disorders refer to any disorder in children who are not acquiring spoken and/or written language skills in accordance with an age appropriate developmental pattern. This will include children with difficulties in comprehension and production of language, including pragmatic aspects of language, at one or more levels. There may or may not be an identifiable aetiology.

Terms commonly used for this client group include specific language disorder/delay, phonological disorder/delay, phonetic disorder/delay, developmental dyspraxia and specific reading and writing difficulties (see section on Written Language Disorders). It should be noted that 'delay' is generally applied to those presenting speech and language difficulties where skills are being acquired in accordance with the known developmental sequence, whereas 'disorder' is generally applied to those presenting speech and language difficulties where skills are not being acquired in accordance with the known developmental sequence. In addition, the terms disability, dysfunction and deviance are all commonly used.

However, diagnostic terms are not always mutually exclusive. Differential diagnosis can be a difficult task. The child who presents with, for example, a phonological disorder, may or may not present with other language difficulties. It may be that disordered phonology causes further language difficulties. For example, in order to convey meaning, the child may choose to use a syntactically/semantically inappropriate structure that will reliably inform the listener, with the result that normal language development may be inhibited and inappropriate language skills rehearsed.

Aims/Principles of Service Delivery:

1 To promote the child's communication skills in order that he/she may achieve optimally:

- in satisfying the child's/others' needs and desires;

- in exchanging information;

- in using language creatively;

- in initiating and maintaining social interaction;

- in learning and in participating in education.

2 To use the child's strengths in communication in order to minimise his/her weaknesses; to work with the child from a baseline of success and to reinforce positively as skills develop.

3 To provide the child with strategies for communication including augmentative communication skills and problem-solving skills for use in situations where he/she is unable to understand or is not understood.

4 To recognise the effects of speech and language difficulties on other areas of development and vice versa. In particular, to acknowledge the effects of speech and

language difficulties on language and on the formation and maintenance of social relationships.

5 To work through the child's carer/nursery staff/education staff in order that a functional approach to intervention may be achieved, ensuring carryover and generalisation into the child's meaningful communication environment.

6 To ensure that, as far as is possible and appropriate, intervention is part of a total programme for the child.

7 To ensure that any intervention programme is seen as the joint responsibility of all parties involved in the child's speech and language development.

8 To access further referral as appropriate, either for specific investigation, e.g. audiology, or for a further opinion regarding speech and language skills.

9 To acknowledge that, where intervention is indicated, it should be offered so that it is both minimal in duration and optimally effective.

10 To contribute to the achievement of educational placement/needs, where appropriate.

11 To access the National Curriculum for the school-age child.

Referral:

1 **A clear referral procedure will be available to potential referring agents.**

2 **An open referral system will operate.**

3 Referrals will be allocated in terms of the most appropriate therapist, with regard to specific responsibilities/duties and location.

4 **Agreement of carer/child will be gained before making referral with due regard to 'consent to treat' as outlined in the Children Act.**

5 Referring agents will be informed as to the type of referral suitable for speech and language therapy.

Assessment:

1 As language skills are interdependent, the child's communicative ability must be considered holistically. For example, it is necessary to assess the receptive skills of a child who presents with any speech and language difficulty, not only to complete a full assessment and facilitate diagnosis and prognosis, but also to ascertain language levels that may be used during the therapeutic process.

2 Assessment will follow similar outline procedures for all children presenting with developmental speech and language difficulties.

3 Assessment must be seen as an ongoing process throughout intervention in order that aims and objectives can be modified to meet the child's needs.

4 Assessment should lead to a differential diagnosis of the child's difficulties in order that an appropriate management decision can be made. This can be difficult with very young children, when ongoing assessment may lead to revised diagnoses during the child's development.

5 Assessment will include taking and recording a full case history, including details of audiological assessment and developmental screening. It must be noted that, when taking the history of the child's pre-verbal speech and language development, the rate of development is particularly significant.

6 Formal and informal assessment of communication skills will include, where appropriate:

■ play;

■ social skills;

■ communication need;

■ communication intent;

■ communication method;

■ verbal comprehension;

■ expressive language:

   - form

   - content

   - use;

■ written comprehension;

■ written expression;

■ oral examination;

■ phonology:

   - assessment of phonological system

   - analysis of phonological processes

- assessment of intelligibility

- assessment of self-monitoring skills;

■ articulation:

- assessment of phonetic system

- analysis of phonetic errors

- assessment of intelligibility

- assessment of self-monitoring skills;

■ voice;

■ fluency;

■ prosody;

■ auditory skills;

■ gross and fine motor skills;

■ non-verbal skills.

7 Information on any of the above areas must include observations from the carer/child and other professionals as well as the speech and language therapist's own evaluation.

8 Assessments should reflect the child's functioning in his/her own communication environment, and therefore may include observations in the home, nursery, school and clinic.

9 Assessment should reflect the child's communication in a variety of situations and therefore should include observations of the child's communication with the carer, siblings, peers and both familiar and unfamiliar adults. Assessment should also include observations of the child on both a group and individual basis.

10 Assessment will include the findings of other professionals involved with the child in relation to other areas of functioning as well as speech and language skills.

11 Assessment may include joint/multi/ inter-disciplinary assessment with other professionals, which may be through a joint visit or by meetings/liaison.

12 Assessment will include looking at the need for, appropriateness of and timing of intervention, which will be established in consultation with the carer, child and other professionals. It should include assessment of the child's need, readiness and ability to change.

13 Assessment may involve specialist advice, which may be through the use of speech and language therapists with specific responsibilities from within the employing authority, involvement of other professionals, and referral to centres of specialism in specific clinical fields. Assessment may require the involvement of speech and language therapists with specific responsibilities from outside the employing authority. These additional services should be introduced in consultation with carers and other professionals, and it is to be noted that this may involve an extra-contractual referral (see the section on Specialist Outpatient Centres in Chapter 2).

14 **Assessment must include reporting and discussing findings with the carer and other professionals, as well as with the child, where appropriate. This should include the formation of a management plan detailing the aims and objectives of a period of intervention.**

Intervention:

1 Intervention should be planned in conjunction with the child/carer and other professionals as appropriate and should be based upon assessment findings.

2 Intervention may be carried out by the therapist directly or indirectly; it may also be facilitated by the therapist and carried out by, for example, the carer. Intervention is the joint responsibility of therapist, child, carer and/or other professionals.

3 Intervention will include the setting of specific aims/goals, which should be recorded as expected outcomes and evaluated as actual outcomes with a specified timescale. Intervention should be modified accordingly.

4 During the process of intervention there must be constant reassessment of the child's performance and need for intervention.

5 Intervention may take the form of individual, paired or group work as appropriate.

6 An episode of intervention must be agreed with the carer and other professionals as appropriate. For those professionals involved with the child but not directly involved in the child's speech and language programme, the therapist should attempt to ensure that they are kept fully informed.

7 The agreement between the therapist and carer/other professionals should outline the location of the contact, the frequency of the contact, the nature of the contact and the respective responsibilities of those involved.

8 Intervention must always include consideration of the child's need to change, readiness to change and ability to change.

9 As part of intervention, consideration must be given to the relevance and appropriateness of materials.

10 As part of intervention, consideration must be given to the child's non-linguistic needs/concerns.

11 Intervention should aim to work from a basis of success, using the child's strengths to counteract weaknesses.

12 Intervention should focus on those areas of speech and language performance in which the child is most likely to effect change and where such change would provide the maximum results in terms of overall communicative competence.

13 Intervention should address the child's total communication needs and may involve the use of support systems e.g. sign, colour coding.

14 Intervention must work towards offering the child strategies, so that he/she is empowered to manage his/her communication difficulties effectively. This may involve educating the carer/other professionals of such strategies locally within the child's functional communication setting.

15 Intervention may involve the child in discussion of his/her difficulties and the effect of communication impairment. For example, as a child's sound system changes, he/she may continue to perceive that his/her system demonstrates errors that no longer exist, and whilst this may be due partly to poor self-monitoring, it may also be due to negative self-imaging.

16 It should also be noted that intervention represents change and the risk of change should be acknowledged. For example, the child who presents with a speech and language difficulty relating to production may feel safe with his/her production/realisations, despite frustration, embarrassment etc., because the child is confident about the level of intelligibility. During intervention the child may feel anxious that intelligibility could lessen, but equally he/she may become anxious that if intelligibility increases, other expectations and demands will be made upon him/her.

17 Intervention within a school setting may include the provision of a written programme outlining areas of strengths and weaknesses as well as specific strategies or ideas for intervention. This should be planned jointly with education staff to fit in with the child's overall educational programme and address educational issues, including access to the National Curriculum, where appropriate.

18 Intervention should include the provision of in-service training to other professionals involved with the child on both a formal and informal basis.

Discharge:

1 The client may be discharged at any point following referral, subsequent to a case management decision to do so. Normally, the decision to discharge will be taken by the therapist responsible for the client's care in the light of progress and/or change in performance, and should always be discussed with clients/carers. The criteria for discharge will be locally agreed and clearly defined.

2 For clients who are discharged for failure to attend, clients/carers will be informed that discharge procedures are to be initiated. A date of discharge will be given.

3 **A discharge report will be written and circulated as appropriate.**

4 **All relevant personnel will be informed of the conclusion of the episode of care, and the reasons for the decision to discharge.**

Interface/Liaison with Other Professionals:

1 Joint assessment, planning and intervention is seen as essential in meeting the needs of the child.

2 Assessment will include non-verbal functioning. This will include the findings of other professionals such as educational psychologists, clinical medical officers and health visitors as appropriate. The therapist should acknowledge the value of discussion with such professionals, in addition to exchanging written information.

3 The programme of intervention may be seen as the joint responsibility of therapists, carer, the child and other professionals, although it will be facilitated by the speech and language therapist.

4 The programme of intervention for the school-aged child will be seen as part of his/her total educational programme, most of which will be determined by other professionals and carers.

5 The programme will be seen as cross-curricular and, therefore, will be relevant to all professionals involved.

6   Speech and language therapy advice will be part of the statementing/recording process for any child with a communication difficulty on whom a statement/record of needs is completed.

Skill Mix:

Children with speech and language delay/disorder may present as part of a specialised and/or general caseload.

Initial presentation will usually be as part of a pre-school/school-age general clinical population and, as such, the child will usually be assessed initially by a speech and language therapist with specific duties. Where this is the case, it is important that the speech and language therapist has access to a speech and language therapist with specific responsibilities, as appropriate. The latter should be available to offer joint assessments and intervention planning.

All speech and language therapists holding a mixed caseload must undertake post-graduate training in order to update themselves on recent research into the identification of developmental speech and language difficulties and intervention programmes.

Speech and language therapists with specific responsibilities:

The speech and language therapist with specific responsibilities will have had a period of experience working with speech and language disordered children for a period of not less than three years.

Speech and language therapists therapist with specific responsibilities must have

attended relevant post-graduate training and education courses pertaining to aspects of speech and language disorder/delay assessment and intervention.

Speech and language therapists with specific responsibilities must act as a point of reference for speech and language therapists with specific duties.

Speech and language therapists with specific responsibilities must keep abreast of current research and literature pertaining to the field and hold membership of relevant College Specific Interest Groups and professional associations e.g. NAPLIC.

Assistants:

Speech and language therapy assistants have an important contribution to make to the management of children with developmental speech and language difficulties. They can be of particular benefit in assisting either with individuals or in group intervention. Assistants appropriately trained with this client group may carry out programmes under the direction of the qualified speech and language therapist. Assistants may also offer support in the preparation of equipment and materials for intervention.

See guidelines on skill mix (Chapter 9).

Resource Requirements:

See general guidelines and standards for accommodation and equipment (Chapter 8).

DYSFLUENCY

Definition/Description of Client Group:

Dysfluency describes a disorder which affects the fluency of speech production. This may also affect the individual's attitude to communication and to themselves. Disorders of fluency are usually characterised by both overt features, e.g. blocking, and covert features, e.g. avoidance behaviours and feelings such as anxiety.

Aims/Principles of Service Delivery:

1 The speech and language therapy service should provide a comprehensive and effective service to pre-school, school-age and adult clients with fluency disorders and associated difficulties.

2 This service should be accessible to clients in a variety of settings.

3 The service should enable the client to manage their dysfluency effectively and communicate more freely.

Referral:

1 **An open referrral system will operate , including self-referrals.**

2 The waiting period between initial referral and assessment should relate to the guidelines agreed by each speech and language therapy department. This should be no more than two months. In the case of children, this should be earlier.

3 Pre-appointment literature may be sent out if appropriate.

Preschool and School aged Children

Assessment of children should include:

1 a full assessment of language, motor skills, fluency across contexts, cognitive skills, word finding difficulties;

2 an assessment of carer-child interaction;

3 interview with carers.

The carer should be given a summary of the interview, a diagnosis and a rationale for the recommended intervention programme.

Referral on to another agency may be appropriate at the assessment stage.

For the school-aged child, additional information should be obtained on the child's attitude towards school, home, peers and friends.

Intervention:

1 Intervention may include the following:

■ support and advice to the nursery, school and carer;

■ interaction therapy for carer and child, either individually or in groups;

■ symptomatic therapy, individually or in groups;

■ language or phonological remediation;

■ carer counselling, individually or in groups;

■ monitoring for up to two years;

■ referral to other professionals.

2 The decision regarding the structure and type of therapy should be based on the assessment results.

3 Clearly identifiable aims of therapy should be drawn up in the case notes.

4 Therapy activities should be recorded.

5 Periodic re-assessment and modification of therapy aims may take place during the course of intervention.

6 Reports should be written and correspondence maintained with all relevant professionals/agencies.

Adolescents and Young Adults

Assessment of adolescents and young adults should include a detailed case history with information on personal, social and emotional development, as well as educational/work background.

1 Assessment should include an analysis of:

- linguistic skills;

- fluency/dysfluency;

- communication skills/social skills;

- attitude, personality, insight;

- motivation to change, client's perception of problem and expectations of therapy;

- carer-client interaction where appropriate.

2 Assessments should include both formal and informal procedures.

3 Pertinent information from other sources should be collected and referrals to other agencies should be made as appropriate.

4 **Clients should be presented with a summary of the assessments, a diagnosis and a rationale for the therapy programme recommended.**

Intervention

1 Intervention may be provided on an individual or group basis. It may be intensive or non-intensive. It may be provided during working hours, evenings or at weekends, and may be residential or non-residential, as appropriate.

2 Intervention may include:

- symptomatic therapy programme;

- attitude change, anxiety reduction, cognitive restructuring;

- social skills, assertiveness training;

- information and advice to school and carer;

- video feedback and role-play.

3 An intervention programme may include any combination of the above. It should be based on the results of assessment and take into account the specific needs and changes associated with the adolescent/young adult.

4 Clearly identifiable aims of therapy should be agreed with the client and recorded in the case notes.

5 Periodic re-assessment and modification of therapy may take place during the course

of intervention.

6 When regular therapy is no longer deemed necessary, this should be discussed and agreed with the client.

7 The client should be able to contact the therapist for further advice or intervention.

8 Reports should be sent to appropriate professionals/agencies.

Adults

Assessment of adults should include a detailed case history with information on personal, social and emotional status as well as educational/work background.

1 Assessment should include an analysis of:

- linguistic skills;
- fluency/dysfluency;
- communication skills/social skills;
- attitude, personality, insight;
- motivation to change, client's perception of problem and expectations of therapy.

2 Assessments should include both formal and informal procedures.

3 Pertinent information from other sources should be collected and referrals to other agencies should be made, as appropriate.

4 **Clients should be presented with a summary of the assessments, a diagnosis and a rationale for the therapy programme recommended.**

Intervention:

1 Intervention may be provided on an individual or group basis. It may be intensive or non-intensive. It may be provided during working hours, evenings or at weekends, and may be residential or non-residential, as appropriate.

2 Intervention may include:

- symptomatic therapy;
- avoidance reduction,anxiety management;
- psychotherapeutic and counselling approaches;
- social skills training.

3 A therapy programme may include any combination of the above and should be based on the results of the assessment.

4 Clearly identifiable aims of therapy should be agreed with the client and recorded in the case notes.

5 Periodic re-assessment and modification of therapy may take place during the course of intervention.

6 When regular therapy is no longer deemed necessary by both the client and therapist, this should be discussed and the client may be placed on review for an agreed period of time.

7 Should the client wish to contact the therapist for further intervention, advice, counselling, etc., he/she should be able to do so.

8 Following the review period, the client should be re-assessed to establish future management.

Discharge:

1 Discharge from either review or regular therapy should be made by the speech and language therapist following discussion with the client and/or carer and other relevant professionals.

2 Clients and carers should be informed of the procedure for re-referrals.

3 A discharge report should be written.

4 Information on self-help groups should be provided if not already given.

Interface/Liaison with Other Professionals:

1 The speech and language therapist should ensure that advice and/or training is available and provided for any individuals, other professionals and voluntary agencies relevant to an individual client or care group.

2 Local general practitioners should be informed of the services available for those with fluency disorders.

Regional Specialist Centres:

1 Regional specialist centres should be created for the use of clients and therapists. They should be equipped to provide specialist assessment, consultations and a variety of therapeutic techniques and approaches.

2 They should instigate and carry out research in relevant areas of interest, provide training at all levels for other speech and language therapists/students, and act as a resource centre.

Resource Requirements:
Accommodation:

A group room should be available alongside a smaller room to be used as an office and for individual therapy. These rooms should have facilities for one-way viewing and wiring for sound and video recording between them.

Rooms for the therapy given to young children will require two group rooms, one for carers and one for the children, a room for individual consultations and one office. Similarly, a video recording system operating between the rooms will be necessary.

If residential therapy is to be offered, appropriate accommodation should be available which will include facilities for sleeping, dining and recreation as well as therapy.

Skill Mix:

Speech and language therapists with specific responsibilities for services to dysfluent clients should have:

- at least 3 years post-qualification experience;

- post-graduate training acquired by advanced study courses, higher degrees or short courses;

- wide knowledge of and skills in therapeutic intervention for children and/or adults who are dysfluent;

- substantive experience of working with a clinical caseload of fluency disorders.

They should also:

- demonstrate skills and abilities necessary to support and teach other therapists in the management of fluency disorders;

- continue to develop their own skills in the field;

- provide support and training for other professionals;

- be members of an appropriate College Special Interest Group;

- establish links with voluntary groups, e.g. The British Stammering Association.

Assistants:

These should only be deployed under the close supervision of the speech and language therapist and would be involved in the management of equipment and other practical aspects of therapy.

See guidelines on skill mix (Chapter 9).

Resource Requirements:

See general guidelines for accommodation and equipment (Chapter 8).

DYSPHAGIA

Definition/Description of Client Group:

The term dysphagia is used here to describe swallowing disorders which may occur in the oral, pharyngeal and oesophageal stages of deglutition. Subsumed in this definition are problems positioning food in the mouth and in oral movements, including suckling, sucking and mastication. These problems may arise from a wide range of neurological, structural and psychological conditions.

Aims/Principles of Service Delivery:

1 Speech and language therapists possess a sound knowledge of the structure and function of the vocal tract. They are skilled in the assessment and remediation of voice and speech disorders arising from neurological, structural and psychological aetiologies.

2 Knowledge and skills developed in this area have been extended and applied to assessment, intervention and management of clients with dysphagia.

3 The College supports the principle that speech and language therapists as a professional group are ideally equipped to take a central role within the multi-disciplinary team in the assessment and remediation of swallowing disorders.

4 The aims of a dysphagia service are:

- to provide a comprehensive and responsive service to clients presenting with eating and swallowing disorders;

- to facilitate intervention as part of the multi-disciplinary team;

- to become engaged in the planning of services to potential clients presenting with eating and swallowing disorder.

Referral:

1 Written information regarding the service will be made available to health service staff, other professionals, relevant agencies and the general public.

2 Clients with dysphagia will gain access to the service via a written referral from the medical practitioner responsible for their care.

The referral should indicate the reason for referral as being dysphagia. In cases where the speech and language therapist identifies a client suspected of having dysphagia, a written referral will be requested prior to assessment.

3 The service is required to respond promptly to new referrals. In-patient referrals will be seen within two working days of receipt of referral, out-patient referrals within two weeks.

4 On receipt of the referral, close liaison with the relevant medical, paramedical and social care team should be instituted in order to gain the maximum information regarding the client and the presenting disorder.

5 Local policies for clear reporting and documentation procedures will be devised and publicised to all appropriate personnel.

6 If the client is to be seen on a domiciliary basis, the appropriate safety guidelines should be followed and due regard given to the 'duty of care' guidelines given in Chapter 6.

Assessment:

1 Effective assessment, intervention and management of clients with dysphagia require expertise from a number of different professionals. Speech and language therapists working with dysphagic clients should function as members of a multi-disciplinary team.

2 Speech and language therapists need to understand the complementary roles of the professions involved and to respect skill boundaries. Close liaison and joint assessment/intervention will further understanding and benefit the client.

3 Clinical procedures: clinicians will need to examine the nature of the client's difficulty, using a variety of methods, e.g. case history, observational and investigative techniques.

4 Where a client has a tracheostomy and/or is ventilation-dependent, speech and language therapists must be acquainted with the different types of tracheostomy tube and the implications for therapy when dealing with such a client.

5 Where a client is already taking some food/liquid orally, speech and language therapists should observe him/her drinking and/or eating, provided it is not contra-indicated by clinical examination. Where a client is being fed non-orally, the team should be consulted before trial swallows are attempted, and amounts given fully documented.

6 Speech and language therapists should be involved in the decision to investigate dysphagia further using, for example, radiographic techniques.

Speech and language therapists should be aware that the use and interpretation of videofluoroscopic investigation must be undertaken in conjunction with radiology colleagues. Speech and language therapists are advised to consult College guidelines on the use of videofluoroscopy.

7 Speech and language therapists' assessment of a client with dysphagia must be fully documented.

8 **Results of investigations, assessment findings and planned management will be discussed with the client and carer and reported in writing to the team. Medical records will be kept up to date.**

Intervention:

1 Speech and language therapists should plan their management after reporting their assessment findings to the team and in the light of the team's assessment findings.

2 **All forms of intervention will be discussed with the team, client and carer at the outset, and a written careplan formulated.**

3 It is necessary to follow guidelines relating to 'consent to treat'.

4 Where there is broad agreement within the team and the client and carer have given their consent, the planned management can proceed.

Where disagreement exists between the client or carer and the team, every effort should be made to resolve it through discussion. It is important to have their full co-operation if management is to be carried out effectively.

If the client or carer refuse to consent to the planned intervention, this should be documented and communicated to the doctor responsible for the client's care.

Where there is disagreement amongst the team, particularly between the doctor responsible for the client's care and other team members, every effort should be made to resolve it through discussion. Where the doctor chooses a course of action contrary to the advice of the speech and language therapist, and the therapist believes that such an action may cause the client harm, the therapist is advised to record her/his opinion in writing to both the doctor and her/his manager and withdraw involvement.

Following agreement with the medical team, it may still be appropriate for the therapist to be involved with some clients where specific problems have been identified, if she/he feels that specific swallowing exercises without oral intake would be beneficial. In such cases, the therapist should continue to fully document that exercises only are recommended and that she/he does not advocate oral intake. Any such intervention should be regularly reviewed.

5 Where intervention is indicated, speech and language therapists should be fully conversant with the range of therapy approaches available, and clear as to the rationale of the approach adopted.

6 Speech and language therapists may choose to delegate tasks to other team members, the client or carer. The decision to delegate must be clinically motivated.

Written and verbal instructions should be given, accompanied by demonstration and observation of the 'proxy' therapist. Where a specified individual has been trained, they should be identified in the instructions. People acting under therapists' instructions must be given written information regarding the expected outcome of their actions, and what to do if difficulties arise.

Speech and language therapists remain responsible for the 'proxy' intervention if a task is delegated.

7 Clients may need to be reviewed:

■ to ensure progress has been maintained;

■ to evaluate their readiness for intervention;

■ to monitor any change in status.

The frequency of review should be carefully considered. Clients presenting with degenerative disorders may need regular review over many months.

8 **Local dysphagia policies will be formulated and published to all interested parties.**

Discharge:

1 Team members, the client and carer should be involved in the decision to discharge a client.

2 **A written discharge summary will be made available to all appropriate personnel.**

3 The procedure for contact with the speech and language therapy department should be made clear to the client and carer.

Safety Procedures:

1 Speech and language therapy staff are advised to adhere to policy information as described under 'Health and Safety' in Chapter 8.

2 Speech and language therapy staff are advised to follow specific local policies on safety procedures, e.g. relating to cross infection, use of suction.

3 Due consideration should be given to the safety of providing therapy in environments without medical support and this should be discussed fully with appropriate medical staff prior to intervention.

4 Speech and language therapists should consult with a representative of the Radiation Protection Group if they are to be present during investigations involving the use of radiation.

Legal Issues:

1 Legal Liability

The employing authority is vicariously liable for torts committed by its employees within the scope of their duties. Where speech and language therapists are working within the scope of their employment, the employing authority should in all normal circumstances (i.e. provided the charge is not a criminal one) support them should there be litigation. However, the authority's support could depend upon whether the speech and language therapist was deemed to be performing duties covered by the job description.

For this reason, speech and language therapists engaged in dysphagia therapy are advised to ensure that this is appropriately reflected in their job descriptions.

Registered members of the College have professional indemnity insurance that specifically cites dysphagia as an area of work carried out by speech and language therapists.

2 Decision-making

The primary responsibility for taking decisions which could bring about a new 'life-threatening' situation rests with the medical practitioner concerned.

3 Duty of Care

Once a duty of care has commenced, it must be discharged in full. Negligence can be either an act or an omission that causes harm. The speech and language therapist remains responsible at all times for her/his own acts and omissions.

Speech and language therapy intervention with clients with dysphagia may be required at short notice, and therapists should ensure their availability to discharge their duty of care according to local guidelines.

4 Duty to Act

In the event of difficulties arising in a life-threatening situation, a positive duty to act arises and therapists are then required to do whatever would be reasonably expected of them in those circumstances. There are a number of difficulties which may arise during speech and language therapy intervention with clients with dysphagia. These include foreseeable events, e.g. the airway may be compromised through aspiration of food/fluid and co-incidental events, i.e. a client may suffer an unrelated medical emergency such as an epileptic fit.

Speech and language therapists should follow the health and safety guidelines and ensure that they are adequately prepared for such events and familiar with emergency procedures.

Competence:

It is recognised that individual speech and language therapists will have varying degrees of experience in treating clients with dysphagia. Circumstances may arise where the therapist will recognise that an intervention should be carried out by someone with greater experience, or a referral should be made to a specialist from another discipline. Failure to recognise such situations may amount to a breach of the duty of care.

See guidelines on skill mix (Chapter 9).

See 'Code of Ethics and Professional Conduct' and 'Clinical Accountability' (Chapter 1).

Interface/Liaison with Other Professionals:

1 Clear local policies should exist regarding the need for close liaison with medical personnel responsible for the client and with others involved in their management. This should include advice on procedures in the event of disputes about client management.

2 Effective team management requires close liaison and co-operation with other professionals involved. Speech and language therapists need to ensure that they have sufficient time available for attending meetings and discussing client cases.

3 It is important that the client and carer are kept fully informed and involved in decision-making as appropriate.

4 The medical personnel in overall charge

of the client must be kept informed of the aims and methods of dysphagia therapy intervention, the possible risks of intervention and the expected outcome. The medical personnel must give consent to the proposed intervention. Speech and language therapists must work as part of a multi-disciplinary team.

Skill Mix:

The speech and language therapist with specific responsibilities for dysphagia must have attended post-graduate education training at a post-basic level which includes a consideration of:

- normal eating behaviour;

- sensori-motor processes involved in self-feeding;

- neuro-physiological mechanisms of swallowing;

- characteristic symptoms of the common causes of dysphagia and associated eating disorders.

Speech and language therapists with specific responsibilities are also required to have attended more advanced training within one or more of the main groups:

- structural;

- neurological

    - developmental

    - acquired;

- psychological.

Guidance on the content of courses in dysphagia are available from the College (RCSLT, 1995).

The speech and language therapist with specific responsibilities may be required to support and supervise less experienced colleagues and work independently within a multi-disciplinary framework. Due to the developing nature of the service, speech and language therapists with specific responsibilities are advised to participate in collaborative clinical and research work with other professionals, as well as in the development of services.

They will be members of the appropriate College Specific Interest Group.

Speech and language therapists with specific duties engaged in dysphagia management will have attended a post-basic course. Therapists will have the ability to refer to colleagues with specific responsibilities and to secure a specialist opinion when required.

Speech and language therapists not trained to the advanced level described previously must gain their clinical experience in a supervised setting.

Assistants:

Assistants working in a hospital department may undertake the elements of swallowing therapy that the therapist would feel able to delegate to carers. These tasks may include assisting in the programme of thermal-tactile stimulation. The therapist is reminded that responsibility cannot be delegated. It is the speech and language therapist's responsibility to ensure that non-specialist support personnel, be they assistants, nursing staff, volunteers or carers are adequately trained in carrying out the task required and in the necessary safety procedures.

It is advised that the speech and language therapy assistants work under the guidance of a speech and language therapist with specific responsibilities.

See guidelines on skill mix (Chapter 9).

Resource Requirements:

Speech and language therapists should have access to the following:

- videofluoroscopy/video-nasendoscopy;

- thickening agents;

- gauze;

- ice;

- spatulas;

- gloves;

- torch;

- laryngeal mirrors;

- range of food and drink;

- suitable straws;

- suitable spoons.

See general guidelines for accommodation and equipment (Chapter 8).

DYSPHONIA

See guidelines under ENT services in Chapter 3.

EATING AND DRINKING DIFFICULTIES IN CHILDREN

Definition/Description of Client Group:

A service provided to children with eating and drinking difficulties which may be associated with a communication difficulty.

Aims/Principles of Service Delivery:

1   The child and his/her carer should be viewed holistically, their overall needs being taken into equal account.

2   The aim of therapy is to ensure safe nutrition in an atmosphere which promotes the development of skills and positive communication.

3   Eating and drinking should be viewed as a pleasurable event.

4   The service will be provided in the context of a multi-disciplinary team with shared assessments, aims and objectives of therapy.

Referral:

1   **Referral to the speech and language therapist will be made with carer consent, and due regard to the 'consent to treat' guidelines as laid down in the Children Act. (Children Act, 1989).**

2   **A published referral procedure will be**

available to potential referring agents.

Assessment:

1 **The assessment will be undertaken in close collaboration with the child's carer and nursery/school staff, where appropriate.**

2 The assessment procedure will be specific to the age and presenting difficulties of the child. It would normally include:

- case history - this should be obtained from the carer and other professionals involved with the child;

- a general overview of the eating/drinking strengths and needs. This may be obtained through discussion with the carer, observation of the child's interaction with the carer and an observation of eating and drinking skills. An indication of the physical, sensory and communication issues will therefore be gained.;

- specific formal and informal assessments carried out as a follow-up to the initial assessment.

3 Specific questions for the carer may include:

- the child's likes/dislikes - flavours, textures, consistencies, temperatures;

- consistency of food eaten;

- quality of food;

- utensils used;

- easy/difficult textures, consistencies;

- eating/drinking positions;

- length of time taken to eat a meal;

- feeding partners;

- food allergies and sensitivities.

4 The assessment will also take into account:

- the physical environment of the child, e.g. seating and positioning;

- the communication environment, e.g. the extent to which the mealtime situation facilitates normal interaction and increased opportunities for communication between the person being fed and the 'feeder';

- the sensory environment of the child - the consistency, texture, temperature of the foods offered and received.

5 The assessment should be carried out in close conjunction with the physiotherapist, occupational therapist and teaching staff involved with the child. In order to view the child as a whole person, and to avoid considering the eating and drinking skills in isolation, the speech and language therapist must ensure close liaison with the other professionals involved with the child.

6 The assessment should include an investigation of the potentialities of intervention.

7 **The assessment results will be compiled in a written report, including a plan of action. This report will be shared with the carer and other professionals involved with the child.**

Intervention:

1 **A summary of the child's strengths and needs will be recorded following assessment.** This summary will be used as a basis for intervention planning.

2 The intervention programme must take into account the physical, emotional and cognitive skills and needs of the child.

3 **Short and long term goals will be formulated in conjunction with the carer and other professionals involved with the child.**

4 The interrelated factors of posture, tone and movement, feeding movements, sensation and communication will be integrated into the intervention programme.

5 In order to plan effective therapy based upon goals with measurable outcomes, the speech and language therapist must set aside sufficient time for assessment and intervention planning.

6 The intervention programme will be sensitive to the changing needs and skills of the child, and take into account the desires of the child where these can be ascertained.

7 The intervention programme should concentrate upon the skills the child possesses thereby building upon strengths. The programmes should also aim to develop the child's motivation, where appropriate.

Discharge:

1 The team members, the client and carer should be involved in the decision to discharge a client.

2 **A written discharge summary will be made available to all appropriate team members.**

3 **The procedure for contact with the speech and language therapy department will be made clear to the client and carer.**

Interface/Liaison with Other Professionals:

The child presenting with eating and drinking difficulties will usually have associated difficulties of movement and function. It is, therefore, important that the speech and language therapist works in close liaison with colleagues in, for example, physiotherapy, occupational therapy, dietetics and health visiting. When tube feeding or nutritional issues are involved, the speech and language therapist should work in close conjunction with the medical team.

The 'dysphagia' guidelines will be followed where appropriate.

Skill Mix:

Services to children with eating and drinking difficulties should be provided by speech and language therapists with specific responsibilities for working with children with special needs and who have post-graduate education in feeding skills. Undergraduate training alone is not considered to be sufficient for a therapist to undertake the assessment and programme planning of a child with eating and drinking difficulties.

Speech and language therapists with specific duties and assistants should work under the direction of a speech and language therapist with specific responsibilities.

See guidelines on skill mix (Chapter 9).

Resource Requirements:
*See general guidelines for accommodation
and equipment (Chapter 8).*

See guidelines on dysphagia above.

WRITTEN LANGUAGE DISORDERS (DEVELOPMENTAL)

Definition/Description of Client Group:
Developmental written language disorders
refer to difficulties with reading, writing
and spelling in childhood. A child may
be considered to have a specific learning
difficulty (dyslexia) if, in spite of adequate
teaching, the child has specific persistent
difficulties with reading and writing in
comparison with his/her abilities in other
spheres, to a degree sufficient to prevent
school work reflecting his/her true ability
and knowledge.

The child may have presented with
difficulties in acquiring spoken language
and may have received help from a speech
and language therapist.

Aims/Principles of Service Delivery:

1 To provide therapy for clients within a
co-ordinated team approach, referring
clients on to other agencies as appropriate
(e.g. psychologists, occupational therapists,

educational establishments and voluntary
bodies).

2 To provide advice and support for clients
and carers.

3 To plan and develop services with
reference to current knowledge and research
findings and to contribute to the theoretical
and scientific development of this speciality.

Referral:

1 Early identification of the child with
specific reading and writing difficulties
is essential if these children are to receive
appropriate help. The earlier difficulties
are identified the greater the likelihood of
successful remediation.

2 **Referral information will indicate the
role of the speech and language therapist
in providing help with reading and writing
difficulties.**

3 The procedure for re-referral of a child
previously seen with a language
delay/disorder should be made explicit
for all potential referring agents.

4 Referral details should include an up-to-
date audiological assessment.

Assessment:

1 A full case history is taken at the time
of assessment. This will include a full
consideration of early speech and language
difficulties and any resulting therapy.

2 The case history of a dyslexic child
may reveal early, previously undiagnosed
language difficulties that only become of

recognised significance in the light of emerging reading and writing difficulties.

3   The assessment of a language disordered child will address both the written and spoken aspects of language. A holistic approach to the disorder should be adopted throughout.

4   The assessment may include an investigation of issues such as:

- birth history;

- family history;

- co-ordination;

- perceptual skills, e.g. shape perception, size perception, colour perception;

- figure/background relationships;

- visual tracking;

- confusions in speech comprehension;

- phonological difficulties and reversals of word order and sentence order;

- auditory perception;

- concentration and attention;

- formal and informal language assessments appropriate to the child.

Other areas of the child's cognitive, social and emotional development.

5   The assessments should be recorded so that monitoring of progress at re-assessment can be achieved.

6   The assessment will form part of a multi-disciplinary assessment which may include the assessment of the child's skills by, for example, an educational psychologist, occupational therapist, pre-school or school teacher, audiologist, orthoptist and paediatrician.

7   The assessment of a school-age child should take into account the educational context of the child.

8   **A full report detailing the child's reading and writing difficulties and their relationship to spoken language difficulties will be compiled and shared with the carer and all relevant agencies.**

9   The speech and language therapist may refer on to another agency or specialist service at any time in the assessment process.

Intervention:

1   **Carers should be fully involved at every stage of the intervention programme.**

2   The intervention programme will be based upon the assessment findings, and will be defined as a series of goals/steps.

3   The intervention programme will be written following the assessment, will incorporate short- and long-term goals, and be evaluated at regular time intervals.

4   In the therapy given for written language disorder, the therapist must be aware of the relationship between spoken and written language disorder.

5   In the management of all pre-school and school-age children, the therapist should be able to foster skills necessary for the

development of written as well as spoken language.

6 Speech and language therapists' knowledge and skills mean that they are ideally placed to contribute to the management of children with specific learning difficulties/dyslexia. Their training in phonetics is essential to the successful management of a dyslexic child. 'Informed phonetics' and linguistic techniques have been proven to be successful in intervention.

In addition, when providing therapy to children with spoken language disorder, the speech and language therapist will consider pre-requisite written language skills and actual written language skills as part of the overall intervention programme. The discharge of a child who is speaking but not reading or writing, or showing the pre-requisite skills appropriate to age, cannot be seen as a successful discharge.

7 Intervention will be offered on a multi-disciplinary basis, utilising the skills of teaching staff at all times.

8 When planning intervention, the speech and language therapist will be aware of the emotional reaction that the existence of a reading and writing difficulty provokes both in the child and carer. Frustration and evasion are understandable sequelae to the educational problems and daily 'ordeal' of school work for these children.

Discharge:

1 **The discharge will be accompanied by a written report detailing the outcome of therapy and future advice.**

2 Following discharge from speech and language therapy, the therapist may keep in contact with the child on a periodic basis. A yearly report from the child's school until the child is known to be reading, writing and spelling at his/her expected level would provide a valuable contribution to early detection and management of the child's special educational needs.

Interface/Liaison with Other Professionals:

The speech and language therapist will work within a multi-disciplinary team which may include: the teacher, paediatrician, occupational therapist, educational psychologist, audiologist and orthoptist. Due to the multi-faceted needs of the child with reading and writing difficulties (dyslexia), the therapist needs to work in close collaboration with the above-named disciplines in order to ensure a holistic and co-ordinated approach to the child's management. The speech and language therapist will have specific skills to offer these children when therapy is delivered in close conjunction with others, in particular, the teaching staff for a school-aged child.

Skill Mix:

The speech and language therapist with specific responsibilities for written language disorders will have undertaken post-graduate education in the subject. Multi-disciplinary courses for therapists and teachers should be undertaken where possible.

Speech and language therapists with specific duties working with children with written language disorders should have the ability to refer to colleagues with specific responsibilities for advice at both the assessment and intervention stages.

Speech and language therapists' assistants will be of value in assisting with carrying out therapy programmes, and in the preparation of equipment.

See guidelines on skill mix (Chapter 9).

Resource Requirements:

See general guidelines for accommodation and equipment (Chapter 8).

WRITTEN LANGUAGE DISORDERS (ACQUIRED)

Definition/Description of Client Group:

Acquired written language disorders include any acquired reading and/or writing disorder which presents as part of an overall aphasic syndrome. If such a disorder occurs, it may receive attention from the speech and language therapist for a number of reasons. These include using written language as an alternative means of communication, focusing on these areas when they are the predominant feature of the disorder. The disorder may also occur in isolation, e.g. letter-by-letter readers, other specific acquired dyslexias such as phonological, surface and deep dyslexia.

Aims/Principles of Service Delivery:

1 To assess and diagnose the nature of the disorder, and to provide therapy for clients in the light of accurate medical and social history and in relation to the client's needs.

2 To provide therapy for clients within a co-ordinated team approach, referring on to other agencies as appropriate (e.g. psychologists, occupational therapists, voluntary bodies and educational establishments).

3 To recognise the effects upon the communication skills, working life and personal confidence of the client.

4 To be sensitive to the needs of the client presenting with acquired reading and writing disorders as the predominant feature of their disability, where intervention is wholly directed towards reading and writing disorders.

5 To provide advice and support for clients and their carers.

6 To provide relevant others (e.g. professionals, employers) with information that will enhance their understanding of the nature of the disorder and to give ongoing advice as required.

7 To plan and develop services with reference to current knowledge and research findings, and to contribute to the theoretical and scientific development of this speciality.

Referral:

1 **A referral procedure will be available to potential referring agents.**

2 **An open referral system will operate, with the proviso that, in the case of in-patients, discussion is held with the medical team prior to speech and language therapy involvement.**

3 A written acknowledgement will be sent to the referring agent and client on receipt of a referral.

4 The speech and language therapist will require access to the client's medical notes in order to obtain pre-assessment information.

Assessment:

1 A screening assessment takes place upon first contact with the client in order to determine the need for full assessment and intervention. Information about reading and writing skills is also essential for the appropriate planning of aphasia therapy in general (i.e. to determine how far these skills can be incorporated and used in therapy).

2 A full assessment can then be made, to include the following:

- full case history, including the client's assessment of his/her own reading and writing needs;

- informal assessments of reading and writing. These assessments may have been constructed by individual therapists, since few published assessments are currently available.

3 Areas to consider in assessment:

- reading of single letters;

- cross-case matching (i.e. lower case vs. capitals);

- reading aloud vs. silent reading;

- lexical decision tasks (i.e. words vs. non-words);

- comprehension of single words/phrases/sentences/passages;

- word frequency;

- imageability;

- word length;

- word class: regular vs. irregular spelling;

- reading aloud of non-words;

- complexity of grammatical structure.

All of the above may also be applied to the assessment of spelling/writing skills and both areas of assessment should always be related to functional abilities and needs of the client.

4 In addition, assessment of the following should be made:

- the comparison between reading and writing skills;

- visual and visuo-spatial skills;

- perceptual skills;

- cognitive skills;

- use of non-preferred hand.

5 Formal assessments using standardised test materials should be undertaken where possible.

6 Assessments should be recorded so that monitoring of progress at re-assessment can be achieved.

7 Assessment may indicate referral to other agencies. This may be to gain further information relevant to therapy (e.g. psychological assessment for information on cognitive skills) or where the intervention of other agencies may be appropriate (e.g. adult education).

8 Clients should be informed of their assessment results and participate in the decisions regarding their future management.

9 **Following assessment, a programme will be outlined, detailing the aims, objectives and methods of therapy, the planned time for re-assessment and the expected duration of intervention.**

10 The assessment findings and the plan for therapy will be reported back to the referring agent and to others involved in the client's care, as appropriate.

Intervention:

1 An agreement will be reached between the client and the speech and language therapist, regarding aims, expectations and responsibilities during the course of therapy.

2 The nature of the therapy programme will be agreed, i.e. number and frequency of sessions, time for re-assessment/review etc.

3 Liaison with other key people will be maintained as appropriate, e.g. carer, other professionals, volunteers etc.

4 Therapy on an individual and group basis may be appropriate.

5 Therapy may include a functional approach for some clients, with the emphasis upon practising the types of tasks

appropriate to the client concerned. However, therapy may follow a cognitive neuropsychological model, where the specific breakdown in the process of reading and/or writing is considered. Therapy may then involve re-training particular skills and relating these to functionally relevant tasks.

6 **Re-assessment and review of progress will be carried out at the agreed time following a course of therapy.** This will either indicate an appropriate end to therapy or a further course of intervention.

Discharge:

1 The decision to discharge will be discussed and agreed with the client, together with the process for re-referral if necessary.

2 Referral on to other agencies will be considered again at this point, e.g. voluntary bodies, adult literacy classes.

3 **A discharge summary will be sent to the referring agent and others involved in the client's care as appropriate.**

Interface/Liaison with Other Professionals:

The speech and language therapist must be aware of the range of other agencies who may need to be involved in both the assessment and therapy of reading and/or writing disorders, e.g.:

- medical team (for in-patients);

- neurologists;

- psychologists;

- occupational therapists;

- voluntary bodies (e.g. ADA/CHSA scheme);

- educational establishments (e.g. where joint initiatives have been undertaken such as adult literacy groups for dysphasics/adult education classes).

Skill Mix:

See guidelines on Aphasia (Chapter 3).

Assistants:

Assistants are of value to this client group in carrying out specific therapy tasks under the direction of the speech and language therapist. This may be in a group or on an individual basis.

See guidelines on skill mix (Chapter 9).

Volunteers:

It may also be possible to involve volunteer organisations with this client group, either to supplement therapy (e.g. as in some Adult Literacy Schemes for Dysphasics) or to follow on from therapy (e.g. CHSA scheme). Careful monitoring should be maintained where the voluntary input is supplementary and, even where the client is referred on to voluntary bodies, support and input may still be necessary, where possible.

Resource Requirements:

See general guidelines for accommodation and equipment (Chapter 8).

5

RECORDS AND
RECORD KEEPING

PERSONAL HEALTH RECORDS

The term Personal Health Records describes all records in the National Health Service held on a client or patient.

Personal Health Records within the National Health Service are the property of the Secretary of State. The employing authority acts as custodian of the records. However, the professional opinions expressed on the record remain the property of the authors concerned.

The Retention of Records:

The Health Circular HC(89)20 recommends minimum periods for the retention of records other than those held by the Family Health Service Authority (FHSA). The term personal health records is not defined with precision in the circular but special considerations applying to records relating to children, young people and people with mental disorders are identified.

Records relating to children and young people should be kept until the client's twenty-fifth birthday or eight years after the death of the client if sooner and for eight years after the conclusion of treatment in most other cases.

Health Records generated within the National Health Service by employees are the property of the Secretary of State and not of the individual practitioner.

ACCESS TO HEALTH RECORDS ACT

The above Act received Royal Assent on 17th July 1990 and came into effect on 1st November 1991. It gives clients:

- a right of access to information recorded in manually-held health records;

- a right of access to computerised health records which already exists under the Data Protection Act 1984.

The system for dealing with application for access is explained in the "Guide to the Access to Health Records Act 1990" (DOH (1990)).

The Royal College of Speech and Language Therapists fully supports the principle of open access to records.

All therapists must be aware of the rights of the client, give careful consideration to the language and terminology they employ and recognize the positive advantages of greater trust and confidence which can result from shared information.

RECORD KEEPING

Records written by health professionals are primary evidence. Primary evidence is defined as the production of an original document or the admission of its contents and, as such, it must be duly authenticated by the maker of the record, by means of a date and signature, not merely by initials. A signature identifies the author of the individual entries in the record.

Records of professional services rendered to the client are kept for one primary purpose:

- To facilitate the delivery of service to the client.

Secondary reasons for keeping records include:

- providing documentary evidence of a service delivered;

- demonstrating clinical decisions relating to client care;

- providing evidence that the therapist's common law duty of care has been understood and honoured;

- contributing to the preparation of reports and statements;

- contributing to the evaluation of the service offered;

- facilitating continuity of care;

- discharging a contractual duty to the employer;

- assisting the mechanism of accountability.

Records should be:

- in black ink;

- accurate;

- comprehensive;

- legible;

- dated and signed;

- confidential;

- contemporaneous.

'Contemporaneous' is defined as follows:

'As soon as possible after contact and within the same working day', although a record made within twenty four hours of the event to which it relates would suffice (DOH (1990)).

Records made after this would suffer from variability of memory, would be difficult to validate and would reduce the status and credibility of the professional on a record.

Information recorded cannot be changed by obliteration. A single line should be drawn through the error and it should be dated and initialed. Obliterating material (Tippex, etc.) must never be used.

Practitioners are advised that records which have been written up contemporaneously cannot later be torn up and discarded. If a record is damaged it must still be retained for legal purposes.

No record = no contact, as the activity cannot be corroborated.

Abbreviations should only be used if a key to their precise meaning is provided on the record.

Trivia should be avoided and pejorative remarks should never be recorded.

Dated records of indirect contacts should be included.

The keeping of records should be seen as an integral part of the delivery of service to theclient and time should be allocated to reflect the importance of the task.

Summary:

- Records must be contemporaneous.

- Records must be legible, accurate, relevant and avoid jargon.

- All entries must be signed with a signature, not initials.

- Errors should be crossed through with a single line, initialed and dated.

- A key should be shown where initials are used.

DIARIES

Diaries issued by the employing authority are the property of that employing authority. This includes the information recorded in them. Diaries are used to record daily activity of the professional in the pursuance of her/his duties. Information recorded about clients form part of the record of that client and as such, may form part of the record in a court, at a disciplinary hearing or inquiry.

The diary may be called in for audit by the employing authority.

Practitioners are reminded that:

- the diary is a document which must be retained for a period of at least 8 years (HC(89) 20);

- the diary should reflect the work undertaken in the course of a working day;

- information relating to the professional

must also be recorded:

- annual leave;
- sick leave;
- overtime;
- meetings attended/cancelled;
- conferences/courses attended;
- study leave;
- supervision of students/assistants;
- administration.;
- research activities;
- court appearances;
- rotas.

This list is not exhaustive.

Alterations:

There will be occasions when alterations will be required. On those occasions, a single line should be drawn through the error. The error should be dated and initialed.

Loss of Diary:

If a diary is lost, the matter must be reported and a report submitted to the manager.

Change of Employment:

The diary and information are the property of the employing authority. To this end, staff leaving the employ of the employing authority must return their diary to their manager so that it can be sent to the archives for storage.

SHARED OR JOINT RECORDS

The College recognises the value of 'shared' records in which all health professionals make entries into a single record of an individual.

When circumstances lend themselves to such practice, local protocols should be agreed:

- each practitioner's record should be of equal importance;

- the same right of access by the client will exist;

- a lead professional should be identified to consider requests for access in particular circumstances.

COMPUTER-HELD RECORDS and CLINICAL SYSTEM SECURITY

Computer-held records must not be allowed to breach the absolute principle of confidentiality.

Professionals must satisfy themselves as to the security of the system and the categories of staff who have access to personal and confidential information. Periodic audits should be carried out to verify the security of the system.

Accountability for Entry Made by Others:

Whether the record is written or computerised, the therapist must recognise personal accountability for entries made by students or others under their supervision.

Professionals should be diligent in guarding the security of their computer equipment, particularly when using laptop computers. Computer equipment should be made secure at all times against theft, loss or damage.

The College shares the concern of other professional bodies that the confidentiality, availability and integrity of client records must be upheld in the context of information technology. It would not support the implementation of an NHS-wide network of client information until such a system could guarantee confidentiality. (BMA, 1996, Anderson, 1996).

Information transferred by telephone or electronic mail

Personal information should be faxed only to a machine that is known to be secure during working hours.

In addition, great care should be taken when transferring information via modem or when using the electronic mail network.

AUDIO/VIDEO/ PHOTOGRAPHIC MATERIAL

As with all written documentation, audio/video/photographic material should be used primarily to facilitate the delivery of a quality service to the client.

- The principle of confidentiality applies.

- Clients must be made aware and understand that recordings are being made.

- Clients must give written consent to use and subsequent publication of recorded material.

- All recordings and photographic materials must be safely stored.

REPORT WRITING

A report is a written account designed to convey information and ideas.
Recommendations and proposals may form part of a report.

Every report must have:

- an introduction, with identifiable objectives, i.e. reason(s) for the report;
- a middle section, which covers past, present and future action or plans;
- a final section, which includes a summary and conclusions to give clear indications of actions.

The language of the report should be easy to read and understandable to the reader.
Sentences should be short and clear. The use of jargon must be avoided.
If abbreviations are used, a key must be clearly shown.

Hallmarks of a good report include:

- clarity .... understanding after first time reading;
- completeness .... relevant and necessary;
- accuracy .... verifiable information;
- consistency .... tables and lists correlate;
- logical progression .... from past to present to future;
- conciseness .... minimum but intelligent and intelligible information.

The report may be:

- an initial report .... following an assessment;
- a closure report .... following discharge;
- an interim report .... as and when necessary following a referral.

Important Points To Remember:

- objectives must be defined;
- date of the report must be shown;
- circulation lists should be specified;
- details should be brief;
- recommendations should be identified;
- local guidelines should be adhered to.

Pitfalls to Avoid:

- unnecessary jargon;
- long sentences;
- omission of important facts;
- lack of headings;
- lack of structure;
- lack of clarity.

Summary:

A report should be checked for dates, facts, grammar and spelling before being submitted.

A report must be 'timely'. If the therapist is making a forward referral, a report should accompany the referral.

Finally, the importance of a report should be recognised. Reports which are incomplete or inaccurate can be misleading or mis-informative. Therefore, a report must be relevant. If reference is made to another discipline or agency, then the relationship between the service of the therapist and the agency/discipline should be apparent. Sources of information must also be given.

THE DATA PROTECTION ACT 1984

The Data Protection Act 1984 received Royal Assent in July 1984 and took effect between 1985 and 1987. HC(89)29 clarifies the position of health professionals under the Data Protection Act. The Data Protection principles are as follows:

■ The information to be contained in personal data shall be obtained and processed lawfully and fairly.

■ Personal data held for any purpose shall not be used or disclosed in any manner incompatible with the purpose or purposes.

■ Personal data held for any purpose shall be adequate, relevant and not excessive in relation to the purpose for which they are held.

■ Personal data shall be accurate and, where necessary, kept up-to-date.

■ Personal data held for any purpose shall not be kept for longer than is necessary.

■ Any individual member of staff should be entitled, at reasonable intervals and without due delay or expense, to be informed by a data user whether he/she holds personal data of which that individual is the subject and have access to any such data held by a data user and, where appropriate, to have such data corrected or erased.

6

WORKING WITHIN A
LEGAL FRAMEWORK

Duty of Care

Power and Duties

Consent to Treatment

Confidentiality

Legal Statements

Appearing in Court as a Witness

Child Abuse

Guardian Ad Litem

Children Act (1989)

Education Act (1981)

Disabled Persons Act (1986)

NHS and Community Care Act (1990)

Professional Insurance

*T*his chapter outlines some of the major legislative influences on the work of speech and language therapists. It explains legal terminology and legal procedures as they apply to professional practice. It outlines key parliamentary Acts and their relevance to work with individuals with communication difficulties.

There are important differences between legislature in different parts of the United Kingdom. For example, speech and language therapists working in Scotland should refer to the Children Act (Scotland)(1995) which is similar to the Children Act (1989) described below, but follows the evolution of Scots law (SLGIU, 1995).

LEGAL TERMINOLOGY

DUTY OF CARE

A 'duty of care' is owed to clients by the employing authority, and discharged by the professionals (or officers).

Therapists discharge a duty of care through assessment and diagnosis of communication disorders, consequent intervention and any decision to the continuance of therapy.

A duty of care arises from the first moment the therapist makes a professional contact with a client and through that contact commences an 'episode' of care.

An 'episode' is taken to mean an interaction with a client at which information, advice, guidance or intervention is offered or commenced.

POWERS AND DUTIES

Employing authorities are empowered by their respective legislation to provide a comprehensive service to their local population. Current legal terminology distinguishes between 'Duties' and 'Powers'. A parliamentary Act places an authority under a 'Duty' to provide a range and level of services. The authority is obliged by law to provide these services to the local population or client group stipulated. If, however, the Act places an authority under a 'Power' to provide a range of services, the authority can provide such services at their discretion and are not obliged to do so.

Speech and language therapists are advised to familiarise themselves with this distinction in relation to all legislation relevant to their practice.

CONSENT TO TREATMENT

A client has the right under common law to give or withdraw consent prior to examination or treatment. Consent to treatment may be implied or expressed. In many cases, clients do not explicitly give express consent but their agreement may be implied by compliant action, e.g. keeping an appointment. Express consent is given when a client confirms their agreement to treatment in clear and explicit terms whether orally or in writing.

Where therapists are practising in environments where consent cannot be assumed as part of a child's placement, carer consent must be obtained to see the child, e.g. screening in nurseries/schools.

Oral or written consent - documentation:

Oral consent may be sufficient for the vast majority of contacts with clients. Written consent should be obtained for any treatment carrying a substantial risk or substantial side effect. Oral or written consent should be recorded in the notes with relevant details of the therapist's explanation. Where written consent is obtained, it should be incorporated into the notes. Where a client is unable to give or withhold consent, e.g. reduced consciousness/dysphasia/dementia, it may still be appropriate to proceed with treatment with the consent of carers.

Duty of Care to the client:

The most important element of consent is the duty to ensure that clients understand the nature and purpose of the proposed treatment. Where the client has not been given appropriate or sufficient information, then consent may not always have been obtained, despite a signature or the assumptions of the therapist. Speech and language therapists must ensure that where a client does not accept assessment or treatment, the therapist should respect that decision and withdraw, recording the situation in the casenotes.

Consent for one form of treatment does not give an automatic right to the therapist to undertake a further episode of care.

Client information and level of understanding:

Consent to treatment must be given freely and without coercion. It must be based on information about the nature, purpose and likely effects of treatment. The information must be understandable to the client. The capacity of the client to understand the information given by the therapist will depend on the client's age, intellectual state and the client's ability to appreciate the significance of the information. All these factors should form part of the assessment of the client before an episode of care/treatment is commenced.

The treatment of children and young people - the legal position:

Wherever a child under the age of sixteen has sufficient understanding of what treatment is being proposed, that child may consent to a therapist giving treatment. The therapist must be satisfied that any such child has sufficient understanding of what is involved in the proposed treatment.

A full record should be made of the factors taken into account by the therapist in the making of her/his assessment of the child's capacity to give a valid consent. Speech and language therapy is one of a few health care situations where a child is sometimes alone. Efforts should be made to encourage the child that his/her carer should be informed (except in circumstances where it is clearly not in the child's interest to do so).

Parental consent should be obtained where a child does not have sufficient understanding and is under the age of sixteen.

A client's right in accepting treatment:

Care must be taken in respect of the client's wishes. This is particularly relevant where clients may be involved in student training and/or research. An explanation should be given of the need for practical experience and/or research, and agreement obtained before proceeding. It should be made clear that a client may refuse to agree without adversely affecting his/her care.

Advising the client:

Where a choice of treatment might reasonably be offered, the therapist must always advise the client of her/his recommendations together with the reasons for selecting a particular course of action. Sufficient information must always be given by the therapist to ensure that the client understands the nature and consequences of the treatment. This is to enable the client to take a decision based on that information. The therapist should assume that all clients would wish to be well-informed.

Treatment without a client's consent:

The following are examples of occasions when treatment may proceed without obtaining the client's consent.

- for life saving procedures where a client is unconscious and cannot indicate his/her wishes;

- where there is a statutory power requiring the examination of a client, for example, under Public Health (Control of Disease) Act (1984). Nevertheless, an explanation should be offered and the client's co-operation should be sought.;

- in certain cases where a minor is a ward of court, the court may make a specific issue order under Section 8 of the Children Act (1989). The court may give directions concerning medical examinations when the court makes an interim care or supervision order, an emergency protection order or a child assessment order.;

- treatment for a mental disorder of a client liable to be detained in hospital under the Mental Health Act 1983;

- treatment for a physical disorder where the client is incapable of giving consent by reason of mental disorder, and the treatment is in the client's best interest.

CONFIDENTIALITY

Confidentiality may be defined as maintaining security of information obtained from an individual in the privileged circumstances of a professional relationship. Breach of confidence is, therefore, unethical, unprofessional and in some cases, unlawful. Confidentiality should not in itself produce problems for those professionals who work within a Code of Conduct. It should, however, be remembered that a breach of confidence cannot occur where prior permission to disclose has been sought and obtained from the individual client or responsible individual.

In a situation where permission has not been sought or obtained, but disclosure of information about a client by a professional is under consideration, the professional must ask the following questions of herself/himself:

■ Was I categorically asked not to disclose?

■ Will withholding information affect the well-being of the client/the child?

■ Is the disclosure relevant?

If the answers to the above are positive, then maintaining confidentiality may actually mitigate against the client.

Therapists should note the following principles in relation to confidentiality:

■ confidentiality does not equate with secrecy;

■ keeping a secret could be construed as collusion.

There may be occasions when a carer or client requests that information is not passed on. On these occasions, the therapist must not make promises. Furthermore, if in the opinion of the therapist the information is requested by another professional authorised to receive that information, and who also owes the client a duty of care, then the information must be passed on.

An example of this would be the general practitioner, to whom the therapist has a responsibility to provide information about actual or planned care specific to the particular speciality, i.e. speech and language disorders.

CONSENT FORM

For treatment by a health professional other than doctors or dentists

Health Authority . . . .   Patient's Surname . . . .

Hospital . . . .   Other Names . . . .

Unit Number. . . . .   Date of Birth . . . .

Sex: *(please tick)*   Male ☐   Female ☐

HEALTH PROFESSIONAL *(This part to be completed by health professional. See notes on the reverse)*

TYPE OF TREATMENT PROPOSED

Complete this part of the form

I confirm that I have explained the treatment proposed and such appropriate options as are available to the patient in terms which in my judgement are suited to the understanding of the patient and/or to one of the parents or guardians of the patient.

Signature . . . .   Date . . . . / . . . . / . . . . .

Name of health professional . . . .

Job title of health professional . . . .

PATIENT/PARENT/GUARDIAN

1. Please read this form and the notes overleaf very carefully.

2. If there is anything that you don't understand about the explanation, or if you want more information, you should ask the health professional who has explained the treatment proposed.

3. Please check that all the information on the form is correct. If it is, and you understand the treatment proposed, then sign the form.

I am the patient/parent/guardian (*delete as necessary*)

I agree   ■   to what is proposed which has been explained to me by the health professional named on this form

Signature   . . . .

Name   . . . .

Address   . . . .

(if not the patient)   . . . .

. . . .

LEGAL STATEMENTS

(Relating to Court (Civic or Criminal) Inquiries).

A statement of fact is an accurate account of a person or professional's involvement with an individual adult, child or family for a professional reason during the course of undertaking their duties.

A statement may be requested by:

■ the employing authority;

■ a solicitor;

■ a social worker;

■ a guardian ad litem (an officer appointed by the court to represent the interests of the child);

■ others.

Before making a statement, the professional should first establish the employing authority's policy for professionals making a statement. This will usually include contacting a line manager in the first instance.

■ The statement should be truthful, accurate and factual.

■ The facts should, to the best knowledge of the therapist, be verifiable.

■ The statement should be made from the records and advice taken from the legal officer retained by the authority.

When writing a statement, the following format should be followed:-

■ date of statement;

■ name, professional address and qualifications, position and employing authority;

■ name, address and relationship of family and member(s) about whom the statement is written;

■ the sequence of events in chronological order, e.g. sub-headings with dates of each contact and an explanation of what took place or was observed. A record of any clinical measurement/treatment should be included.

■ include, in chronological order, any other communication or attempted communication, e.g. telephone calls, visits, failed appointments, contact with other agencies/disciplines.

The above should be in short paragraphs to facilitate reading.

APPEARING IN COURT AS A WITNESS

Therapists who anticipate any involvement with regard to the making of statements, medico-legal reports or appearing in court should seek help from their employing authority's legal department.

Before giving evidence, the witness is required to swear an oath or to affirm that the evidence that she/he will give is the truth. Questions will be asked on the basis of the written statement which the professional will have been asked to make prior to appearing in court. Professionals will not have a copy of their statement while giving evidence.

In some cases, the statement will have been written months earlier. Under these circumstances, a witness may wish to refresh her/his memory by referring to contemporaneous records.

It is necessary to obtain permission from the employing authority to take the records to court. Under normal circumstances, permission is given as the witness summons or the subpoena may stipulate that the practitioner attend court with the relevant records.

A witness should not attempt to give evidence from memory in the absence of a record in an attempt to be helpful.

A witness who has no relevant records available but who has received a witness summons or subpoena should attend court. Refusal to attend could be seen as contempt of court.

If it is necessary to refer to contemporaneous records or notes whilst giving evidence, a witness must ask leave of the judge or magistrate. If there are no objections, the witness may refresh her/his memory.

It is important to note that if the records or notes are referred to in court, they become part of the evidence in the case and may be examined by the other solicitor and the judge/magistrate.

The professional can be cross-examined by the solicitor of the defendant on matters contained in the records which may not have been referred to orally.

When giving evidence, technique is important. A witness is advised to:-

- speak slowly and clearly, in a loud voice;

- address all answers to the judge;

- remember everyone is nervous in court.

The therapist may be asked to explain any clinical terms used. The evidence given by the therapists may be weighed against that of an expert witness (independent therapist) or the therapist may be called as an expert witness. In such instances, it is vital to be clear and specific when giving evidence.

(Further guidelines are available from the College/ASTIIP).

CHILD ABUSE

Child abuse is usually defined in terms of the conditions of the child or the actions of the carer, where a child has suffered, or is likely to suffer, 'significant harm'. Child abuse is the outcome of a highly complex set of factors, both psychological and social.

Three requirements for establishing child abuse are identified:

- There must be some definable or avoidable behaviour by the parent or carer in relation to the child. This may be an act of commission or omission and it can either be physical or emotional.

- A causal link needs to be established between the behaviour of the parent or carer and harm to the child (or the behaviour is such that harm will very likely occur).

- The harm is currently demonstrable or confidently expected on the basis of professional judgement or research evidence.

The categories of abuse for which a child may be placed on the Child Protection Register are given below (DHSS (1988), (1991)).

Neglect

The persistent or severe neglect of a child, or the failure to protect a child from exposure to any kind of danger, including cold and starvation, or extreme failure to carry out important aspects of care, resulting in the significant impairment of the child's health or development, including non-organic failure to thrive.

Physical Injury

Actual or likely physical injury to a child, or a failure to prevent physical injury (or suffering) to a child, including deliberate poisoning, suffocation and Munchausen's Syndrome by Proxy.

Sexual Abuse

Actual or likely sexual exploitation of a child or adolescent. The child may be dependent and/or developmentally immature.

Emotional Abuse

Actual or likely severe adverse effect on the emotional and behavioural development of a child caused by persistent or severe emotional ill-treatment or rejection. All abuse involves some emotional ill-treatment. This category applies where it is the main or sole form of abuse.

Child Protection

The aim of child protection is to safeguard the proper development of the child (Children and Young Persons Act (1969), Section 1.2(a), Children Act (1989) Children Act (Scotland) (1995)). The protection of the child is vital. Therefore, the therapist must always act positively to protect the child. Any relationship to the parent or carer is secondary to the protection of the child.

The Role of the Speech and Language Therapist in Child Protection:

From time to time, through observations or by information received through disclosure, therapists may discover actual or suspected child abuse. It is important on these occasions that therapists are clear about what actions to take and are sufficiently informed to understand the implications and ramifications of these 'discoveries'.

Therapists are in a privileged position and may be 'chosen' by the child to be given information in such matters as sexual abuse or other forms of abuse or neglect. The opportunity for this disclosure may be provided by the 'climate of communication' which exists between the therapist and the child. In addition, the therapist may be the only trusted worker whom the child sees alone. A third reason may be the category of client the therapist sees, i.e. children with articulation difficulties, children with learning disabilities, children with hearing impairment. These children will have difficulty expressing themselves verbally to others. The therapy situation may allow the child to share sensitive information. The speech and language therapist may also discover information relating to abuse through therapeutic activities, such as play and drawing.

Therapists must recognise the limits of their competency and not attempt to interpret such information passed on in isolation. However, if a speech and language therapist has any concerns regarding a child or thinks there has been any disclosure, she/he must discuss the matter with her/his manager and follow the Child Protection procedures of the employing authority for actual or suspected child abuse.

Knowledge of the procedures and the process of referral is the responsibility of every therapist. Protection of the child is part of the duty of care owed by the therapist.

All speech and language therapists must be informed about:

- the interlocking factors which predispose to child abuse;

- the signs and symptoms of potential abuse;

- the signs and symptoms of actual abuse;

- what specific action must be taken for potential and actual abuse (i.e. the procedures dealing with these);

- the possible outcomes of the abuse and the therapist's role in these;

- the role of the child protection conference (or meeting) and the therapist's contribution to this;

- the criteria for registration in respect of Child Protection.

GUARDIAN AD LITEM

A guardian ad litem is an independent advisor appointed by the court for the purposes of advising the court regarding the best interests of the child.

The Children Act (1989) heralded many changes in the legal status of children and brought with it increased responsibilities for those professions which are required to implement part or parts of the Act. An example of this in public law is the Guardian ad Litem. In private law, the advisor will be the court Welfare Officer.

The Guardian ad Litem has, among other responsibilities, a right to access the health records of those children who come before the court. The Guardian ad Litem no longer seeks permission or co-operation to obtain information from the records. Their remit is to obtain the record to access information. Professionals are, therefore, required to carry out a legal instruction and provide all relevant documentation to the Guardian ad Litem.

Therapists need to be aware that information given to a Guardian ad Litem verbally, as well as on record, can be used in court.

Therapists working in Scotland need to refer to the role of the Curator ad Litem, who has a similar function to the Guardian ad Litem.

THE CHILDREN ACT
(England and Wales) (1989)

see Children Act (Scotland) (1995)
see Children (Northern Ireland) Order (1995)

The Children Act (1989) for England
and Wales came into force in October 1991.
It involved a major reform and rationalisation
of child care law and sought to strike a
balance between the rights of parents and
the welfare of the child. The Act also had
important implications for health authorities
in relation to child health and welfare, as it
established that such authorities had a duty
to liaise with local authorities and social
services departments (SSDs). The Children
Act (Scotland) (1995) and the Children
(Northern Ireland) Order (1995) are
due for implementation in late 1996.

Key issues of relevance to health service staff:

■ health service professionals have key
role in identifying children in need
and liaising with social services
departments;

■ regulations requiring health service
professionals to be involved and
consulted by social services departments
about the health needs of the children
they are looking after;

■ court orders relating to child protection
with which relevant health service staff
need to be familiar;

■ a duty for health service professionals
to assist social services departments
in safeguarding the welfare of children
in long-stay health authority
establishments;

■ the opportunity for co-ordinated
planning of services and collaboration
between professionals in specific areas,
such as work with children with
disabilities, and the power to hold
joint assessments.

Initial awareness of the Act was achieved
by the publication of 'An Introduction to
the Children Act' (HMSO, (1990)) a booklet
distributed to health authorities, local
authorities and other relevant organisations.

In addition, the Children Act simplifies and
increases accessibility of child care law and
reduces the likelihood of children's safety or
welfare being imperilled simply as a function
of professional ignorance of powers and
duties.

In more substantive terms, the Act represents
a major assessment of the delicate balance
between 'the need to protect children and
the need to enable parents to challenge
intervention in the upbringing of their
children'.

The balance has been struck on the child's
side at several points which make clear, for
example, that child protection has to be the
priority; that courts must regard the child's
welfare as the paramount consideration; and
that both courts and local authorities have a
duty to ascertain the wishes and feelings of
the child.

On the other side, the Act emphasises the
principle that the upbringing of children is
primarily the responsibility of parents. For
example, even if the grounds for a care order
are proved, it is now necessary also to be
satisfied that making an order is better for
the child than not making an order (and thus
leaving him/her within the family). A second

example of this principle is that the Emergency Protection Order, replacing the Place of Safety Order, can be used, 'if, but only if, ... there is reasonable cause to believe that the child is likely to suffer significant harm'. Furthermore, the new order can last no more than eight days and can only be extended once, for a period of seven days. Thirdly, working in partnership with parents is now required of professionals by law and is no longer simply a matter of good practice.

The Act also makes it a duty for relevant local authority departments and health authorities to co-operate with each other and to keep each other informed in specific ways in relation to children in need (including children with disabilities).

Equal opportunities are explicitly advanced at a number of points in the Act. For instance, local authorities are required to have regard to 'the religious persuasion, racial origin and cultural and linguistic background' of any child in their care. In addition, the concept of a child 'in need' specifically includes children with disabilities.

Despite the simplification in the law which this Act brings, there is a need for training and re-training amongst professionals working with children. This involves not only acquiring knowledge and understanding of the Act, but also, in some cases, developing new attitudes and practices, for instance, in relation to partnership with parents, equal opportunities and developing closer collaboration between agencies.

The following sections of the Children Act relate to the protection of children:

Section 37, Children Act 1989.
Section 47(1), Children Act 1989.
Section 47(8), Children Act 1989.
Schedule 2, paragraph 4, Children Act 1989.

These procedures provide a mechanism whereby any agency concerned that a child may be at risk, can share information with other agencies.

EDUCATION ACT (1981)
Education Act (Scotland) (1981)

Historical Background:
1944:

Education Act (1944) made local education authorities responsible for identifying, assessing and meeting the needs of handicapped children.

Categories of handicap were introduced for which different forms of education were to be provided. Medical officers were employed to determine special education need and any children deemed ineducable were excluded from the school system and dealt with under the Mental Deficiency Act.

1970:

Education (Handicapped Children) Act (1970) abolished the category "ineducable" and local authorities became responsible for all children regardless of type or degree of disability.

1974:

The Warnock Committee was established with the following brief:

'To review educational provision in England, Scotland and Wales for children and young people handicapped by disabilities of body and mind, taking account of the medical aspects of their needs, together with arrangements to prepare them for entry into employment; to consider the most effective use of resources for these purposes, and to make recommendations'.

1975:

Special education forms introduced. Procedures put the emphasis on multi-professional approach to assessment.

1978:

Warnock Report published.
Its recommendations were:

■ abolition of categories of 'handicap', and focus on the education implications of a disability;

■ common provision for all children where handicapped and non-handicapped would be educated in the same setting as far as possible;

■ greater involvement of parents in the process of assessing educational need;

■ improved communication between health, education and social services, with adequate resources to be made available by health authorities to ensure effective child health service.

The Government consulted widely about the recommendations made by the Warnock Committee, and, based on the central themes of the Report, passed the 1981 Education Act which was finally implemented in April 1983. DES Circular 1/83 made detailed recommendations concerning the implementation of the Act.

EDUCATION ACT (1981)
Principles of the Act:

Principles relating to the nature of Special Educational Need:

■ Categories of 'handicap' were abolished and replaced by the term 'learning difficulties'.

■ A learning difficulty related to:

- the child having significantly greater difficulty in learning than the majority of children his/her age.

- the child having a disability which prevents or hinders him/her from making use of the educational facilities generally provided in his/her particular local education authority.

■ A child, therefore, has a special educational need if he/she is identified as having learning difficulty for which special educational provision must be made. This provision must be in addition to, and different from, the provision made for children of the same age in the local authority.

- The definition of special educational need is applied to children under five who are likely to have a learning difficulty when over this age. There is a distinction between children over and under the age of two. Under the age of two, any educational provision is deemed to be special educational provision and flexibility is allowed in how assessment and provision are undertaken by the education authority. Between the ages of two and five, the formal procedures of the Act apply.

Principles relating to the rights of children with special educational needs and their parents:

- It is the duty of the LEA to make provision for the child in ordinary school provided that:

  - the child thereby receives the special education he/she needs;

  - it allows for the efficient education of children with whom he/she will be educated;

  - it represents an efficient use of resources.

- Parents have the right to participate in the process of assessment and respond to decisions about provision and placement, and also to initiate the process of assessment.

- Parents have the right to appeal:

  - if after an assessment the local authority decides not to proceed with the record;

  - after the record, if they disagree with provision made.

Principles relating to the effectiveness of the identification, assessment and meeting of special educational need:

- Where the LEA is required to determine the special educational provision, a thorough multi-professional assessment is required in order that appropriate allocation of resources can be made.

- Once the record has been made, it must be reviewed annually. There is special provision made for statutory reassessment of the child in his/her early teens.

1993:

The Education Act (1993) builds upon the principles and practices first set out in the 1981 Education Act. It places duties and responsibilities on the education authorities, schools, health and social services towards all children with special educational needs.

Statutory Procedures:

The Education Act (1993) laid down that a Code of Practice would be established with effect from 1 September 1994. This document covered all statutory procedures as follows:

Section One:
Introduction - principles and procedures.
Section Two:
School-based stages of assessment and provision.
Section Three:
Statutory assessment of special educational needs.
Section Four:
Statement of special educational needs.

Section Five:
Assessment and statements for under-fives.
Section Six:
Annual review.

Part 3 of the Code of Practice set out a stage approach to assessment and provision for school-age children.

Stage One: involves the initial identification and registration of child's special educational needs, taking early action to meet the child's needs within the normal classroom work, monitoring and reviewing progress.

Stage Two: special educational needs (SEN) co-ordinator is responsible for taking the lead in assessing the learning difficulty; planning, monitoring and reviewing provision, working with teachers and consulting parents.

Stage Three: the school involves the Local Education Authority. Teachers and the SEN co-ordinator are supported by specialists from outside the school.

Stage Four: statutory assessments are the focus of Stage 4, and Part 3 of the Code of Practice describes the statutory assessment of special educational needs.

Stage Five: the Local Educational Authority considers the need for a statement of special educational needs.

Page 3.45 of the Code summarises the time limits for making assessments and statements. Statements must be completed within 26 weeks.

All speech and language therapists will abide by the Code of Practice and should have Part 3 easily available for reference.

ASSESSMENTS AND STATEMENTS FOR UNDER FIVES

The Code of Practice Section 5 is subdivided into two parts, relating to the assessment of children under two years, and other children under five years.

Section 176 of the Education Act (1993) states that it is the responsibility of DHAs and NHS Trusts to inform the parents and the appropriate LEA when they form the opinion that a child under the age of five may have special educational needs. They must also inform the parents if they believe that a particular voluntary organisation is likely to be able to give the parents advice or assistance in connection with any special educational needs that the child may have.

Assessment:

The continuous nature of assessment has been emphasised throughout the guidance on assessment for the under fives. Before formal procedures are considered, there should be a gradual process of assessing need by all those involved with the child. For example, 'Assessment should be seen as a partnership between teachers, other professionals and parents, in a joint endeavour to discover and understand the nature of the difficulties and needs of individual children' (DES Circular 1/83, para 6).

Professionals or parents may draw the attention of the Local Educational Authority (LEA) to a child who seems to have learning difficulties. It is recommended that speech and language therapists work in consultation with other professional colleagues when raising their concerns. The LEA, having established grounds to proceed with assessment, is responsible for initiating the formal procedures. Its decision to do so will be based on local factors such as the range of facilities already being provided in ordinary schools.

Children under two may be assessed by the LEA with the agreement of the parent, or must be assessed if the parent requests it. There are no formal procedures for assessing needs or making provision for these very young children so that a flexible approach can be adopted by the LEA. Assessment of children over the age of two must follow procedures as laid down in the Act.

For children under five, health authorities have a duty to inform parents when they are concerned about their child and to bring the child to the attention of the LEA. Health authorities also have a responsibility to inform parents of any particular voluntary organisation that is likely to be able to give the parents advice or assistance in connection with any special educational needs that the child may have.

The parents have the right to be present at examinations carried out for the purpose of assessment, although this right does not apply if assessment is by observation only for a period of time. However, professionals are advised that 'it will be part of the process of maintaining good relations with parents for all professionals to involve them in the process of assessment even where some part of the assessment is undertaken in privacy or by observation' (1/83, para 36).

It is recommended that interpreting facilities be made for non-English speaking parents.

(See also Welsh Language Act, (1993).

EDUCATION (SCOTLAND) ACT (1981)

Although the Education Act, (1981) and the Education (Scotland) Act, (1980) share much in the way of background and philosophy, there are differences in the legislation which result in variations of terminology, procedure and statutory obligations.

In addition, the Report on the Education of Pupils with Learning Difficulties in Scottish Schools (HMSO, 1978), had a seminal effect upon arrangements for special education and learning support in schools in Scotland, and, nearly twenty years later, still underpins some of the significant differences in provision between the English and Scottish systems.

Summary of the Assessment, Recording and Review of Special Educational Needs in Scotland:

1 Assessment - the education authority initiates formal assessment of the child's special needs and notifies the parents who have twenty one days in which to send in views about the child's needs. The education authority considers reports from psychological, medical, educational and other services and considers the parents' views.

2 Recording - following formal assessment, the education authority reaches a decision on whether to open a Record of Special

Educational Needs. If the decision is made not to open a record, the parents are informed and have twenty eight days to appeal. If the decision is made to open a record, the parents are given a draft record and have fourteen days in which to comment on the decision and the contents of the draft record. The education authority opens a record and the parents receive a copy and have twenty eight days to appeal.

3 Review - the education authority initiates a review of the child's needs either of its own accord or if parents request it (so long as the initial recording or review decision was not made within the past twelve months).

4. Further Needs Assessment - when the child is between fourteen and fifteen and a quarter years, the education authority must prepare a report on the child's future educational and training needs and whether the child should continue to be recorded at sixteen plus. Parents are given twenty one days in which to give views before the future needs assessment. Parents are asked to comment on the draft report.

5. Ending of Record - Recorded Needs are discontinued if:

■ on appeal, the Secretary of State orders this to be done;

■ child is sixteen plus and leaves school;

■ child is sixteen plus and wants the record discontinued.

The record is preserved for another five years if the child/parents request it, otherwise it is destroyed.

Relevant Legislation:

■ Education (Scotland) Act (1945)

■ Education (Scotland) Act (1969)

■ Education (Scotland) Act (1980)

■ Scottish Education Department Circulars 1083, 1087

■ Mental Health (Scotland) Act (1984)

■ Disabled Persons Act (1986)

■ Education Reform Act (1988)

■ Self-governing Schools, etc. (Scotland) Act (1989)

■ The Children Act (1989)

■ Education (Schools) Act (1992)

■ The Education Act (1993)

■ Code of Practice (September 1994)

■ Children Act (Scotland) (1995)

Implications of the Education Acts for Speech and Language Therapists

The following guidelines are intended as a basis for good practice.

Procedures:

The Local Education Authority (LEA) England and Wales, the Education Authority (EA) Scotland, will seek advice through the designated medical officer in the health authority/trust/DMU (Directly Managed Unit) on children to be assessed.

Speech and language therapy managers should be routinely informed of all children to be assessed by the (L)EA. They will ascertain if they are known to the speech and language therapist and request advice from the appropriate therapist.

Because some of these children may have speech and language difficulties and may not be known to the speech and language therapy service, it is essential that there is some mechanism for ensuring that children in need of a speech and language therapy opinion are referred. Good communication with other professionals assessing children is needed to ensure that appropriate referrals are made.

The speech and language therapist should send her/his advice to the speech and language therapy manager. The speech and language therapist's advice should be attached in full to the medical advice and unaltered when sent through the designated medical officer. The speech and language therapy manager should keep a copy of the advice.

The speech and language therapy manager should see a copy of both the proposed and final statement/record and there should be the opportunity to discuss with the (L)EA the resources available to meet the needs identified.

A speech and language therapist should participate in the annual review of any statement/record to which a speech and language therapy contribution has been made. The first annual review after the child's fourteenth birthday, and any subsequent review, is particularly significant under the requirements of the Disabled Persons Act (1986), the NHS and Community Care Act (1990) and The Chronically Sick and Disabled Persons Act (1970).

When a child transfers from another authority with speech and language therapy needs identified as part of the statement/record, it is recommended a re-assessment of these needs be made and discussed with the education and health authorities.

Content of Speech and Language Therapy Advice:

DES Circular 1/83 gave guidance concerning the advice prepared by professionals for the statement.

Advice should be full enough and clear enough to give other professionals and particularly the child's parents an understanding of the child's needs. Language used in reports must be unambiguous and jargon is to be avoided. Each professional must only advise within their sphere of work and not seek to pre-empt the decisions of the education authority. Therapists should be aware that any advice given for the statement/record may be challenged in the event of an appeal and they may be called upon to justify what they have written.

The speech and language therapist's view of the child's needs should cover:

1 A clear analysis of the child's communication, both in terms of abilities and disabilities.

- Include a positive statement about the child's strengths.

- Specific test scores and age levels should be avoided. However, clear evidence of the nature and degree of the child's overall communication difficulty should be given. This can be supported with examples.

- It may be appropriate to include a description of the child's rate of progress.

- The implication of the child's difficulties should be briefly described. The child's communication disabilities should be related to the educational environment.

- Where the child has experience of two/more languages, the first language should be noted and whether or not an assessment has been made in that language.

2 A summary of the speech and language therapy aims required to help the child develop educationally and in achieving independence.

3. The facilities and resources recommended to achieve these aims.

There is a wide diversity of opinion amongst the profession as to the way in which speech and language therapy needs should be specified. However, terminology should be clear and unambiguous and should be agreed locally. The facilities and resources recommended must relate to the communication needs of the child and not to the speech and language therapy resources available.

'Children may need regular and continuing help from a speech therapist, either individually or in a group. In other cases, it may be appropriate for staff at the child's school to deliver a programme of support under the guidance and supervision of a speech therapist' (para 4.36 Code of Practice 1994).

Parents:

The Warnock Report stressed the need to make parents partners in the process of identifying, assisting and providing for the special education needs of the child. As the circular advises: 'The relations between professional advisers and parents are of crucial importance. Parent involvement in assessment provides the opportunity to reach an agreed understanding of the nature of the child's learning difficulties'(para 36).

Parents may also be helped by referral to a voluntary agency appropriate to their child's needs which can assist them with the procedures.

Resources:

This issue is obviously of concern to speech and language therapists and their managers. The local education authority is legally bound to provide for the recommendations made on a statement. The local authority is legally bound to provide for the recommendations made in Part 3 of the statement (educational provision). Speech and language therapy provision may be described in Part 3 (educational) or Part 6 (non-educational provision). The Code of Practice (para 4.35 and 4.36) states that the prime responsibility for speech and language therapy provision is with the NHS but 'where the NHS does not provide for a child whose statement specified speech and language therapy as educational provision the ultimate responsibility for ensuring that provision is made rests with the LEA'. In addition, amendment 537 of the Education Reform Act (1988) enabled local authorities to provide for non-educational provision which is specified in a child's statement of special educational needs. It is recommended that the speech and language therapy manager be part of the discussion about available speech and language therapy resources for any particular child. Any mismatch between need and resources should be recorded and monitored. The integration of children with special needs into mainstream school has significant resource implications and should be monitored.

This information should be brought to the attention of both education and health authorities to be part of the planning process.

Communication and Liaison:

The importance of good communication and liaison cannot be overstated. This was highlighted by the Warnock Committee and was emphasised by the DES Circulars 1/83, 22/89, and more recently in the Code of Practice (1994). The procedures of the Acts enable speech and language therapists to be consulted but effective involvement in the process will only come through good communication. Such liaison with other colleagues will:

- allow the therapist to share concern about a child who may have special educational needs;

- ensure weight is given to the therapist's view about the child;

- enhance the effectiveness of provision.

Effective action on behalf of children with special educational needs will often depend upon close co-operation between schools, LEAs, health and social services. The

Children Act (1989) and the Education Act (1993) place duties on these bodies to help each other (para 2.38 Code of Practice, 1994).

The DISABLED PERSONS ACT (1986)

The Disabled Person's Act (1986) , also known as the Tom Clarke Bill, provides people with disabilities with additional rights in relation to decisions regarding their present and future needs. It has implications for the delivery of health and social care, and the assessment of people with disabilities living in community and hospital settings.

The Act outlines four rights which allow people with disabilities to claim more control over their own lives. These are:

- the right to representation;

- the right to assessment;

- the right to information;

- the right to consultation.

It also gives carers two specific rights:

- the right to ask for an assessment of a disabled person's needs;

- the right to have their ability to care taken into account.

It makes no provision for additional services or additional funding, nor does it make any reference to rights to public facilities or transport.

Under the Act, a disabled person can appoint a representative to assist in putting forward his or her views to local authority and health service personnel. The authority must ensure that a disabled person with communication difficulties resulting from mental, physical or sensory impairment receives appropriate assistance in such negotiations. Such assistance could be provided by a speech and language therapist.

The Act also stipulates three categories of people with disabilities who have a right to assessment. These are:

- any disabled person who asks for services from the local authority listed under Section 2 of the Chronically Sick and Disabled Persons Act (1970);

- any disabled child or young person leaving full time education;

- any person discharged from hospital who has been receiving treatment for a mental health problem or learning disability for six months or more.

Following the assessment, the local authority must provide the disabled person with written statements detailing the needs that have been identified, the services that will be provided, and an explanation of any identified need that the local authority does not intend to meet. The disabled person has a right to appeal against any aspect of the assessment. Health service personnel must be involved in making appropriate assessments, and must cooperate fully with local authority personnel in ensuring that the assessment is undertaken.

This legislation gives disabled people more control over decisions regarding provision of services and transition from hospital to community settings, or from school to community settings, whichever is appropriate.

In addition, the Act gives disabled people the right to information on services which are relevant to their needs, whether or not they are receiving those services. It also encourages greater representation of people with disabilities and their organisations on local authority councils and committees concerned with disabled people.

NHS AND COMMUNITY CARE ACT (1990)

The NHS and Community Care Act (1990) sets out the government's proposals for the future delivery of health and social care in the United Kingdom. It puts into place significant structural and organisational changes to the delivery of health and social care. The Act makes clear the respective responsibilities of health agencies and social services agencies and brings into focus the separation of those responsible for purchasing health and social care and those responsible for providing health and social care. The Act was originally published in the form of two working papers 'Working for Patients' (DOH, 1989) and 'Caring for People: the Next Decade and Beyond' (DOH, 1989). The working paper 'Working for Patients' predominantly dealt with hospital and family practitioner services whilst 'Caring for People: the Next Decade and Beyond' concentrated upon social services and community health services.

Health Care

The Act sets out the roles of purchasing authorities and general practitioner (GP) fundholding practices in purchasing health care on behalf of an identified population. Their responsibilities as purchasers include the identification of need, drawing up service specifications, negotiating and agreeing contracts, monitoring and evaluating provider performance and quality indicators. Purchasing arrangements also include the development of locality-based commissioning groups and GP sub-groups. GP fundholding practices are increasingly organising themselves into commissioning consortia in order to purchase services in sufficient quantities and thereby affect the quality of services they receive. Provider organisations, such as trusts and independent groups, are responsible for delivering the health care negotiated and agreed within the contract, and for monitoring the effectiveness and quality of that care.

In addition to setting out the NHS hospitals' responsibilities, the Act makes reference to joint responsibilities for the delivery of health and social care with, for example, the development of continuing care arrangements and the setting of eligibility criteria. The Act pays particular attention to the shift from secondary care settings to primary care settings in the provision of services.

Health authorities, through their contracts with provider agencies, are responsible for ensuring, whenever possible, the provision of community-based staff to carry out assessments and resulting treatment programmes for clients falling within the target groups of elderly and disabled, learning disabled clients and clients with mental health problems. Where clients have identified social needs provided for at home, the health authority has a responsibility for meeting their health care needs within that setting.

Community Care

The Act makes a distinction between clients with health care needs and clients with social care needs. In its simplest form, those with health care needs have their needs met by health service agencies and those with social care needs have their needs met by social care agencies. This requires collaboration and communication between the various groups involved. Joint commissioning between health and social services organised via locality-commissioning groups is one method by which such collaboration can be achieved. The Act operates from the premise that for the majority, care in the community offers the best choice of care available. The Act states that people should be able to live as normal a life as possible in their own homes or a homely environment of their choice. People should be provided with the optimum amount of support to help them realise their full potential and increase their quality of life. Emphasis is placed on promoting advocacy and choice for individuals.

Needs Assessment:

Social services are responsible for undertaking a comprehensive needs assessment of clients either living at home or being discharged from hospital. The assessments are organised by specially appointed case managers who co-ordinate the assessment plan on behalf of the local authority. The Act makes reference to the need for the assessments to be multi-disciplinary and, where possible, to be undertaken in the client's own home. The result of each assessment is that the client will have a care plan designed to address the needs identified in the assessment stage. The local authority and health authorities will be obliged to publish clear public plans detailing the local arrangements. These arrangements are published in the form of a 'community care plan'.

The local authority is largely an 'enabling agency' responsible for arranging and purchasing care services but no longer a major provider of service. The Act requires local authorities to spend 82% of their revenue in the independent and 'not for profit' sector.

The local authority is responsible for:

- assessment of social need;

- designing a package of care to meet the needs of clients and carers;

- purchasing services to meet these needs;

- monitoring and evaluating quality of provision.

The Act makes particular reference to four priority groups: elderly and disabled people, people with a mental health problem and people with learning disabilities. It sets out a number of key objectives for the delivery of care to these groups:

Elderly and Disabled People:

1 the promotion of positive and healthy life styles through the delivery of primary health care;

2 the avoidance of unnecessary institutional care wherever possible;

3 health authority provision of the full range of acute services, geriatric medicine and therapy services;

4 locally-based planning agreements maximising the elderly or disabled person's local networks.

People with Learning Disabilities:

1 services to be designed from collaborative multi-disciplinary assessments;

2 clients to have their health care needs met by the local health authority with their needs for residential and day services met within the context of social care provision;

3 children should not grow up in an institutional setting;

4 people with a learning disability should only be in NHS facilities when they have a medical need.

People with Mental Health Problems:

1 the care programme approach should be adopted for all individuals with mental health problems;

2 partnership capital schemes should be developed with the private sector;

3 a Code of Practice on compulsory admission should be laid before Parliament.

4 special assistance should be given to those who are mentally ill amongst the homeless population.

5 research on 'Emergency Care' should be developed.

Implications of the NHS and Community Care Act for Speech and Language Therapists:

The NHS and Community Care Act has implications for the delivery of speech and language therapy services in both health and social care domains.

Providers at a local level need to ensure that local health authorities make provision for continuity of care to be achieved. Assumptions should not be made as to their understanding of the role of the profession in this respect or indeed the availability of resources to provide such community care.

The Act makes it clear that health providers like speech and language therapists have a responsibility to work in tandem with local authorities by contributing to multi-disciplinary care assessments, where possible in the client's own home.

The profession needs to ensure that it is able to comply with these requirements. The profession should pay due regard to the priority groups and alert local purchasing authorities to the need to commission speech and language therapy services for these groups in accordance with professional guidance.

Speech and language therapists will need to ensure that they are in a position to contribute fully to the achievement of the principles of the Act as they relate to direct client care.

PROFESSIONAL INSURANCE

The College has taken out a Legal Liability policy for its members. The following comments on the terms of the policy have been agreed with the brokers.

Terms

The Policy has the following features:

- Legal Liability (with Property Damage excess of £100 each and every loss);

- Professional Indemnity for a total of £500,000 covering any malpractice or negligence during diagnosis or treatment.

1 The policy is in the name of the College for all registered subscribing members who are practising speech and language therapists (including in private practice) or who have practised speech and language therapy and have paid the requisite subscription.

2 It covers claims arising from alleged professional negligence, breach of professional conduct and damage to property.

3 It covers claims advised during the policy period regardless of when the actual incident giving rise to the claim occurred.

4 The policy is worldwide but excluding the USA and Canada.

5 It would be the responsibility of the Council of College to certify who is, or is not, a member and to decide on what is, or is not,

within the scope of professional activities when any notice of, or actual, claim is received.

6   Retired members can, if they wish to carry forward cover, pay one sum on retirement for cover against a claim arising from an incident when they were practising. They may obtain cover for occasional practice (i.e. not amounting to a business) on payment of a small premium.

7   Students (including student members) are not included. However, members would be indemnified for acts of students and/or others while under their supervision, providing the member is legally liable.

8   Newly qualified members are covered as soon as their application for membership has been approved.

9   The Policy covers the Legal Liability for injury to a client occurring during a domiciliary visit.

10 Whenever a member is aware of circumstances likely to give rise to a claim, immediate notice must be given to the College Office. No liability must be admitted, no admission, arrangement or promise of payment made.

Members working from their own homes are recommended to so advise their Home Insurers, particularly in respect of the General Public Liability Risk.

Copies of the policies and details of current premiums are held at the College Offices and may be obtained by any member (associate member) on request during normal working hours.

7

PROFESSIONAL DEVELOPMENT

Educational Framework

Pre-Qualification Education and Training

Transition to full clinical autonomy

Continuing Education and Professional Development

Research

EDUCATIONAL FRAMEWORK

 One of the central concerns of the College is to further the development of the profession into the 21st century. As such, it plays a key role in determining and establishing national policy in the education of speech and language therapists.

The College has established the following guidelines on undergraduate and post-graduate pre-qualification education, professional development and continuing education.

PRE-QUALIFICATION EDUCATION AND TRAINING

Course Content:

Through its Academic Board, the College provides definitions of what a speech and language therapist is or should be. The Board is actively involved in determining the knowledge base, skills and therapeutic competence of speech and language therapists with a view to evaluating the syllabus of all courses accredited by the College in line with the relevant statutory instruments (NHS Regulations (1974; amended 1985).

The Board does not consider it desirable to prescribe set hours for the teaching of specific subjects. The development of a competent speech and language therapist is not dependent upon following an identical prescribed routine of teaching. The Board therefore welcomes and supports diversity of approach to course planning, but provides certain basic criteria for the core subjects, which are agreed nationally and internationally.

1. The Board sets baseline criteria for the length of courses:

- the normal route to qualification will be by a three or four year full-time or equivalent part-time undergraduate course;

- an honours undergraduate course which includes a dissertation must extend over a minimum of three years full-time or the equivalent part-time study; such three year Honours courses must average at least 35 weeks per year;

- a post-graduate qualifying course must take place over two extended academic years of full-time study, i.e. 80 weeks or the equivalent part-time study.

2. The Board determines the baseline criteria for clinical experience required of all students successfully completing an accredited course.

- A minimum number of sessions of tutored clinical experience that should be spent in a clinic setting working under the supervision of a qualified speech and language therapist is laid down. Full details of the range of service locations, client groups and types of disorder that should be covered are contained in an annex to the College guidelines on accreditation of qualifying courses (RCSLT, 1995a).

The Education Process:

The goal of education is to develop relevant theoretical knowledge and skills, together with an ability to integrate and apply these in dealing with the pathologies encountered in the clinical setting. This forms the basis for understanding and taking on the multiplicity of roles of the speech and language therapist.

The academic component of the course should equip students to analyse and respond appropriately to any disorder they might meet. It is not necessary to have observed, experienced or studied in any depth every disorder or every theoretical approach. The goal is for students to be able to recognise when they need additional information, and to seek out and utilise such information.

The purpose of studying the core disciplines of language pathology, linguistics and phonetics, anatomy and physiology, audiology, psychology and research methodology is:

- to understand those principles in each subject which are relevant in analysing communication and related cognitive disorders, and to understand their role in the speech and language therapy context;

- to understand research within these disciplines which relates to the cognitive, emotional and social dimensions of communication disorders.

This does not necessitate a detailed study of the history or theoretical debates internal to each discipline. Rather, it depends on a critical appraisal of concepts and methods which contribute to the analysis of disorders and which should be taken into account in assessment and intervention.

It is important to recognise that such concepts and methods provide crucial directions in speech and language therapy, but do not themselves constitute theories of assessment or intervention and do not necessarily have immediate application to clinical practice. Furthermore, the relevant theoretical skills may be developed in different ways. Courses may vary in the balance of subjects and the depth to which each subject is covered, and still achieve similar skills in critical appraisal.

The clinical component of the course should provide the opportunity for students to integrate and apply their theoretical knowledge with a range of disorders in a variety of settings.

Students successfully completing a course accredited by the College are eligible for a certificate to practise. This is conditional on passing both the clinical and theoretical components of the course. The certificate is the guarantee of competence at the stage of entry to the profession.

At the conclusion of a qualifying course, a successful student is expected to be able to demonstrate the following:

- a core theoretical understanding of a range of communication and related disorders, and the theoretical frameworks underlying the principles of assessment, intervention and management of individuals with these disorders;

- a core of generally applicable clinical skills. It should be accepted that students cannot be expected to have developed a high level of clinical expertise in all areas and that such expertise is necessarily developed post-qualification.;

■ a grasp of the principles of research and research methodology which underpin:

- an analytical approach to clinical practice;

- the ability to access current literature and research, to evaluate it, and to apply the information where appropriate.;

■ skills in locating additional research and knowledge when needed in the clinical setting;

■ recognition of the scope and limits of the speech and language therapist's role, and knowledge of when to refer a client to other specialists;

■ ability to take an appropriate level of responsibility for professional and clinical actions;

■ ability to make use of information technology and AAC equipment in client intervention;

■ skill in maintaining clients' clinical records and an understanding of the legal implications of these records;

■ good interpersonal clinical skills which are developed through clinical observation and experience, and can only be assessed in the clinical context;

■ ability to plan and carry out individually appropriate management strategies:

- to set realistic objectives and

targets, and to devise means for achieving these;

- to justify objectives and targets;

- to evaluate therapy outcomes critically and modify therapy appropriately;

- to provide support, information and appropriate feedback to clients and carers.;

■ ability to prioritise clients for therapy and skills in caseload management;

■ an awareness of the administrative duties that are routinely undertaken in clinical practice;

■ an understanding of the importance of working in a multi-disciplinary team and appreciation of all professional roles within such a team.

The quality of the educational process will be assessed in terms of specific student achievements and also in terms of the totality of the learning experience for students.

Defining roles and responsibilities
Introduction:

The profession has analysed the shared responsibilities for providing opportunities and activities for the development of therapists during their pre-qualifying course and during their employment as newly qualified Grade 1 therapists. These responsibilities are set out the section entitled Bridging the Gap (see below).

Bridging the Gap – Shared Responsibilities for Providing Opportunities for the Development of Speech and Language Therapists

These guidelines have been produced after extensive consultations with educators, managers, experienced and recently qualified therapists. They are intended for use by these groups, as well as final year students and clinical teachers.

They are designed to provide guidance for those involved in the education of speech and language therapists and those employing graduates as Grade 1 therapists, in order that the development of the graduating therapist should continue after qualification. These guidelines should give valuable information to students and graduates on realistic expectations related to their development as therapists and their progress to full clinical autonomy. They will also inform the process of transition from graduate to fully registered status on the College register.

The guidelines are outlined in the Table below. The Table consists of a list of activities and development of skills which newly qualified speech and language therapists should experience during their qualifying course and/or during their employment as a Grade 1 therapist, normally for a period of about one year. The star (*) rating indicates where the balance of responsibility lies for providing that experience, or for supervising the acquisition of a particular skill:

- one star (*) indicates that the activity or skill is either introduced to a limited degree or needs to be continued during the first year of employment;

- two stars (**) indicate that a great deal

of experience or training needs to be provided during the designated period and by the designated person (or persons) responsible for the therapist before or after qualification.

It should be noted that these are guidelines only and, although the College strongly recommends that they are followed, it recognises that a number of points may be either difficult to implement in individual cases or inappropriate because of local circumstances. For example, it is recognised that:

- under I(a) it may be local policy that Grade 1 therapists work with a limited range of clients and/or in a limited number of locations;

- under I(c), while all graduating therapists should be well equipped to collect and keep accurate and detailed clinical data, they would be involved in more formal research only through choice and with guidance and supervision.

Students and newly qualified therapists themselves are expected to take a major responsibility for their own learning, and to make maximum use of the opportunities provided for them to develop as professionals.

BRIDGING THE GAP – Shared responsibility for providing opportunities for the development of speech and language therapists

One star (*) indicates that the activity or skill is either introduced to a limited degree or requires to be continued to some extent during the first year of employment.

Two stars (**) indicate that a great deal of experience or training needs to be provided during the designated period and by the designated person (or persons) responsible for the therapist before or after qualification.

	EDUCATION ESTABLISHMENT	CLINIC TEACHER (during qualifying course)	CLINICIAN/ MANAGER (during first year Grade 1 post)
I CLINICAL MANAGEMENT			
(a) CLINICAL CASELOAD			
- Caseload management		*	* *
- Therapy techniques/guidelines	* *	* *	*
- Case study skills including:			
case history taking;			
setting long- & short-term aims;			
ongoing evaluation and			
management, discharge of patients	* *	* *	*
- Quality assurance, audit and			
standard of practice	*	*	* *
- Provision of opportunity for clinical			
experience with a wide range of child			
and adult clients/rotation of Grade			
1 posts to complete clinical			
experience/interests	* *	* *	* *
- Case discussions	*	*	* *
- Joint sessions with experienced			
clinicians or specialist advisers		* *	* *
- Provision of identifiable base clinic			
and consideration of number of			
different sites covered per week			* *
(b) CLINICAL PLANNING			
- Time management	*	*	* *
- Time allowance for planning/preparation	*	*	* *
(c) CAREER DEVELOPMENT/RESEARCH			
- Research methodology	* *		
- Research opportunities	*		* *
- Career guidance			
(i) Advice re first job applications	* *	*	
(ii) Further education, in-service training,			
attendance at courses, research	*		* *

II CLINICAL ADMINISTRATION			
(a) INFORMATION - GENERAL			
- Organisation of speech and language therapy services, including trust policies (e.g. child abuse, dysphagia, violence, health & safety), referral procedures, etc.	*	*	* *
- Working with clerical staff			* *
(b) CLIENT RELATED			
- Principles of administration, including statistical returns, case notes, appointment system, filing etc.	*	*	* *
- Report writing	* *	* *	*
- Information technology	* *	*	*
III PROFESSIONAL RELATIONSHIPS			
(a) CLINICAL ORIENTATION			
- Induction period, including visits to all clinics in District or Trust, and other relevant departments (e.g. PT, OT, Health Visitors)			* *
- Introduction to NHS structures	*	*	* *
- Conditions of employment			* *
- Organisation of health care provision in UK	*	*	* *
- Organisation of educational system, including Education Acts, statementing/ recording procedure	* *	* *	* *
- Legal aspects, including health & safety, personal well-being, etc.	*	*	* *
- Current political issues	*		*
- Role of College	*		*
- Role of Union (MSF)	*		*
(b) PERSONAL SKILLS			
- Speech pathology knowledge base	* *	*	*
- Problem-solving skills that can be widely applied	* *	*	*
- Communication and self-presentation skills	* *	*	*
- Counselling skills	* *	* *	* *
- Advising and informing other staff groups including carers, volunteers, assistants (on a one-to-one basis, in meetings/conferences etc. .	*	*	*
- Assertiveness	*	*	* *
- Regular and frequent access to designated member for support/counselling			* *

Clinical Placements:

The organisation of clinical placements during a qualifying course is a crucial element in the preparation of a competent clinician.

Speech and language therapists undertaking clinical teaching of students should normally have at least one year's post-qualification experience. Therapists employed in posts Grade 2 and above, remuneration for the supervision of students on clinical placement is incorporated into their salary scales. The College therefore expects members to take on this responsibility for assuring the future of the profession and the provision of services. Speech and language therapists should be appropriately trained and supported to undertake clinical teaching. This is the joint responsibility of education establishments and services providing placements.

Induction:

1 An induction programme should be arranged for the student. The broad aims of induction are as follows:

- to help the student to have realistic expectations of her/his placement;

- to help the student settle into the clinic as quickly as possible;

- to outline the clinician's expectations of the student;

- to help the student understand speech and language therapy procedures;

- to open up clear lines of communication from the start of the clinical placement;

- to ensure the safety of the student and any clients being seen by the student in the clinic.

Good practice in clinical placements:

The elements of ongoing supervision can be identified under the following headings:

- clinician's responsibilities;

- student's responsibilities;

- education establishment's responsibilities.

Clinician's responsibilities towards the student speech and language therapist

General

1 Once the clinician has confirmed their student placement they should send the student an information sheet.

2 Clinicians should set aside time for induction on the first day of a placement, before introducing student speech and language therapists to clients.

3 To complement the induction programme, each department or clinical base should develop a student information pack containing routine information regarding the clinic, school, hospital, etc. Parts of this pack should be made available to the student before the placement begins.

Health and Safety

1 To ensure that the student speech and language therapist is aware of the clinic's

Health and Safety policy and of all relevant emergency procedures.

2   To ensure that the student is aware of the need for confidentiality, clinical teachers should clarify guidelines for the sharing of written and oral information.

Organisational

1   The clinical teacher should clarify the allocation of time for:

- clinician's observation of the student;

- student observation of the clinician;

- discussion/feedback of observation and/or therapy.

2   The clinical teacher must ensure that the student speech and language therapist and clinician agree arrangements for cancellation of attendance by either clinician or student.

3   Should the clinician be absent from the clinic she/he must ensure appropriate supervision for the student speech and language therapist.

4   The clinician should discuss the number of clients the student speech and language therapist will be responsible for, and agree this within the objectives set with the student.

Administration

1   The clinician should be aware of the need to provide clear information and support with regard to administrative tasks.

2   Administrative tasks should be described and, wherever possible, an opportunity to

undertake procedures should be given for:

- appointment booking;

- transport booking;

- waiting list management;

- portering system;

- postal system;

- referring clients to others;

- telephone system/message taking;

- data collection;

- discharge of clients.

Development of Clinical Skills

1   The clinician should ensure the student speech and language therapist has access to relevant information about the client.

2   The clinician should ensure that the student speech and language therapist has an opportunity to carry out agreed objectives for:

- observation;

- assessment;

- therapy;

- management.

3   The clinician should help the student speech and language therapist to develop skills for case note records and report writing, perhaps providing examples of standard reports and notes.

4   The clinician should explain the legal implications of case notes/reports and supervise and sign any notes/reports that

student speech and language therapists are involved in producing.

5 Where possible, arrangements should be made for student speech and language therapists to observe other related client care, e.g. physiotherapy, occupational therapy.

6 The clinician should ensure that feedback to the student speech and language therapist is constructive, and should aim to:

- encourage students to feel that they are contributing significantly to client care;

- help students to evaluate their interaction objectively;

- encourage students to feel able to bring new ideas to the clinic;

- encourage students to discuss anxieties/concerns openly and to provide support where appropriate;

- assist the student to become an independent professional.

7 The clinician should enable students to focus on and develop knowledge, skills and attitudes which are appropriate to professional practice, and take account of client care, working with carers and team working.

Clinician's Responsibilities Towards the Clients/Service

1 The clinician remains responsible for the provision of the service to clients and their carers and for the adequate supervision of students working with them.

2 The clinician should always request and obtain permission of the client or relevant unit head before a student speech and language therapist observes or undertakes therapy with them.

3 The clinician is responsible for ensuring the appropriate supervision of student speech and language therapist contact with clients.

4 The clinician should sign the case notes, reports etc. that a student speech and language therapist produces in relation to a client, and must ensure confidentiality at all times.

Clinician's Responsibilities Towards the Education Establishment

1 The clinician should:

- organise a clinical placement that is in line with the requirement of the particular course;

- be responsible for the allocation of adequate time for student speech and language therapist's supervision, including time for the visiting tutor to discuss the placement;

- provide the student speech and language therapist with a positive and realistic experience of clinical practice;

- if appropriate, discuss any problems with the education establishment at an early date so that necessary support can be given to both the student and the clinician.

Student Speech and Language Therapist's Responsibilities

1 The student should:

- confirm the placement arrangements with the clinician before the start of the placement;

- work within the guidance of the supervising clinician;

- maintain the confidentiality of client information and be familiar with Health and Safety procedures;

- inform the clinician as early as possible if they are unable to attend clinic or are delayed, and advise the clinician about clients they are managing;

- discuss concerns with the clinician and seek support in areas of uncertainty;

- be punctual;

- be professional in all dealings with clients and colleagues.

Education Establishment Responsibilities

1 The education establishment should:

- provide clear learning objectives which have been agreed with the student for each placement;

- provide the clinician with current information regarding the course content;

- ensure that clinicians are given information about their student speech and language therapist's placement;

- after consultation with the student, inform the clinician about any relevant problems the student may have that might affect their participation in clinical work and provide support when appropriate.

A Guide to Information that could be contained in a Student Information Pack:

1 Legal/Professional Accountability - for information

2 HIV virus - Guidelines for speech and language therapists

3 Data forms and procedures, with examples

4 Health and Safety Policy and Emergency procedures for specific clinics

5 Fire Policy

6 Child Abuse: Guidelines for speech and language therapists

7 Guidelines for gifts

8 Guidelines for sick leave

9 Speech and language therapy structure

10 Clinic description/outline

11 Administrative procedures - brief description for reference

12 A-Z map of Clinic/Hospital

13 Bibliography/reference list, if appropriate to clinical base.

General Operational Guidelines for Clinical Placements

There will be times when students will be observing proceedings in the clinic and the clinical teacher as she/he carries out the full range of professional duties. Students should be given adequate opportunity to question, and to participate within the level of skills and knowledge they have already acquired. Students should always be encouraged to make notes on their observations for later discussion and be encouraged to transcribe utterances where they can and where this may be significant or useful. It may also be helpful to ask students why certain therapies or recommendations are made, before an explanation is given.

Placements give students the opportunity to tackle real problems in a working environment. The degree to which students wholly or partly carry out clinical procedures themselves will depend on their ability and experience.

1 Caseload

This will depend on the type of placement, the student, and the way that the supervising therapist works. The caseload number should be agreed with the relevant education establishment based upon local guidelines.

2 Case Selection

In clinical settings, a range of factors will affect the choice of case selection available to students. These include consideration of the client's needs, the length of time that the student will be available, the pattern of placement and the likelihood of attendance.

3 Report Forms

Report forms have two major purposes:

to provide feedback to clinical tutors on students clinical progress, and to provide feedback to each student on their developing competence.

Ideally, by the time students reach the end of their course they should be their own assessors and evaluators. For this reason, students should be encouraged to self-assess and compare their own assessment with those of their clinical teachers. This makes the assessment procedure much more accessible to students, and ensures that it does not appear as an arbitrary judgement over which the student has little control.

It is desirable that each service identifies a key clinical teacher in the speech and language therapy team with overall responsibility for placements, and for communicating with the education establishment and the clinical teaching team.

TRANSITION TO FULL CLINICAL AUTONOMY

The College accepts the need for all entrants into the profession to serve at least one year in clinical settings before being accepted as clinically autonomous practitioners registered as full members of the College.

Good management of newly qualified staff is critical to their successful development into clinical autonomy and successful integration into existing services. This also applies to 'returners' to the profession (i.e. speech and language therapists who have not practised for five years), who may present the speech and language therapy manager with similar challenges.

It is important that newly qualified staff and returners be given a balanced induction to the employing authority's services, management structure and areas of specialist expertise. New staff must be aware of the expectations placed upon them and the standards to which they are required to work.

The induction period should include an assessment of the speech and language therapist's skills and knowledge in the context of the workplace. Managers should not rely on assumptions based on academic achievements.

Newly qualified staff and returners may benefit from the support of a 'mentor' colleague, whose role it is to offer advice and guidance outside of the management line. Specifically, the role of the mentor will be to assist her/his colleague in integrating theory and practice, in building self confidence as a practitioner, and in developing and implementing skills in critical appraisal (RCSLT, PSB, 1996).

In addition, regular line management supervision is essential in order to ensure that ongoing support and training is provided and that potential difficulties are avoided. Such meetings should be held on no less than a monthly basis, with weekly meetings during the first three months of appointment.

These meetings can be divided into two parts, the first part focusing on any queries the therapist may have, and the second part discussing specific topics.

Suggested topics may include:

- setting up a caseload and caseload management;

- organisational skills in the clinic;

- different treatment modes, i.e. group/individual;

- structuring treatment contracts;

- interviewing skills;

- administrative skills:
  - referral systems
  - report writing
  - statistical collection
  - record keeping
  - discharge systems;

- assessment and intervention strategies;

- research initiatives;

- communication and communication skills:
  - interdepartmental liaison
  - attending and participating in meetings
  - case conferences;

- areas identified for formal/informal training.

It may be useful to supply the new staff member with an induction folder containing notes on the general procedures for the department under the following headings:

*Location of policies, procedures
and protocols;
Annual leave; Time keeping;
Travel; Expenses;
Sickness; Statistics; Library;
Courses/In-service training;
Supplies; Health and Safety;
Students; Time Sheets;
Reports and letters for typing;
Clerical check list;
Useful names and addresses.*

It should also include specimen forms used in the clinics, as well as a copy of the organisational structure for the employing authority and a timetable showing when and where staff are located.

During the first two weeks the mentor therapist should arrange to see the new member of staff on a daily basis at a mutually agreed time. In addition, the therapist should be available by phone. Subsequent meetings should be by arrangement, but should be held frequently during the first six weeks.

At the end of the first six weeks, the mentor therapist should ensure that the new member of staff:

- is familiar with all that is included in the induction folder;

- is able to deal with new referrals;

- knows how to write reports and where to send them;

- has been introduced to collection of statistics;

- knows where to go to resolve problems;

- knows the main professional people with whom they are likely to have regular contact;

- has been introduced to local Health and Safety policies;

- knows how to discharge a client.

It is suggested that during the first year of practice, newly qualified staff/returners join with their peers in order to discuss on a small group basis specific topics of interest. These groups may or may not be led by senior colleagues.

The transition to full clinical autonomy, normally after approximately one year of post-qualification clinical work, should not be seen as an automatic progression based upon time in post, but on an assessment of competence and the application of learning to clinical practice within a planned programme of experience.

Employing authorities are responsible for establishing criteria by which the newly qualified staff member moves to full clinical autonomy. The profession, through the College, has established guidelines in order to enable employing authorities to act consistently.

The guidelines are summarised in the following criteria. The newly qualified staff member must have:

- significant knowledge of the role and composition of the employing authority;

- an understanding of the administrative and managerial system and their implications for speech and language therapy service delivery;

- an ability to organise and operate a clinic and the associated caseload;

- an ability to provide professional input into a multi-disciplinary service and achieve service delivery through other non-speech and language therapy caseworkers;

- an ability to access specialist advice and to develop an understanding of current clinical issues and debates;

- opportunities for involvement in meetings of professionals and other planned development opportunities;

- an ability to maintain adequate systems of recording and communicating relevant data.

The decision to recommend to the employing authority that a therapist transfer to the clinically autonomous grade should be taken by a speech and language therapist acting in a management capacity. This therapist is required to countersign the newly qualified therapist as 'competent' in relation to the categories outlined in 'Bridging the Gap'. which forms the basis for the College procedure for transfer from the Graduate to the Full Practice Register. The decision will be the outcome of performance appraisal, which in turn will draw on information gained through the formal supervision sessions.

The newly qualified/returner therapist

should be made aware, at the outset, of the purpose of the programme and the methods of evaluation to be used.

Where performance difficulties become apparent, they should be addressed immediately, giving time and an opportunity for improvement to occur. An assessment of the additional support needs of the individual should be made.

Where an individual is experiencing difficulties in achieving performance targets, in spite of professional support, the therapist should be counselled using local and/or College resources. This may include career advice where appropriate. These facts should be communicated in a clear but sensitive way, and support offered regarding career planning.

The professional body does not consider it appropriate to prescribe time-scales for establishing competency for newly qualified/returner programmes. However, it is unlikely that a speech and language therapist will have established competence across a range of services in less than twelve months, but should have done so within two years.

CONTINUING EDUCATION AND PROFESSIONAL DEVELOPMENT

Introduction
Speech and language therapists work within a climate of rapid change in health, education, social services and voluntary sector settings. In order to maintain a skilled

and motivated workforce, who are able to plan and deliver an appropriate high quality service to purchasers, and thus to clients, it is crucial that individuals continue to expand their knowledge base and to enhance their skills following qualification.

Continuing professional development [CPD] refers to the process whereby practitioners - within a structure of identified goals - seek to increase their level of knowledge, to refine or learn new skills and to apply these in the workplace. Continuing education [CE] describes the activities undertaken to acquire this knowledge and skills. The aim of both is to allow practitioners to remain competent to provide an appropriate high quality service to clients, and to offer a greater level of expertise.

Regular up-dating is required:

■ to become familiar with the requirements of new legislation;

■ to deal with the consequences of changes in public policy or shifts in client profile;

■ to equip individuals to provide support and advice to purchasers, providers and the profession;

■ to move forward the frontiers of knowledge within the discipline and ensure practice is evidence-based;

■ to ensure that all clinicians entering a new or expanding field have the knowledge and skills that are essential to safeguarding their duty of care;

■ to satisfy demands for improved standards.

The professional body distinguishes between two periods for the developing clinician:

■ the immediate post-qualification period (which will only exceptionally be less than one year, and may be longer), during which newly-qualified therapists [NQT] consolidate their previous knowledge and apply their learning to clinical practice (see Section on Transition to Full Clinical Autonomy);

■ the remainder of clinicians' careers which, in many cases, is likely to be characterised by periods of practice and of non-practice, and by movement into a variety of posts in different locations and with different responsibilities.

Policy framework

The responsibility for engaging in ongoing CPD/CE activities should be shared by practitioners and employers. Such activities should be ongoing throughout the working life of every speech and language therapist. It is important that a range of opportunities should be widely available to therapists who are prepared to take advantage of them.

CPD/CE policy for the profession should be practicable, acceptable, credible and affordable. It must be flexible enough to respond both to service needs and also to changes in professional practice and educational thinking. It must provide evidence for purchasers that the CE/CPD activities are essential and cost-effective in order to justify use of limited resources.

The College has taken the initiative in defining a national CE/CPD policy (RCSLT, 1995b), as part of its role in setting standards for the profession. These necessarily involve standards and guidelines for ensuring the initial and continuing competence of its members.

Individuals should also make a commitment to effective appraisal, self-monitoring, reflection and by actively seeking learning opportunities. As professionals, speech and language therapists are responsible for ensuring that they work within their level of competence and that they contribute to identifying their own development needs.

Speech and language therapy departments should have a clear policy for CE/CPD and employers should ensure that managers have access to advice so that appropriate assessment, counselling and mentoring can be offered to clinicians.

Speech and language therapists working outside a management structure are advised to enlist the support and advice of colleagues in creating their own system of self- and peer-appraisal.

Scope of CPD/CE activities

A programme of CE/CPD should not be a series of isolated courses, seminars or other training events but should exist within a framework of initiatives that includes regular appraisal with objective setting, briefing groups, case review and presentation.

Of particular relevance are:

- advanced clinical studies courses run in centres of excellence, which equip therapists for posts with specific responsibilities (e.g. in working with deaf people, dysphasics, the elderly or severe learning disabled);

- approved short courses in subjects where there is a general need to raise the knowledge base of the profession (e.g. dysphagia, clinical supervision);

- Specific Interest Group meetings, workshops, seminars and conferences which provide a wealth of CE/CPD opportunities at all levels.

The minimum required personal commitment by practising therapists to continuing education activities covering specific areas of clinical interest is the equivalent of 10 (half-day) sessions per year. The needs of those working part-time and on short-term contracts, as well as of returners to the profession, should be taken into account in local policies. Since 1991, all registered members of the College have been requested to complete a personal record (log) of appropriate activities. These have been defined as widely as possible to take in all activities which can be considered as ultimately contributing to the enhancement of therapy services and client care. The range of suggested and acceptable activities and their approximate time value are set out in the log. These are defined as flexibly as possible so that all opportunities can be exploited. Many types of self-directed learning can be included, as well as more formal courses.

Annual re-registration by the professional body for practising members depends on fulfilling these CPD/CE requirements.

Speech and language therapists are also encouraged to initiate or participate in research projects, to study for relevant higher degrees, and to take advantage of more general health service management and other appropriate continuing education programmes.

The professional body maintains an up-to-date list of appropriate higher degrees and other educational and research opportunities. Information on providers and funding sources is disseminated to the membership. Guidance is available to clinicians on pursuing research activities within both uni- and multi-disciplinary settings.

Supervision

A key factor in delivering a quality speech and language therapy service is good professional supervision. Supervision refers to a formal arrangement which enables a speech and language therapist to discuss her/his work regularly with someone who is experienced and qualified. Two forms of supervision are recommended for speech and language therapists:

- management-directed supervision; and

- non-managerial supervision.

Management-directed supervision:

Managers need to ensure that the system of supervision used in their department is understood by all staff, that it is offered on a regular basis with adequate time available and necessary recording and follow-up actions taking place.

The supervision process should, in general terms, allow the 'supervisee' to consider her/his strengths and needs. The process may involve case review, either on a random selection or case selection basis.

The supervision sessions should provide information and data which contributes to the formal appraisal, whilst dealing with day-to-day challenges in a positive way.

In instances where significant difficulties are encountered in achieving acceptable standards of conduct or performance, and where opportunities have been offered to improve, the supervisor needs to know her/his level of authority in the use of a disciplinary procedure. It is essential that speech and language therapy managers are trained in managing these situations in order to prevent punitive use of these procedures, and only after all other avenues have been exhausted.

In summary, management supervision aims to:

- enable the speech and language therapist to fulfil her/his job description;

- provide information for carrying out individual performance reviews;

- encourage and support staff in following through objectives set during the formal appraisal;

- give advice on managing caseloads and any problems that may cause problems in the day-to-day functioning of the service;

- ensure that the speech and language therapist is aware of the professional standards and codes of conduct expected of them, and to facilitate their adherence to such professional standards;

- discuss professional development needs in relation to service delivery;

- assist the speech and language therapist in relating practice to theory and theory to practice thereby promoting continuing education and development.

Non-managerial supervision:

Non-managerial supervision provides an opportunity for therapists to obtain case supervision outside the line management structure. It is a formal arrangement in which therapists can discuss their work, and their feelings about their work, regularly with another person or in a group.

The aims are to:

- help the speech and language therapist overcome some of the considerable demands created by the nature of the work by helping to develop understanding of the interactive processes in relationships with clients;

- help the therapist deal with issues of over-involvement, avoidance or confusion by directing attention to factors affecting the client's situation;

- reinforce and offer feedback on good clinical skills;

- assist in the management of issues arising out of the location of delivery and the speech and language therapist's confidence in managing complex inter-disciplinary situations;

- offer support to therapists and thereby prevent crises or disillusionment arising;

- challenge therapists on their practice in

a supportive, trusting environment.

Issues of confidentiality should be fully addressed in the context of non-managerial supervision. The speech and language therapist must feel assured that discussions which take place are strictly confidential.

Non-managerial supervision can take place individually, in pairs and in a group. The criteria for making supervision contracts are as important in a group context as in an individual context. The frequency should not be less than monthly and the meetings should be regular. It may be important for a newly qualified speech and language therapist to have a supervisor who shares a similar type of caseload. A more experienced therapist may well benefit from having a supervisor who has a different speciality. Experienced speech and language therapists may at times find peer group supervision sufficient. The supervisor or group facilitator should encourage a learning environment which promotes critical appraisal and problem solving skills.

Training should be available for supervisors and facilitators. In the case of manager-directed supervision, training in individual performance review and disciplinary proceedings should be provided.

Support

The College recognises that speech and language therapists require easy access to support networks both from within and outside of the profession. Good clinical practice relies upon therapists' recognition of their limits of expertise and their ability to secure clinical support in the delivery of their services.

Therapists at all levels of expertise and management require support in order to exchange information and share expertise thereby raising the overall quality of the delivery of client care.

Professional support should be available through:

- the management structure of the employing authority;

- colleagues;

- the College local groups;

- the College Specific Interest Groups;

- regional professional networks for speech and language therapy managers and clinicians;

- the managers associations.

The College acknowledges the potential for pressures arising from professional practice where the unique relationship with the client is paramount. The College suggests that adequate provision of support leads to reduced stress levels and the enhanced ability to 'manage' distressing or complex situations. This is especially important for newly qualified therapists and therapists who may find themselves working in isolation. The College recommends that, wherever possible, joint initiatives and close collaboration should be a normal part of service delivery in order to prevent isolation and resulting difficulties.

It is important for speech and language therapists working in a service structure to be confident in their manager's ability to offer responsive and sensitive support in times of difficulty.

The speech and language therapy manager recognises that her/his commitment to staff will at times extend to facilitating personal support. It is likely that the support will be more appropriately offered outside of the management line. However the therapist may need help in accessing the appropriate support.

In situations where especially high levels of stress are likely owing to the nature of the speech and language therapist's caseload or work environment, it is important to enable groups to offer mutual support in order to prevent individual isolation, and facilitate group learning and problem solving. If speech and language therapists find themselves in work situations which generate stress and emotional vulnerability, it is important that the work context also creates opportunities to deal with these.

Support may also be available from within the resources of the employing authority, e.g. from the occupational health department or staff counsellors.

In summary, the professional body recognises that speech and language therapists may require support of both a professional and personal nature throughout their career and urges employing authorities, speech and language therapists managers and clinicians to deal sensitively and effectively with these needs as they arise.

Appraisal

Appraisal is a process aimed at managing performance in the work setting. Information regarding individual performance is provided to staff in order to allow comparisons with previously-agreed expectations to be made.

The College supports such appraisal when it is based on a explicit system, clearly understood and capable of gaining staff commitment. It should be carried out regularly and thoroughly by supervisors who will have appropriate experience and training. This should ensure a positive and motivating experience capable of enhancing performance.

An appraisal system following these principles is less likely to be dependent upon documentation than the skills with which it is carried out. As with supervision, it is essential that the necessary time is committed to the appraisal/interview. Its aim should be to identify the strengths and needs of the individual, and set clear objectives for the following year. There should also be a commitment to professional career development.

The College supports initiatives which seek to use appraisal to enhance quality of service rather than management control.

The appraisal system relies upon the information gained throughout the supervision sessions.

There should be no surprises for either the appraiser or the appraisee at the interview. Appraisal which occurs in the absence of regular supervision will be non-productive and potentially demotivating.

This is particularly important in professions such as speech and language therapy, where therapists do not usually work alongside their managers.

Where a speech and language therapist is

managed by more than one person, one senior must assume the responsibility for undertaking the appraisal.

In these instances, the appraisee would have a meeting with the second manager during which new objectives and development plans would be formed. These would be fed into the formal appraisal interview.

Following the appraisal, the performance outcome and a plan for the following twelve months should be drawn up and agreed. The information may be shared with the appraiser's line manager.

The College supports appraisal systems that follow these guidelines, as a positive mechanism for quality assurance and continuous development.

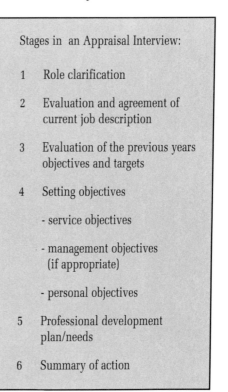

Stages in an Appraisal Interview:

1   Role clarification

2   Evaluation and agreement of
    current job description

3   Evaluation of the previous years
    objectives and targets

4   Setting objectives

    - service objectives

    - management objectives
      (if appropriate)

    - personal objectives

5   Professional development
    plan/needs

6   Summary of action

RESEARCH

The College is committed to the development of high standards of clinical practice through the systematic evaluation of therapeutic approaches and outcomes and the development of evidence-based practice. It gives full support to the NHS Research and Development Strategy, which aims to integrate research into practice and to nurture a knowledge-based and reflective workforce (DOH, 1993). If the profession is to continue to develop its expertise and apply this expertise to new and challenging areas of service delivery, research aimed specifically at informing clinical practice must be undertaken. Speech and language therapy research should be grounded in the concerns of the communication-disabled population and seek to answer questions relevant to their needs.

Clinical research is fundamental to future clinical practice and therefore requires investment. In order to be successful, research needs to be properly planned and adequately funded.

One of the requirements for effective clinical research is adequate time for preparation and reflection. This can be only be achieved if the speech and language therapist is not undertaking a full time clinical commitment. The College therefore recommends that research is carried out during time designated for research and separated from clinical commitments.

Speech and language therapists carrying out research require contact with colleagues for peer discussion and supervision. They need to build up a network of colleagues who can provide support in selecting appropriate methodologies and evaluating outcomes.

Resourcing needs to take into account the necessary finance required to facilitate both research supervision and peer support.

Research should be supervised. In order to ensure that research addresses clinically relevant issues, it is important that close collaboration is developed with clinical departments relevant to the research topic.

Due to the multi-dimensional nature of communication, it is likely that the necessary collaboration will involve close links with members of other professions and consumer organisations. Where a speech and language component is part of a larger study, an appropriate advisor should be available to the research team.

Research should at all times follow the employing authority's Ethical Committee requirements and the College Ethical Guidelines for Research as laid down in the Code of Professional Conduct.

The speech and language therapist undertaking research must ensure that clients participating in any research or teaching activity are fully informed and understand the nature, course and possible effects of these activities. Despite the potential difficulties of working with a communication-disabled population, clinician researchers should at all times ensure that clients are kept informed of the research programme as it unfolds. It must be made clear that any decision taken by the client and/or carer not to take part in a research study will not in any way affect the therapy which the client may receive.

Research findings should be made public and disseminated fully within the relevant client and professional groups. Researchers are encouraged to share their research proposals, progress and results with the College Research Committee.

All therapists are encouraged to share their findings with the professional body, regardless of the size of their study.

Research in speech and language therapy is eclectic, encompassing methodologies from social and natural sciences. It should be conducted with an open mind and a broad vision, adhering to the research principles of verification, objectivity and critical appraisal. In order to facilitate an interest and expertise in clinical research, training in research methodology should be available to therapists at both an undergraduate and post-graduate level.

In 1994, the Department of Health published a Position Statement on Research and Development in the Therapy Professions. This report was prepared by a working group consisting of occupational therapists, physiotherapists and speech and language therapists with research experience. Key recommendations in the report included:

- an increase in the number of doctoral and post-doctoral research awards for speech and language therapists;

- an increase in the number of joint appointments by university departments and trusts to facilitate the development of research expertise within the profession and research which is rooted in clinical experience;

- service managers were urged to facilitate the development of clinical research in their departments in order to progress the knowledge and skills of the services

provided to communication-disabled clients.

- purchasers were encouraged to write research components into contracts and to place more value on research activities undertaken by clinician researchers;

- the report suggested that protection against salary differentials for experienced clinicians wishing to return to clinical practice following completion of a specific piece of research would also contribute to a more established and attractive career infrastructure for researcher clinicians.

The full report is available from the College (DOH, 1994).

8

A STRATEGY FOR
SERVICE MANAGEMENT

THE SPEECH AND LANGUAGE THERAPY MANAGER

Effective management at every level of the speech and language therapy service is essential in order to ensure provision of a quality service to clients with a communication difficulty.

The role of the speech and language therapy manager is to facilitate the provision, delivery and development of an effective and efficient service.

In addition to managerial skills, a professional manager of speech and language therapy services must have an appropriate theoretical knowledge base and relevant clinical experience, in order to ensure that the most appropriate clinical advice and standards are available to purchasers and service users.

The Manager's Role encompasses:

■ Identification of epidemiological and demographic needs:

- these will relate to local, regional and national policies from health, social services, education, voluntary and private agencies.

■ Provision of Services:

- to monitor both supply and demand to ensure the most efficient use of

resources, financial and manpower, in accordance with national and local professional standards, statutory requirements and purchasing intentions.

- to monitor the service provided, evaluate outcomes, modify and devise clear policy statements for service delivery.

- to be involved in the provision of service development plans, business planning and contracting.

■ Quality and Effectiveness of Service:

- to provide leadership and direction for the service.

- to provide local standards for the service which adhere to national and regional professional standards

- to develop appropriate quality assurance initiatives.

■ Quality Strategy:

- to produce a strategic plan including a review of the service and appropriate service and quality objectives.

- to develop and maintain audit.

- to carry out critical analysis and interpretation of service data in order to inform purchasers and to ensure maintenance of clinical standards.

■ Recruitment and Retention of Staff:

- to recommend appropriate conditions for employment.

- to ensure the availability of appropriate levels of competence and skill mix within the staff group to meet local needs. This requires appropriate recruitment policies with knowledge of the professional market and staff expectations.

- to allocate appropriate workloads within an overall career structure.

- to provide professional and personal continuous development programmes, through effective supervision, personal appraisal system and provision of appropriate informal and formal training.

- to encourage and facilitate clinical research and provision of clinical training for speech and language therapy students.

- to provide leadership to speech and language therapy staff and foster good multi-disciplinary team work.

■ Cost and Value:

- to relate costs of service to input and outcomes and to identify areas of concern and effective remediation.

- to ensure that costs of equipment and training are related to needs of the service and provide value for money.

■ Income Generation:

- to recommend activities or products which can generate income without disturbing quality of service.

■ Flexibility:

- to ensure that resources are used flexibly for maximum effect.

- to identify where and when changes in service need to be made and appraise line management structures accordingly.

The Resources:

In order to be effective the manager must have:

■ access to a good information system;

■ support of experienced personnel managers and staff;

■ good financial information and easy access to finance staff/managers;

■ good communication and liaison with other services and senior managers;

■ access to professional networks;

■ regular feedback from staff and clients.

Standards For Management Practice:

Professional speech and language therapy managers will;

1 **have a certificate to practice as issued by the Royal College of Speech and Language Therapists.**

2 **undergo post-graduate management training and education and/or research experience in all areas of management activity.**

3 **undertake ongoing management training in order to update knowledge and skills.**

SERVICE PLANNING AND DEVELOPMENT

Epidemiology

Population Data

Epidemiological data makes an important contribution to service planning and development. It should provide information which enhances the organisation and distribution of services. However, establishing reliable and useful data on the varied populations of individuals with communication disorders can be difficult, as prevalence figures are subject to local variations and changes in referral patterns as well as differences in terminology and methodology.

In 1986, Enderby & Philipp (1986) reviewed the available literature and estimated the number of people in the United Kingdom with speech and language disorders associated with a range of developmental problems and medical conditions. These authors acknowledged that the estimates were sometimes difficult to derive because definitions in the literature were not uniform, available information was sparse and information was often based on specific hospital populations rather than on community-based populations. Despite these limitations, the authors estimated that 2.3 million people in the United Kingdom had some speech or language disorder. The 1983 mid-year population of the United Kingdom (56,377,000 persons) was used to derive this estimate (OPCS 1984). Enderby and Phillipp suggested that 800,000 of this population had a severe communication disorder (i.e.. have difficulty making themselves understood by anyone other than their immediate family)

and 1.5 million have a moderate communication disorder (i.e.. have a speech and language defect which is noticeable to the lay person but who may nevertheless remain intelligible). The figures presented in this paper did not include data on autism, mutism, stammering, psychological speech loss, familial dystonias and psychiatric speech disturbances.

Enderby & Philipp's estimates were much larger than those of the Quirk Report (Quirk, 1972), which suggested 324,180 persons in the United Kingdom were 'needing help' from a speech and language therapist. This is partly attributable to the broader range of disorders and client groups reviewed by Enderby & Philipp. Moreover, whereas the figures in the Quirk Report were an estimate of the number of people 'needing help' from speech therapy services, the estimates arrived at in the Enderby and Phillipp study were of the number of people with severe and moderate speech and language disorders. No reference was made to the numbers requiring speech therapy services.

In 1989, Enderby & Davies (1989) revisited existing data and reviewed more recent epidemiological studies. They confirmed that the figures published in the Quirk Report were a considerable underestimate. Their estimates have been summarised in Table 1.

Enderby and Davies acknowledge that their calculations were based upon a combination of empirical data, reported professional standards and consensus treatment regimens. Consequently, the figures may not constitute representative sampling across all the client groups served by speech and language therapists (Bryan et al, 1991). The authors also acknowledged that they did not address the diversity of models of service provision which characterises current speech and language therapy provision (Davies and Enderby, 1991). Enderby and Davies therefore concluded that their estimates would 'require revision in the light of yet further evidence' (Enderby and Davies, 1989, p328). Analyses of population data should become more widespread as speech and language therapy services utilise appropriate computerised information systems.

Other methodologies employed in this complex area include the use of notional and actual caseload analyses and workload analysis. (Gordon, 1993, Scottish Office, 1993, TASLTM, 1995) Notional and actual caseload analysis involves calculating staffing levels based on caseload/staffing ratios. Workload analysis involves calculating staffing levels on the basis of workload activity surveys. Increasingly, a combination of methods are used. The Professional Standards Board of the College acknowledges the difficulties in this area, and suggests that a prescriptive staffing formula, regardless of which methodology has been applied, may not be possible or even desirable. Managers are therefore challenged to choose and apply whichever methods provide the greatest advantage for local needs. The greater the accuracy of baseline data collection, the more representative the staffing prediction or estimate (RCSLT, PSB, 1996).

TABLE 1

INCIDENCE & PREVALENCE TABLE

Disorder	Incidence of disorder per 100,000 population	Prevalence of disorder per 100,000 population	Percent with disorder causing speech or language problem	Number of speech/lang handicapped per 100,000 population	Number of severely speech/lang handicapped per 100,000 population	Number with moderate speech/lang handicap 100,000 population
Mental handicap (all ages)	NK	2,500.0	55.0	1375.0	800.0	575.0
Stammering	3495.0	1,070.0	100.0	1070.0	70.0	1000.0
Pre-school age speech & lang**	NK	691.2	100.0	691.2	230.4	460.8
School age speech & lang**	NK	400.0	100.0	400.0	200.0	200.0
CVA	200.0	500.0	30.0	150.0	70.0	80.0
Deafness	1.6	200.0	60.0	120.0	45.0	75.0
Cerebral Palsy***	2.0	175.0	60.0	105.0	20.0	85.0
Cleft Palate***	2.0	NK (>142.0)	40.0	57.0	19.0	38.0
Parkinson's Disease	20.0	125.0	55.0	69.0	23.0	46.0
Multiple Sclerosis	3.0	60.0	55.0	33.0	10.0	23.0
Dysphonia	28.0	28.0	100.0	28.0	10.0	18.0
Muscular Dystrophy	1.2	20.0	25.0	5.0	2.0	3.0
Motor Neurone Disease	1.6	6.0	57.5	3.5	1.2	2.3
Myasthenia Gravis	3.0	6.0	25.0	1.5	0.5	1.0
Huntingdon's Chorea	0.4	5.0	60.0	3.0	1.0	2.0
Laryngectomy	0.9	3.0	100.0	3.0	2.0	1.0
Friedreich's Ataxia	0.4	2.0	60.0	1.2	0.6	0.6
Head Injury	286.0	NK (800)	20.0	NK (160)	NK (60)	NK (100)

*   *Many of the figures in this table are estimated from references cited in the text. They should be used as a guide rather than a definitive statement.*

**   *The incidence and prevalence estimates are derived from the number of pre-school children per 100,000 general population.*

***   *Based on the numbers per 100,000 new born population.*

NK   *Not known*

Service Profiles

In order to ensure the delivery of appropriate and responsive speech and language therapy services, an effective system of assessing need and undertaking forward planning requires identification and implementation. The assessment of need is a central function of purchasing authorities/boards.

The role of the purchasing authority in assessing needs and securing services to meet those needs has been well documented in the NHS and Community Care Act (1990). Planners at a national and local level have been exploring a range of models around which this task may be focused. It remains, however, a complex task.

Purchasers are increasingly buying 'packages of care' for individual clients or client groups. This change in purchasing will have major implications for the profile of speech and language therapy services.

Speech and language therapy services can be placed within the context of three needs-based assessment models:

- problem-based assessment;

- client -based assessment;

- geographically-based assessment.

The problem-based assessment takes the presenting disorder, for example, language disorder or a swallowing disorder, and relates the incidence and prevalence of the disorder in a given population to the local circumstance. This number then forms the anticipated baseline annual demand. (See diagram A).

The client-based assessment takes a particular client group and extracts the incidence and prevalence of a speech and/or language disorder in that group. (See diagram B).

The geographically-based assessment reviews a given geographical (or otherwise defined) area and establishes the existence of 'factors' in the area which create a service demand. It then works through a series of stages as represented on diagram C, until an assessment of the incidence and prevalence of speech and language disorders has been established for that defined area.

In practice, the most effective way of identifying the need for speech and language therapy services and thereby planning an effective level and type of delivery, will depend upon integrating the three models.

An assessment of a range of factors will therefore be undertaken.

1 At a geographical assessment level, these factors may include:

- rural/urban considerations;

- population size;

- epidemiology of the area, eg.

  - age/sex breakdown

  - social indices

  - health status

  - bilingual considerations

- the number, type and distribution of relevant locations, eg.

  - clinics

  - hospitals

- special schools

- day nurseries

- regional/supra regional specialities

2 At a 'client' or care package assessment level, these factors may include the presence of clients with, for example, a communication problem associated with:

■ autism

■ learning disability

■ stroke

■ mental illness

and their anticipated incidence relative to population.

3 At a problem assessment level, these factors may include the incidence of, for example:

■ language disorder

■ stammering

■ dysphasia

Additional factors will require consideration such as:

■ the local educational policy on issues such as integration, language disorder provision, support teacher, statementing/recording;

■ the local authority's pre-school provision;

■ the care in the community developments for example for the elderly, mentally ill, learning disabled.

Internal factors within the speech and language therapy service will affect the planning of services and the identified resource requirements.

The organisational model of care will be a major influencing factor.

The resource requirements of a service will depend upon the locations of delivery, the model of care adopted and the skill mix of the staff appointed to deliver a service.

Service profiles A + B highlight as examples the wide-ranging factors which need to be addressed in designing appropriate services.

The complexity of a service, both in terms of identifying that need and forward planning, cannot be determined by one set of factors. A comprehensive range of factors must be taken into account in drawing up service profile plans.

Local planning, undertaken with the combined knowledge of the local circumstances and professional issues, will prove the most successful formula for planning appropriate, high quality services.

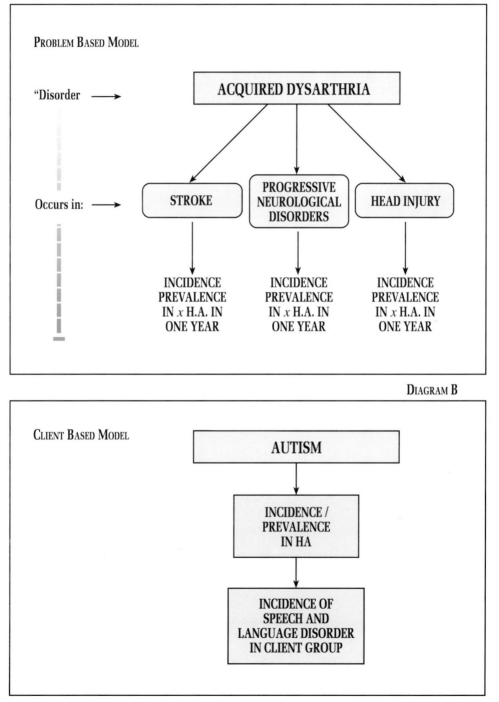

PROBLEM BASED MODEL

"Disorder ⟶

ACQUIRED DYSARTHRIA

Occurs in: ⟶

STROKE

PROGRESSIVE NEUROLOGICAL DISORDERS

HEAD INJURY

INCIDENCE PREVALENCE IN x H.A. IN ONE YEAR

INCIDENCE PREVALENCE IN x H.A. IN ONE YEAR

INCIDENCE PREVALENCE IN x H.A. IN ONE YEAR

DIAGRAM B

CLIENT BASED MODEL

AUTISM

INCIDENCE / PREVALENCE IN HA

INCIDENCE OF SPEECH AND LANGUAGE DISORDER IN CLIENT GROUP

Diagram C

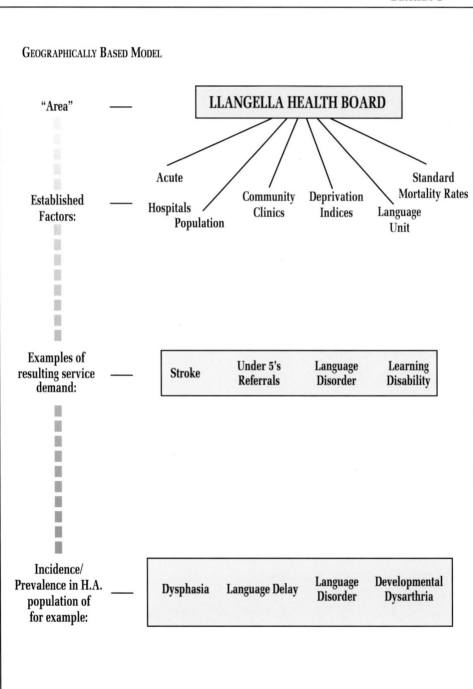

Geographically Based Model

"Area" — LLANGELLA HEALTH BOARD

Established Factors: —

Acute Hospitals   Population   Community Clinics   Deprivation Indices   Standard Mortality Rates   Language Unit

Examples of resulting service demand: —

Stroke   Under 5's Referrals   Language Disorder   Learning Disability

Incidence/ Prevalence in H.A. population of for example: —

Dysphasia   Language Delay   Language Disorder   Developmental Dysarthria

Service Profile A

XANADU HEALTH AUTHORITY
Large rural district
200,000 Population - 40% over 75
3 Special Schools
1 school for children with severe learning disabilities
1 school for children with mild learning disabilities
1 school for children with physical disabilities
1 acute hospital
Elderly Enhanced Care Homes (4)
2 Clinics
Child development centre - assessment only
Full integration policy held by local education authority
Learning disability population in neighbouring hospital - closing

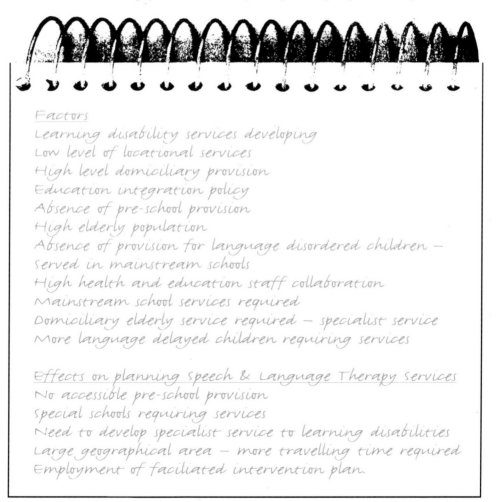

Factors
Learning disability services developing
Low level of locational services
High level domiciliary provision
Education integration policy
Absence of pre-school provision
High elderly population
Absence of provision for language disordered children – served in mainstream schools
High health and education staff collaboration
Mainstream school services required
Domiciliary elderly service required – specialist service
More language delayed children requiring services

Effects on planning Speech & Language Therapy Services
No accessible pre-school provision
Special schools requiring services
Need to develop specialist service to learning disabilities
Large geographical area – more travelling time required
Employment of faciliated intervention plan.

Service Profile B

GEORGETOWN HEALTH AUTHORITY

Small urban district

200,000 Population - 40% under 5's

10 special schools

2 acute hospitals

Higher incidence of infant mortality than the national average

3 adult training centres - 4 clinics

Community Team for People with Disabilities - good pre-school provision

Regional specialities

: ENT

: Neurosciences

: Child Development Centre

: Integrated Paediatric Service

Factors
small size
High number of special schools
Large number of locations
Good pre-school provisions
Well trained Health Visiting staff
High pre-school population
Three major Regional Specialities
Large learning disabilities resettlement population

Effects on planning Speech & Language Therapy
Services
A comprehensive special education service required
Specialist services required for each of the regional
specialities
Good pre-school provision and well trained health
visiting staff leading to fewer pre-school children
requiring active speech and language therapy
management.

Service Specifications

Introduction

The National Health Service and Community Care Act (1990) introduced the concept of a 'service specification'. This is the statement from the purchasing authority or GP fund-holder which outlines the services they wish to secure for their resident population. The actual content of the specification will vary from authority to authority. It will, however, generally follow the following format:

Parties

Description/Service Heading

Philosophy/Aims for the service

Objectives for 199- - 199-

Population to be served

Range of services to be provided

Volumes

Quality Indicators

Monitoring arrangements

Reporting arrangements

Type of contract

The actual content of the specification will be agreed locally and may vary from authority to authority.

Supply Proposals

The speech and language therapy service will formulate a supply proposal as a response to the service specification issued by the purchasing authority. This supply proposal will reflect the headings as outlined in the specification.

Through a process of negotiation, the specification and supply proposal will be refined and integrated to form a Service Level Agreement/Contract.

The service level agreement will reflect the headings of the original specification. The details will reflect the agreement reached between the purchaser and provider.

Due to the size of the speech and language therapy departments and the high incidence of cross-unit working, it is appropriate to view a speech and language therapy service as one group.

If this is to be the case, the speech and language therapy department hosted within one unit will set 'service agreements' with units outside of the host unit. See Diagram D.

This model is characterised by an integrated service under the professional leadership of a qualified speech and language therapy manager who is able to fulfil the aims and objectives of the management task on behalf of the purchasing authority. It is clear that within resource restrictions, staffing groups need to work in close collaboration, not only on an employing authority/board basis, but also on a regional basis, in order that the service is able to achieve the standards as described in this document.

It is recognised that as resource management initiatives gain momentum, speech and language therapy services may form component parts of one or more clinical directorates. The model as described in Diagram E would then pertain.

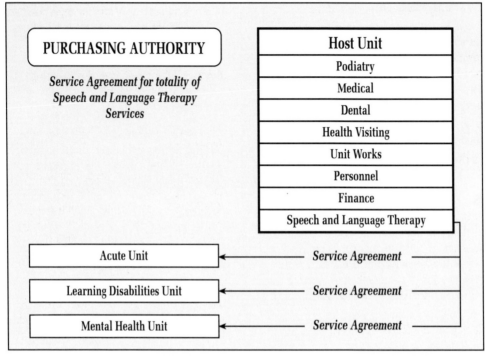

PURCHASING AUTHORITY

Service Agreement for totality of Speech and Language Therapy Services

Host Unit
Podiatry
Medical
Dental
Health Visiting
Unit Works
Personnel
Finance
Speech and Language Therapy

Acute Unit	←	*Service Agreement*
Learning Disabilities Unit	←	*Service Agreement*
Mental Health Unit	←	*Service Agreement*

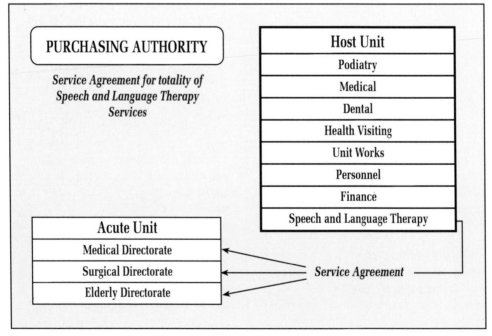

PURCHASING AUTHORITY

Service Agreement for totality of Speech and Language Therapy Services

Host Unit
Podiatry
Medical
Dental
Health Visiting
Unit Works
Personnel
Finance
Speech and Language Therapy

Acute Unit
Medical Directorate
Surgical Directorate
Elderly Directorate

Service Agreement

The College supports models of service organisation which meet locally-defined needs and facilitate the delivery of high quality client care. The model selected will allow for easy access and the creation of a seamless service for the communication impaired client.

BUSINESS PLANNING

A business plan is the internal document that is drawn up by the provider service. It should not be confused with the service agreement. If the service agreement is the 'what', the business plan is the 'how'. The business plan describes the way in which the service agreement will be fulfilled.

It may use the following model:

BUSINESS PLAN

Service Heading/Description
Key Objectives of the Organisation
Referral Patterns
Range of Services Provided
Programmes of Care
Planned Improvements
Quality Strategy
Efficiency Measures
Target Manpower/Costs for Planned Level of Service
Contingency Plans   - Manpower
                     - Funding
Volumes
Sensitivity Analysis
Monitoring
Reporting Mechanisms

The service agreement and the Business Plan will need to be monitored on a regular basis with particular attention being paid to adherence to the quality standards as described. This will be achieved through a system of clinical audit.

AUDIT

Audit is the formal mechanism for measuring the quality of care provided by a service (CSLT, 1993). The purpose of audit is to improve the quality of care (Normand Report, 1991).Speech and language therapists are committed to this process on an ongoing basis. As audit procedures become widespread, clinicians become more confident in applying such procedures on a routine basis. Increasingly, speech and language therapists work closely with their colleagues and clinical audit departments in implementing audit. A variety of resource centres are available to assist them in developing audits, including the National Centre for Clinical Audit, the UK Clearing House for Information on the Assessment of Health Outcomes, the NHS Centre for Reviews and Dissemination and the Cochrane Centre. Published materials are also available (for example, CSLT, 1993; Crombie et al 1993; Farrer et al, 1994; Moving to Audit, 1995).

'Communicating Quality' contains standards and guidelines against which a service may be audited. These standards and guidelines have been incorporated into 'Clinical Guidelines for the Management of Speech and Language Impairments' to be released by the Department of Health in 1996. This document has been prepared according to nationally approved criteria for outlining clinical guidelines throughout the health service. These criteria include epidemiological data, research evidence of effectiveness as well as professional consensus on what constitutes good practice (DOH, EL (93) 115, DOH, EL (94)74).

A range of procedures may be implemented in order to audit the quality of a service. 'Audit; a Manual for Speech and Language Therapists (CSLT, 1993) provides a detailed account of audit procedures and how they can be applied to speech and language therapy services. It outlines several options for initiating audit and recommends a systematic approach based upon the key question: 'How will this audit lead to an improvement in the quality of care?'

The College Audit Manual does not specify which areas of a service should be audited, as this will depend on local circumstances. It suggests that audit begins with a careful monitoring of the standards outlined in 'Communicating Quality'. It recommends the adoption of a client-based approach to data collection, which includes routine collection of information on client group, admissions, discharges and waiting times. This allows for analysis of caseload figures, efficacy of referral procedures, the different stages of waiting times, the length and frequency of intervention, and discharge information. Staff activity analysis should also be implemented on an ongoing basis in order to inform decisions on staffing and identifying the needs of individual staff members.

Clinical audit also includes the evaluation of clinical outcomes. The College Audit Manual recommends the use of two types of outcome measure:

1   consumer outcome measures;
2   clinical outcome measures.

Consumer outcome measures include consumer satisfaction surveys, consumer forums and the implementation of complaints procedures in line with local directives.

Clinical outcome measures include standardised and non-standardised assessments, goal plans, rating scales, and questionnaires determined by the client group and type of service provision. All these methods can be used to audit the actual outcome of a therapeutic intervention against the expected outcomes as hypothesised at the outset of the intervention. The aims of an intervention programme may vary from, for example, seeking to effect a complete remediation of a presenting difficulty, to assisting the client and carers in adjusting to an altered communication status. All aims along this continuum are equally valid, providing a clear evaluation procedure is in effect.

Additional Audit methods
Peer review

Peer review has been described as a 'frank discussion between two peers on a regular basis' (Enderby, 1992). Such discussions focus on clinical management issues. Peer review is a useful way of sharing skills and expertise and assisting the process of ongoing monitoring of individual case management.

Staff Appraisal

Staff appraisal systems provide a valuable

audit system for speech and language therapists. In general, they include a systematic appraisal of individual staff member's achievements on a regular basis. By evaluating a staff member's ability to achieve stated objectives, the speech and language therapy manager is in a position to draw conclusions about the ability of the service to move forward and develop.

Summary of Audit Procedures Relevant to Speech and Language Therapy

Setting standards
Process measurement
    -client group data
    -admissions\waiting times
    -discharges
Outcome measurement
    -consumer outcome measures
    -clinical outcome measures
Peer Review
Staff Appraisal

Regional Committees

Regional committees to discuss, share and estimate audit systems and outcomes may prove beneficial to locally based services.

Multi-disciplinary Audit

The College recommends the implementation of multi-disciplinary audit systems where this is possible. Particular attention should be paid to multi-disciplinary audit in settings where there is potential for joint planning

and record keeping.

Independent Practice

It is recommended that private practitioners actively seek out opportunities to engage in audit activities.

In summary, the professional body recommends that clear audit mechanisms are devised and implemented. Where appropriate, the speech and language therapy service should consider the possibility of uni- and multi-disciplinary audit through local audit committees and regionally based audit committees of speech and language therapists.

SERVICE PRIORITISATION

The College recognises the right of every individual to have equal access to the services provided by speech and language therapists.

It also acknowledges the requirement for service prioritisation.

The College does not support the policy of prioritising one client group above another. The professional body considers it inappropriate to make relative judgements regarding the effects of experiencing a potential, or actual communication disorder on any particular group of clients.

Within any group of clients, there will exist a continuum of need and an optimum time to deliver therapy. The exclusion of an identified group of clients by, for example, age, disorder or location does not allow for an efficient assessment of need to be made.

The College considers that prioritisation of the caseload should be a routine part of good clinical practice and recommends that a local prioritisation policy should be formulated which defines a range of criteria, upon which the decision to fulfil a duty of care will be made.

The range of criteria will depend to some extent on whether the policy is being implemented across client groups, or in relation to one identified group of clients.

However, the criteria would normally include:

- time post onset;

- optimum timing of the intervention;

- client, carer or parental anxiety;

- effect upon a client's communicative function;

- client/carer's ability to co-operate with therapy;

- expected outcome;

- availability of appropriately skilled staff;

- potential for change;

- commitment and motivation;

- research evidence of effectiveness.

No one single factor should be taken as an indicator of priority rating, or alternatively as a reason not to prioritise a client for therapy.

The College, in accordance with the Patient's Charter, recommends that in any clinical situation, priority should be given to the 'unseen caseload' ie. clients on the waiting list who, without a service, remain 'unseen'. In order to plan a service effectively, for example, to enable clients to access a range of therapy programmes or a secondary referral, it may be necessary to assess the previously unseen clients on a regular basis.

This also ensures that any subsequent prioritisation deals with known clients. Speech and language therapy services must be aware of other facilities within their locality that can support, enhance and assist with the management of those with communication disorders. Knowledge of these local facilities should be borne in mind when drawing up local policies.

The College recognises that many services operate within a framework of insufficient resource in relation to demand. It is in these circumstances that a clear prioritisation policy is particularly necessary. The College supports the need to focus resources where they are able to prove most effective, both in terms of the speech and language therapist's contribution to the client's quality of life and ensuring a positive outcome in relation to prognosis.

This will, at times, mean that some clients do not receive a service. The College does not believe that the alternative strategy to be an appropriate one; ie. allocating a scarce resource across a greater number of clients, thereby diluting the service and resulting in clinical inefficiency, poor outcomes and low staff morale.

In times of acute resource restrictions, it may become necessary to re-evaluate the services currently provided and re-assess the needs of the whole population on the basis of the published prioritisation policy.

In this way, the policy takes account of the whole population requiring access to speech and language therapy and does not discriminate against any one group or individual.

The College recommends that services develop pro-active policies and reviews of service in conjunction with their employing authority and purchasers.

MANPOWER

The professional body has considered carefully the need to describe and advise on the manpower requirements for a speech and language therapy service.

In 1972, Sir Randolf Quirk's review of speech therapy services recommended manpower levels of 6.0 whole-time equivalent speech and language therapists per 100,000 population (Quirk, 1972).

In 1989, Enderby and Davies identified a need for 26 whole-time equivalent speech and language therapists per 100,000 population based upon the service delivery models reviewed (Enderby and Davies,1989). It became apparent in follow-up debate that these figures needed to be balanced against the range of models of service delivery increasingly used by speech and language therapists which have proved to be of clinical significance, i.e. programme planning, facilitated intervention, intensive therapy, group therapy and the use of assistants and volunteers (Bryan et al, 1991, Davies and

Enderby,1991).

In 1991, the Manpower Planning Advisory group (MPAG,1991) reported that, across the United Kingdom, speech and language therapy establishment was 5.9 whole-time equivalent therapists per 100,000 population. These figures remain below those recommended in the Quirk Report. There is no evidence to suggest that services with these low establishment figures can adequately meet the needs of their communication impaired population to the level and complexity described in this text.

However, services do exist providing high quality levels of care which may be surprising in the light of recommended establishment levels. Clearly, other factors must be considered in the debate.

Population has long been viewed as an inadequate measure of establishment calculation. The demography and epidemiology of the geographical area are of paramount significance.

As discussed under the section 'Service Profiles and Service Planning', the manpower requirements will not only depend upon the number of potential clients but also upon the range of service locations available, the type and level of health, education, social service provision and the social factors within the population and provision.

The professional body, therefore, considers it to be inappropriate and misleading to indicate recommended establishment levels or recommended caseload size. Manpower requirements, both in terms of numbers and skill mix, will vary with a range of factors as indicated. Establishment levels, therefore, tend to be negotiated locally and, in principle, should reflect locally identified needs.

The model of care will influence service delivery. For example, in a special educational setting with a school roll of ninety children, the speech and language therapist, engaged in a direct face-to-face model will hold a caseload significantly smaller than a therapist working in the same location but delivering a model of care which utilises indirect intervention, group therapy and classroom programmes. This second model should not be implemented because of resource restrictions, but because the speech and language therapist considers it to be clinically appropriate. It will, however, lead to a larger caseload. As both models may be equally appropriate, recommended manpower levels could prove misleading.

The professional body does, however, recommend that all clients referred to the service receive a speech and language therapy model of care which reflects the model outlined under the clinically relevant section of this text. Every client referred to the service should have equal access to the appropriate model. The manpower levels of any one service should, therefore, reflect the ability of the service to deliver an appropriate model of care in terms of access, effectiveness and equity.

PROFESSIONAL ADVICE TO PURCHASERS

In February 1991, the Department of Health issued guidance relating to professional advice for Purchasing Authorities (DOH Circular EL(91)21). This paper described how purchasing arrangements might evolve to reflect and accommodate the separation of the purchaser and provider functions.

The paper's emphasis was on balance and continuity. It described two types of professional advice to which the purchaser would require access:

- independent advice

- advice from providers with whom the purchaser has a contract.

This advice was confirmed in a subsequent paper issued by the Department of Health in 1995 (DOH Circular HSG (95)11).

'Working for Patients' ((DOH, 1990, para 2.11) also made clear the need for health authorities to find the means to secure professional advice to ensure that the health needs of local residents are reflected in the contracts they place.

The DOH report on service specifications - 'Starting specifications' (DOH Circular EL (90), 161, August 90) took this a stage further, identifying the principle that:

'Specifications should be shared in collaboration with providers and their clinical staff'.

In applying this principle, the Department of Health has indicated that:

'Providers, to include all clinical staff, have a key role in offering perspectives on professional and practical issues. District Health Authorities may in addition require access to independent professional advice but this should not substitute for the expertise based in local providers'. (para 6.3)

Health authorities/commissions are advised to devise simple arrangements to secure independent advice in order to stimulate local dialogue.

The increase in the number of purchasers, GP fundholders, social services, education services and other provider units has created more complex arrangements. However, the need to secure advice has not diminished.

Professional advice, both local and independent, is likely to figure prominently in:

- the assessment of the health needs of the local population;

- judgement as to the merits of different services and competing priorities;

- development of service specifications;

- advice regarding the interface between health and other services;

- negotiation of contracts;

- monitoring of contract compliance by providers.

The Department of Health has stressed the need to avoid disrupting existing relationships with purchasers focusing on) the extent to which established sources of advice, in the case of speech and language therapy, the Head of Service, can be adapted to meet new demands.

Local advice may be provided via:
- the head of speech and language therapy utilising the results of clinical audit in

order to provide the purchaser with useful information on good practice;

- local advisors groups made up of colleagues from a range of professions: including for example, speech and language therapy, physiotherapy, podiatry, occupational therapy, psychology and dietetics;

- 'cluster' arrangements of locally based heads of service.

Advice should be based on evidence-based practice wherever possible. However, lack of evidence from published research should not lead purchasers to the view that evidence does not exist in clinical experience. As with other areas of health care and social care, evidence-based practice is still in its infancy and awaits the outcome of ongoing research.

Independent advice may be provided:

- from Regional Machinery; heads of speech and language therapy services meet regularly on a regional basis. This group is in a position to offer individual purchasing authorities a broader perspective than that available locally and to arrange a network for independent advice;

- from National Advice: the College is able to offer advice and support to purchasing authorities through its central office and professional networks which include The Association of Speech and Language Therapy Managers.

The College provides purchasing and providing authorities with information on clinical practice and service organisation through 'Communicating Quality: Professional Standards for Speech and Language Therapists,'. This document is supported by a network of on-site advice and support upon request to the College.

The College supports recent Department of Health guidance relating to professional advice and seeks to contribute to the quality of advice and information available to purchasing authorities.

RECRUITMENT AND RETENTION

RECRUITMENT

In the section on Equal Opportunities, reference is made to the importance of ensuring that speech and language therapists with responsibilities for recruitment and selection of staff receive the necessary training and at all times employ objective procedures. The use of fair and effective recruitment practices can only enhance the employer's success in recruitment.

This is particularly important in situations where recruitment is problematic. It may seem appropriate to reduce the requirements of the post when faced with prospective employees who do not reach the requirements of the person specification. In order to avoid this, it is essential that a full and systematic job evaluation is carried out prior to advertisement, in order to define the potential ways of filling the role required.

The speech and language therapy manager will need to consider the market of prospective employees at this stage, and

make any necessary adjustments. Managers should guard against reducing the post-graduate qualification requirements of staff without ensuring that they can be offered the necessary professional support.

Speech and language therapy managers will need to consider a range of options for recruiting staff. These may include:

- part-time posts;

- job sharing;

- job splits;

- term time only posts;

- annual hours/session contracts;

- flexible hours;

- provision of child care either through:

    - work-placed nurseries;

    - setting up 'nursery networks' ie. developing a register of child minders possibly from existing part-time staff or non-working speech and language therapists;

    - after-school groups;

    - holiday scheme provision;

- rotational posts;

- developing the use of assistant grade, where appropriate;

- returners' courses;

- non-practising speech and language therapists' work experience opportunities.

Supervising students is a professional

responsibility and can contribute to successful recruitment.

RETENTION

Retention of staff can also be problematic. Avoidable staff loss may be prevented through a well-developed programme of continuous development and staff appraisal. These systems will ensure that speech and language therapists' professional development needs are recognised and catered for within the service.

Coaching and mentoring skills will prove essential in the positive development of individual staff skills.

The initiatives mentioned above in relation to the recruitment of staff will also be appropriate in relation to retention.

In summary, in order to be maximally effective in recruitment, selection and retention of staff, the manager of speech and language therapy services will need to be flexible and innovative whilst keeping the needs of the service foremost in her/his mind (Bebbington, 1995).

**Recruitment and Selection:
The Process**

Assess the requirements of the post
■
Prepare job and person specification
■
Prepare information pack
■
Plan selection dates
■
Advertise
■
Receive completed application forms
■
Take up References
■
Short-list
■
Send for candidates
■
Interview
■
Select candidate
■
Make Appointment
■

There may be local variations/legislative requirements on the model produced by the Institute of Personnel Management (shown above) which managers are required to follow.

TERMS AND CONDITIONS OF EMPLOYMENT

In March 1996, Whitley Council terms and conditions of employment were superseded by locally agreed terms and conditions. In practice, many of these follow the Whitley directives. They do offer opportunities for locally negotiable salaries. It is important that speech and language therapists employed by any authority are clearly advised at the time of their employment and subsequently updated, if necessary, of changes in the terms and conditions of their employment. The process of review negotiations should also be made clear.

Speech and language therapists are advised to take the full advice of their trades union bodies with regard to their employment status.

EQUAL OPPORTUNITIES

The College is committed to the promotion of equal opportunities through professional conduct and practice as it relates to employment practice and access to appropriate services for clients and carers.

Key concerns are those of possible discrimination on the grounds of race, gender, sexual orientation and religion. In addition, obligations towards people with a disability and the rehabilitation of criminal offenders should not be overlooked. In all these areas, professional practice should be sensitive and responsive in relation to employment and clinical practice. Services should be planned and evaluated with relevant ethnicity and gender criteria in

mind. Services should ensure the existence of non-discriminatory practice towards carers and relatives.

Individual employers provide their own policy and procedures. However, there are principles and standards which speech and language therapists should take into account.

Speech and language therapy managers involved in recruitment must receive training and have access to personnel advice on promoting equal opportunities. They must recruit using only explicit procedures and practices which use criteria related to the identified requirements of the job, eg. full documentation and information used. Job descriptions and person specifications should be clear, concise, accurate and updated. Selection criteria should not be inflated to reflect the supply of candidates. Speech and language therapists should be aware of the legislation relevant to recruitment.

In offering training and professional development opportunities, managers of speech and language therapy services should use as much care in selection as in initial recruitment in order to prevent discrimination. Good practice points to the need for explicit and consistent performance appraisal, which has as one of its objectives the assessment of professional development.

Success in optimising equality of opportunity depends on strategies which are understood and workable. There will be a need to audit the workforce and the service users in terms of gender and ethnicity.

Finally, opportunities to develop equal opportunities awareness, to access advice which can inform speech and language therapy practice and to promote access to speech and language services from all sectors of the community, is to be encouraged.

HEALTH AND SAFETY AT WORK

The Health and Safety at Work Act (1974) requires employers and employees to fulfil a number of requirements, including an awareness of their responsibilities for health and safety at work as employees and as managers or supervisors. Each employing authority will have a Health and Safety policy statement outlining the levels of responsibility within its own management structures.

It is the responsibility of the Speech and Language Therapy Manager to ensure that the department develops a Health and Safety statement, giving relevant local information about:

- fire safety and fire prevention;

- first aid facilities;

- incident reporting and recording;

- access to occupational health services;

- control of substances hazardous to health (COSHH);

- control of infection;

- arrangements for maintenance of equipment;

- name of safety representative;

- management of medical emergencies;

- risk assessment and control procedures.

Such guidance should inform a visitor or a new member of staff of identifiable local Health and Safety issues and risks, and give advice on good practice. The policy will provide the name, post and location of responsible health and safety officers. It is the speech and language therapy manager's responsibility to make all staff aware of these arrangements and to update them regularly.

Special consideration should also be given in reviewing clinical practice in terms of basic hygiene and arrangements for clients in high-risk categories.

Speech and language therapists involved in care plans which have an element of travel or community activity (e.g. an assignment with non-fluent clients) should make an assessment of risks involved and ensure that their actions are within the practice and policy of the employer and, where necessary, are covered by appropriate insurance.

Therapists using visual display units in their work should be aware of health and safety guidance in relation to usage and positioning.

Therapists have a responsibility to ensure that equipment used in the delivery of therapy is at all times safe and does not place the client or his/her carer at risk. Equipment must conform to health and safety standards.

Notifiable Diseases

Speech and language therapists need to be informed of those diseases which require notification under the Public Health (Control of Disease) Act (1984).

A 'notifiable disease' is legally defined as one of the five diseases referred to in Section 10 of the Act. In addition, food poisoning is made notifiable in Section 11 of the Act.

There are a further twenty four diseases which have to be notified by the doctor who diagnoses them. The term 'notifiable disease' is commonly used for all thirty diseases.

Should a speech and language therapist come in contact with a client suffering or suspected to be suffering from a notifiable disease, the therapist must ensure that this is appropriately reported and seek the guidance of a general practitioner or occupational health department.

Diseases which have acquired a high profile, such as Hepatitis B and HIV and AIDS, also require vigilance both to protect the client and the therapist.

It is the responsibility of managers to ensure that local policies and procedures regarding control of infection are adhered to and that staff are aware of these policies.

HIV DISEASE AND AIDS

Introduction

These guidelines are intended to advise speech and language therapists on issues affecting the safety of themselves and their clients in the work situation. It is also hoped they may help reduce some of the known anxieties regarding the risk of working with someone affected by HIV disease.

More detailed information about infection control and the management of people with HIV disease should be sought from local and regional guidelines. (ACDP, 1990, DOH, 1995, NAM, 1995).

HIV Disease is a term used to cover the full range of possible consequences of the damage to the immune system caused by the human immunodeficiency virus (HIV), from no problems, or minor infections through to AIDS.

AIDS (Acquired Immune Deficiency Syndrome) is a collection of specific illnesses and conditions which occur because of the body's immune system has been damaged.

An individual is said to be 'seropositive' when antibodies to HIV are found in their blood. This situation is irreversible.

Mechanics of HIV transmission

1 The live virus has to be present either in the body of an infected person, or in a contaminated body fluid or body tissue.

2 There has to be a sufficient amount of the virus present.

3 It has to enter the body of the uninfected person through an effective route for transmission.

HIV is not present in urine,faeces, vomit, or sweat.

HIV is not present in sufficient quantities in saliva, tears, or blister fluid.

However, there have been a small number of reported instances of HIV transmission via these routes. Therefore it is prudent to conclude that the likelihood of infection by these routes is remote, but still possible. (This is an important factor to consider when planning infection control).

HIV is present in sufficient quantities in blood and blood derived products, semen and pre-semen, vaginal secretions.

HIV has also been detected in sufficient quantities in amniotic fluid, cerebro-spinal fluid, tissue and organs donated, skin transplants, bone marrow transplants, breast milk.

Effective routes for transmission include;

- parenterally (directly into the blood via wound);

- through a cut or sore, or damaged skin;

- an injection using contaminated and unsterilised injection equipment;

- an invasive surgical procedure such as organ transplant or blood transfusion.

Established routes of HIV transmission include;

- unprotected intercourse with someone who is infected;

- sharing unsterilised injection equipment which has been previously used by someone who is infected;

- injection or transfusion of contaminated blood, blood products and donations of semen, skin grafts and organ transplants taken from someone who is infected;

- from a mother, who is infected, to her baby.

Infection Control

Universal precautions are the only effective way to ensure that the risk of HIV infection is minimised.

Summary of Infection Control Plan

In order to implement an effective infection control strategy, the following procedures should be followed. Breakdown in infection control occurs when the full range of procedures are not adhered to.

1   Accurate assessment of risks .

   This involves identifying real risks and working to ensure risk reduction.

2   Identification of appropriate practical procedures:

   - use of barriers such as gloves, goggles, etc;

   - use of disinfection procedures - safe disposal of sharps, use of chemical or heat sterilisation of reusable instruments and materials;

   - accident prevention;

   - care procedures following accidents.

3   The strategy for the implementation of procedures will include the following:

   - commitment to planning and implementing universal precautions;

   - identifying implications for existing working practices;

   - addressing resource implications;

   - training for all staff;

- monitoring and review of infection control plan;

- regular refresher courses;

- assessment and evaluations of the success of procedures.

Confidentiality

The following guidelines are based upon the guidelines in the National AIDS Manual, (NAM,1995). The basic principle of confidentiality is simple :

There should be no disclosure of an individual's HIV antibody status without their direct consent.

The duty to obey this principle of confidentiality is a statutory obligation upon Health Authorities and their staff under the Venereal Disease Regulations (1974).

The principle of no disclosure should be regarded as inviolable unless :

1 the health of another is at risk

(e.g. in the case of a husband who is unable to tell his wife and cannot or will not initiate safer sex. If there are serious grounds to believe that such a risk exists, permission should be sought from the individual concerned. Individuals usually give consent to proper, humane notification procedures.);

2 disclosure can be proved to be in the overriding public interest;

3 the individual with HIV is not in a fit mental state to be able to understand the principles involved.

Guarding against accidental or unintentional breaches confidentiality.

1 Training is a key strategy.

2 Inadvertent ways of breaching confidentiality include leaving files around, asking leading questions in front of others.

3. Asking key questions such as;
-who will have access to records?
-does information need to be recorded by name?
-does the individual know who has access to files?

HEPATITIS B

Introduction

These guidelines are intended to advise speech and language therapists working with people carrying hepatitis B, eg. speech and language therapists working in residential care units or providing services to carriers at home.

Hepatitis B

Hepatitis B is a virus infection affecting the liver. It can range from a relatively mild illness with diarrhoea, vomiting, loss of appetite, aches and pains and mild jaundice, to a serious infection resulting in liver failure and death. Although some sense of being unwell can go on for some months after the initial infection, about nineteen out of twenty people eventually make a full recovery. However, a small number go on to carry the virus in their bloodstream for many years and may then infect others. Carriers can have an increased chance of developing liver disease in later life.

In the United Kingdom, about one person in every five hundred is a Hepatitis B carrier. The risk of infection is therefore very low indeed under normal circumstances. However, some groups of people have a higher probability of carrying the virus.

Risks

The virus can be transferred from the blood or body fluids of a carrier into the bloodstream of a recipient who is not immune to Hepatitis B.

Once infection has occurred, it can take from forty to one hundred and sixty days for symptoms to develop.

Hepatitis B cannot be transmitted by coughing or sneezing, or by sharing eating and drinking utensils, or by sharing toilet facilities.

Prevention

There are three ways in which transmission can be prevented.

1   Physical measures, which prevent infected blood or body fluids from coming into contact with people who are not immune.

Detailed information should be sought from district, area or regional health information and promotion programmes, usually known as 'Control of Infection Guidelines'. They are very important in the prevention of infection.

2   Passive Immunisation
'Passive' immunisation, although it confers immediate immunity in one dose, lasts for only three months. A booster vaccination

can be given which extends protection for up to five months. Passive immunisation works by conferring a dose of already formed antibodies. It is given in situations where a definite inoculation incident has occurred. Passive immunisation is used to confer immediate immunity in circumstances in which a non-immune person is at high risk of contracting Hepatitis B.

3   Active Immunisation
This is the method of choice for those people who may have prolonged close or intimate contact with carriers or potential carriers. This group will include staff working with client groups who have a high prevalence of Hepatitis B.

Active immunisation stimulates the recipients to make their own antibodies and immunity is longer lasting than in passive immunisation. Protection may last up to five years. Three injections are necessary into the muscle of the upper arm, over the course of six months. It is essential that a blood test is taken two months after the last injection to ensure that the vaccination has been successful. A booster vaccination may be necessary from time to time.

Both active and passive immunisation against Hepatitis B can be administered safely during pregnancy. Since Hepatitis B is a serious disease in newborn children, immunisation should not be withheld from pregnant women at risk of contracting the infection.

First Aid

If an injury occurs which may infect the speech and language therapist with Hepatitis B, the wound should be washed with soap and water and bleeding allowed to occur.

If the eyes are involved, they should be copiously flushed with warm water.

The speech and language therapist should immediately inform their appropriate senior manager.

The independent speech and language therapist is advised to inform her/his general practitioner.

The usual procedure is that a blood sample is taken from both the suspected carrier and the recipient. If the carrier status is confirmed and the recipient is not immune, passive immunisation is then given to the recipient. This MUST be given within forty eight hours of the incident (it is ineffective if given more than seventy two hours after the incident).

Further information

Advice and arrangement for immunisation and testing can be obtained from Local Consultant Microbiologists (Infection Control Officers), Directors of Public Health, Environmental Health Standards Departments and Occupational Health Service Departments.

Confidentiality

All speech and language therapists have a legal and professional responsibility to maintain confidentiality of information divulged to them in their contact with clients or via recorded information.

PERSONAL SAFETY

These guidelines are intended to remind speech and language therapists that care must be taken in respect of personal safety at work.

Some aspects of the speech and language therapist's work can make the practitioner more vulnerable than others, due to the nature or location of the work.

Managers are responsible for producing guidelines in accordance with local policies on personal safety for staff at work on-site as well as off-site. Managers should ensure that all staff are aware of such policies and also appreciate their vulnerability, particularly in relation to domiciliary visits and out-of-hours work.

At Work

1 When interviewing a client and/or carer alone, staff should make known their whereabouts to their manager or designated officer.

2 If there is evidence prior to interview that the client or carer is extremely disturbed and/or the available information indicates that there may be concerns about the person's hostility or aggression, staff should not interview the client alone but with another member of staff present.

3 If a staff member is unavoidably alone, wherever the location, it is her/his responsibility to ensure personal safety and security, e.g. by locking the entrance door and having a 'Please ring the bell', 'Please knock' sign; by working in a room with a telephone etc.

4 Staff are urged to record planned interviews in an open diary in a separate office. Records in the diary should state the time and duration of the appointment, the name(s) of the individuals to be seen and the specific room to be used if not the therapist's own personal office.

5   All staff should be alert to security issues and use alarm/security systems, wherever possible.

Domiciliary Settings

1   Clients who may place colleagues at risk should be made known by the referring agent. If such information is available, for example, if a visit is known to be potentially difficult, it should be made in daylight and with another member of staff.

2   It is recommended that a record of the visit is submitted (See Point 4, Personal Safety above).Where information is lacking, every effort should be made to gain more detail from the referring agent. Staff have the right to decide not to enter a home if they feel that personal safety may be at risk and should inform their manager of the action.

3   In every case, staff are advised to inform the manager at the end of the visit.

4   Should staff be delayed for any reason, they should notify their base/line manager/colleague. If further time is required with the client than was originally planned staff should either:

ring base/colleague/Visit Sheet holder and confirm this;

terminate the interview at the pre-arranged time, and arrange a further appointment with the client.

5   Staff required to visit in the evening should consider whether it will be safer to do so with another member of staff.

6   Staff should be aware of potential problems which may arise when visiting members of the opposite sex. If on arrival at a client's home a member of staff meets a situation other than the one anticipated, e.g, a lone male parent, that member of staff may need to explain that both parents were expected and make alternative arrangements to visit again. In a case where potential or actual threatening behaviour or sexual harassment is occurring, the member of staff should always err on the side of caution in her/his response and leave immediately.

7   Staff who are not car owners are advised to use a transport service to and from home visits, and ensure that the return journey is arranged prior to the visit. The driver should be instructed to knock at the front door rather than wait on the road outside.

8   Staff are urged not to accept lifts from strangers, should avoid walking in dark or ill-lit places and should carry a personal alarm. Staff should avoid accepting a lift from a suspicious person or a lone member of the opposite sex.

9   Staff must not knowingly place themselves in a hazardous situation.

10 Staff should plan visits according to area of risk. When this is not possible and visits need to be made in 'at risk' areas, staff are urged to use their discretion and take the following precautions:

go with a colleague, if possible;

walk in well lit populated areas, avoiding short cuts through subways, parks or waste ground;

when driving, keep all car doors locked.
Do not leave handbags on the passenger seat.
Lock personal items, briefcases and folders
etc. in the boot and/or place out of sight.
Avoid parking in dark secluded areas;

do not wear excessive jewellery or carry
unnecessary amounts of money or valuables
such as credit cards or cheque books.

11 During domiciliary visits, carry a personal
alarm and maintain it in working order.

12 Avoid wearing inappropriate clothing.

13 Be aware of danger signs, e.g, agitation,
restless movements, abusive language.
Do not appear flippant or uninterested.
A professional, calm but firm approach is
essential. Choose to sit in the chair nearest
the door from the start of the visit.

14 Domestic pets may be a hazard. Consider
requesting that they are removed from the
room when visiting.

15 If a serious incident occurs call the
police/ambulance.

16 Report incident in accordance with
employer's accident/incident reporting
procedure.

Guidelines for the Management of Violent or Potentially Violent Behaviour

During the course of a working day, staff may
be faced with a potentially violent situation.
Staff whose work regularly requires them to
come into contact with potentially violent
clients should undergo appropriate training.

Three different types of tactic are helpful:

Avoidance

If someone appears to be becoming angry
and aggressive, use any means to avoid
confrontation. For example, if a client has
become very angry because he/she does
not want to do something and may become
violent, staff should back down or leave
the room if this seems the most appropriate
course of action. This allows the
member of staff time to consult with others
and try to understand why the client has
reacted in a violent or aggressive manner.

Distraction

Distraction can also be helpful, but it is
important not be patronising when adopting
this strategy. For example, if a client is
reacting very aggressively to being told
he/she can not have something, it may
be useful to offer to make him/her a cup
of tea/coffee before attempting to discuss
the problem further.

Defusing

Defusing strategies can help in averting
a confrontation. For example,disclosing
personal experiences of anger can be helpful
if a client is becoming angry or
aggressive.

Whatever approach is appropriate:

it is important to behave calmly, to use
a firm, non-threatening and unhesitating
manner, communicating self-control and
confidence;

be conscious of your own body language and
tone of voice. How you say something can be

more important then what you say. Listening, talking and explaining must be the first approach and, if used properly, can often avert an incident;

help the client to be aware that you are trying to solve the immediate problem and be truthful about this;

approach the client slowly, speaking to them calmly. Do not surprise him/her, for example, by approaching from behind. Be sensitive to the individual's personal space and do not encroach on it. Beware of 'cornering' the client and blocking his/ her exit as you approach.

ACCOMMODATION AND EQUIPMENT GUIDELINES

General Functional and Design Requirements

1 **Accommodation should comply with Health and Safety requirements.**

2 **Therapy rooms should have a good standard of daylight and artificial light.**

3 Therapy rooms should have good ventilation.

4 Therapy rooms should have adequate space to allow for a variety of activities.

5 The temperature in therapy rooms should be well regulated.

6 Carpets in therapy rooms should be clean, stain-resistant and securely fixed.

Access

1 Out-patient clinics should have good access to speech and language therapy departments by public transport.

2 The external entrance used by clients should have an easy approach for vehicles.

3 There should be adequate parking facilities for clients and staff.

4 The therapy area should be located in an appropriate part of the hospital/clinic/school according to client groups etc. with reasonable access for clients attending other departments.

5 External and internal access should be convenient for individuals with wheelchairs/pushchairs/walking aids.

Staff Office

1 **An office area where case records can be stored and general administrative work carried out will be required.** In a small department, the office area and therapy room may be combined.

2 There should be desk space for each therapist using the accommodation.

3 **There should be sufficient lockable filing space to accommodate current and review case records, administrative information, forms etc.**

4 There should be a notice board in the department.

5 The office should provide privacy to make phone calls.

Staff Room

1 Therapists should have access to a room with facilities for bringing or making drinks and preparing snacks.

Clinic Areas

1 Individual Therapy Room

One room should be available for each whole-time equivalent therapist. Allowances may also need to be made for students and assistants. The room should be large enough to accommodate the therapist, client (possibly in a wheelchair), carer, observer. Minimum size 15 square metres.

The room must be quiet with sufficiently low background noise to make it suitable for recording and sound-sensitive equipment. It may be necessary for it to be sound-attenuated.

The room should have a wash basin.

The room should contain a table and sufficient number of chairs, of a size and design suitable for the particular client group. Sharp corners and edges of furniture should be protected.

There should be lockable storage space for equipment.

There should be a full length mirror attached to the wall.

There should be a sufficient number of accessible power points. In children's clinics, these should have protected sockets.

2 Group Therapy Room
There should be regular and reliable access to a room suitable for group work. 39 square metres.

The room should be sufficiently large to accommodate up to eight clients plus a therapist and two assistants. Specific needs should be taken into consideration e.g. space for wheelchairs, play area etc.

Tables and chairs suitable for the needs of the client group should be available and accessible.

Reception Facilities

Suitable reception facilities should be available.

Waiting Room

1 There should be a suitable waiting area near the therapy rooms, large enough and with sufficient comfortable chairs to accommodate the number of people likely to be waiting at any one time. The waiting area should be more than a corridor.

2 The therapy room and waiting area should be sufficiently separated that noise from the waiting area does not disturb treatment and that privacy is maintained in the therapy room.

3 Appropriate toys and materials should be available for children.

Secretarial/Recruitment

1 Reliable and regular secretarial support should be available to type, copy and send out reports and letters within one week of completion.

2 There needs to be a reliable method of taking messages. This may be by a receptionist, secretary, assistant or ansaphone.

3   Administrative tasks should, where possible, be carried out by administration/secretarial personnel.

Equipment

1. Electrical Equipment
Speech and language therapists must have access to an appropriate range of electrical equipment for the client group.

2. Assessment Materials
Assessment materials will include a range of formal and informal assessments appropriate to the client group. Materials should be age-appropriate and non-discriminatory in terms of culture, gender or religious background of the client.

3. Therapy Materials
A range of published and individual prepared therapeutic materials will be required as appropriate to the client group. These items should be age appropriate and non-discriminatory in terms of the client's culture, gender or religious background. Equipment used in therapy must be non-hazardous to the client and conform with Health and Safety standards.

4. AAC Equipment
A range of augmentative and alternative communication systems should be available for assessment, training and long and short term loan.

DOH Circular HSG (95) 19 provides an approved list of goods and services which can be purchased by GP fundholders and Community Fundholders in England and Wales. This list includes the provision of 'communication aids', but it does not include wheelchairs and environmental control aids, which must be purchased centrally. This may make the provision of integrated systems for people with disabilities more complicated. These fundholders hold budgets for the purchase of AAC equipment up to a maximum of £6,000 per client. The document does not, however, specify the need for expert assessment, ongoing support and training in the use of AAC equipment. However, a subsequent DOH Circular HSG (95) 64 does make reference to 'the merits of equipment being part of a care package which includes specialist assessment, training and aftercare', and encourages fundholders to take account of local agreements between established providers and purchasers and social services departments. These guidelines may help to underline the importance of ensuring support services accompany provision of AAC equipment.

5. Stationery
A range of stationery items should be available to the therapist and clerical staff.

PRESS/MEDIA
Every employing authority has a policy to deal with enquiries from the above. Staff are reminded that unless authorised to do so, speaking to press or media may contravene their contract and could result in disciplinary action by the employing authority.

9

SKILL MIX

 The speech and language therapy profession recognises professionally qualified practitioners and non-professional support personnel as being part of the speech and language therapy service. Terminology regarding skill mix helps to identify the differing ways in which the client might expect to receive the service. Qualifications have also now been formalised for assistants, and the breadth of their work and that of volunteers has increased.

The terms bilingual co-workers, speech and language therapists' assistants and volunteer helpers continue to be used to describe members of the speech and language therapy team who are not professionally qualified.

For professionally qualified practitioners, the terms 'specialist', 'generalist' and "specialised" have been superseded to mirror more clearly the changing nature of employment. The terminology which the profession now recognises as the most appropriate description of current practice distinguishes between speech and language therapists with **specific responsibilities**, and speech and language therapists with **specific duties** (following Miller et al, 1996).

The College draws no parallels with these professionally defined descriptions of working practice and any current or future grading structure for clinicians used by the employing authorities. The College recognises that clinicians may hold posts which use this same terminology in the job title, but which do not reflect the criteria of professional activity as described in this chapter. (RCSLT, PSB, 1996).

This chapter describes the different types of clinical activity assigned to each member of the team and the expectations of individuals in each category. The description includes an additional comment on training opportunities for those individuals who are not professionally qualified. See Chapter 7 for details of professional development for speech and language therapists.

THE SPEECH AND LANGUAGE THERAPIST WITH SPECIFIC RESPONSIBILITIES

The speech and language therapist with **specific responsibilities** is a clinician performing her/his duties at a level of competency which serves as a senior reference point for colleagues both within the profession and in related disciplines.

The concept of **specific responsibility** may apply to a location, a client group, a presenting disorder, or another aspect of the speech and language therapist's work in which she/he has expertise.

The speech and language therapist with **specific responsibilities** will:

■ have undertaken a range of professional development activities in subjects related to the field of responsibility. This serves to extend the knowledge base of the therapist considerably beyond that acquired at an undergraduate level. It will also extend the speech and language therapist's skills beyond the core skills directly related to the area of responsibility. For example:

- the speech and language therapist with specific responsibility in the field of learning disability may have undertaken post-graduate education and training in the management of challenging behaviour or learning theory;

- the speech and language therapist with specific responsibility for a geographical area will have accrued a high level of diagnostic and intervention skills across a range of service groups and will be familiar with a range of service models and may have studied local culture or language patterns;

- the speech and language therapist with specific responsibility for student placements may have collaborated with an educational establishment in researching new patterns of clinical teaching and learning;

■ have undertaken a period of post-qualification experience of at least three years. This is considered the minimum amount of time required for the therapist to have experienced a sufficient breadth as well as depth of knowledge in the field of specific responsibility;

■ have delivered or participated in the delivery of a service in a range of locations and in a range of organisational models in this field of work;

■ have a high level of awareness of the broad range of factors relating to the work with which she/he is concerned;

■ offer advice and support to other clinicians and to a range of other professionals who have duties in the same area of work;

■ through the professional body enjoy membership of Specific Interest Groups and access to professional publications and networks.

In summary, the speech and language therapist with **specific responsibilities** will have attained a high level of skill and a comprehensive knowledge-base of a particular service, client or disorder group accrued through a programme of professional development activities and clinical experience. The clinician with specific responsibilities will have the capability to act in an advisory capacity to members of the speech and language therapy profession and other professional groups.

THE SPEECH AND LANGUAGE THERAPIST WITH SPECIFIC DUTIES

All speech and language therapists have a range of professional duties which are delineated in the core standards outlined in Chapter 1. A speech and language therapist enters the profession with sufficient competence to practise, developing proficiency and eventually expertise through a programme of continuing professional development and through clinical experience (Roulstone,1994). In addition, dependent upon the nature of the individual's employment, therapists will also carry out a number of **specific duties**. These therapists will be entering the profession as newly qualified practitioners, while others will already have held a number of posts with a range of differing **specific duties**.

The concept of **specific duties** may apply to a location, a client group, a presenting disorder, or another aspect of the speech and language therapist's work in which she/he has competence or proficiency.

A speech and language therapist with **specific duties** will:

- be developing specific knowledge in subjects related to the field of **specific duties**;

- be gaining experience in the delivery of a service in a range of locations and organisational models in the field of work;

- be gaining an awareness of the factors influencing service delivery in the field of **specific duties**;

- consult with other clinicians and a range of other professionals who have duties in the same area of work;

- refer to colleagues with **specific responsibilities** in the same field of work for advice, information and support;

- be advised to be a member of the professional body thereby enjoying membership of Specific Interest Groups and access to professional publications and networks;

In summary, the speech and language therapist with **specific duties** is a therapist who is extending her/his level of skill and knowledge of a particular service, client or disorder group through a programme of continuing professional development and clinical practice.

BILINGUAL CO-WORKERS

A bilingual co-working service acknowledges the rights of all individuals who are referred to the speech and language therapy service to receive that service in a language of their choice.

Bilingual co-workers will be members of the local community and reflect its demography. They are employed and trained within the speech and language therapy department.

Bilingual co-workers are trained by the speech and language therapy service :

- to take the case history in the client's/carer's home language;

- to assess the client in his/her home language including, with children, to advise on play observation as appropriate to the culture;

- to contribute to the process of diagnosis between primary language difficulties and English as a second language;

- to contribute to the management of bilingual clients;

- to interpret information between client and professional;

- to offer written translations as and when appropriate.

Apart from their specific role in client interaction, bilingual co-workers have a key role within the department in offering relevant training on cultural and linguistic issues and acting as an information resource for materials and cultural matters.

As bilingual co-workers are more accessible to the carers of bilingual clients, they play a vital role in empowering carers to participate in management of the client's speech and language difficulties.

The co-working service should be seen as an integral part of the speech and language therapy department, i.e. accessible to all clients and to all members of the speech and language therapy department. The co-working service will follow the aims and principles of the care groups that exist within the department and may therefore be cross-referenced with all client/service groups.

SPEECH AND LANGUAGE THERAPISTS' ASSISTANTS

A speech and language therapists' assistant is an employed member of the speech and language therapy service who does not hold a speech and language therapy professional qualification and who works under the direction of a qualified clinician. Speech and language therapists' assistants are employed to support, and not to replace, qualified therapists. As such, the balance between professionally qualified and other personnel employed within a service should be reviewed on a regular basis.

The post of speech and language therapy assistant was first introduced on a widespread scale by employing authorities in 1988. (TASLTMS,1993), although assistants have been employed in a small number of authorities since the late 1970s.

Assistants are now engaged routinely in a wide range of clinical settings, with a range of client groups, activities and duties.

Speech and language therapists' assistants are not required to complete a qualification **before** they take up employment. However, assistants may bring a variety of existing skills or qualifications from other areas which can be of direct benefit to the speech and language therapy service. Specific qualifications or experience may be of great value in work with certain client groups (e.g. knowledge of other languages, nursery nurse qualifications, etc.).

In-service training for assistants varies from basic health and safety and first aid courses, to more therapy-orientated packages such as information on types of acquired communication disorders, or stages of language development. This aspect of training depends largely on the resources of the speech and language department in which the assistant works.

National occupational standards for speech and language therapy support have now been defined (Care Sector Consortium,1996). These are the basis of a formal qualification for assistants, which has been developed within the National Vocational Qualifications and the Scottish Vocational Qualifications Care Awards at Level 3. Information is available to the profession on training initiatives and assessment of competence.

The speech and language therapists' assistant will:

- be aware of issues of confidentiality within the workplace;

- understand the range and boundaries of

her/his duties to be defined by the qualified practitioner;

- participate in the delivery of a service within one or more locations or organisational models in a defined field of work;

- use initiative to maximise work activities within the range and boundaries of her/his duties;

- refer to colleagues with specific responsibilities or duties in the same field of work for direction, advice, information and support.

The speech and language therapists' assistant may:

- have skills or qualifications which are complementary to those held by the speech and language therapist. For example;

    - have experience in an area of care of children or the elderly;

    - be able to communicate in a language not shared by the speech and language therapist;

    - have an understanding of a local area or culture unfamiliar to the speech and language therapist;

- gain qualifications through employment as an assistant which allow a greater degree of responsibility within the range and boundaries of her/his duties.

In summary, the speech and language therapists' assistant is an integral member of the speech and language therapy team employed to act in a supporting role and under the direction of a qualified speech and language therapist.

VOLUNTEER HELPERS

The use of volunteers has a long and valued history in speech and language therapy. Volunteer helpers may be individuals who have an interest in helping in the field of speech and language therapy, or may be part of a volunteer scheme such as AFASIC or the Stroke Association. The volunteer is unpaid.

It is suggested that all new volunteers should have an induction period which allows them to become familiar with the service or scheme which they are joining. Subsequently, training opportunities should reflect the expectations of the volunteers' role.

Individual volunteers may carry out similar activities to those of assistants. Where this is the case, the selection procedure should be rigorous.

The individual volunteer will:

- be aware of issues of confidentiality within the workplace;

- understand the range and boundaries of her/his activities to be defined by the qualified practitioner;

- refer to speech and language therapists with **specific responsibilities or duties** in the same field of work for direction, advice, information and support.

The individual volunteer may:

- participate in the delivery of a service

within one or more locations or organisational models in a defined field of activity;

- use initiative within the boundaries of her/his activities;

- have skills or qualifications which are complementary to those held by the speech and language therapist, for example:

  - have experience of living with an individual with a communication difficulty;

  - be able to communicate in a ethnic minority language or language other than English;

  - have an understanding of a local area or specific culture.

Volunteer schemes are separate from the speech and language therapy service. They are responsible for their own volunteer recruitment and organise activities for a group of clients who may or may not have been referred through the speech and language therapy service. It is expected that such schemes will enjoy the support of the speech and language therapy service.

Volunteer schemes may provide friendship and support for people with communication impairments. They may also provide opportunities for people with communication impairments to socialise, to maintain existing levels of communication, to increase confidence in communicating and to develop new interests or rediscover old ones. In this way they can complement the work of the speech and language therapy service (Spencer,1996).

Conclusion

A speech and language service may require a balanced skill mix. The clinical skill mix includes professionally qualified staff, clinical support staff and volunteer helpers. In addition the provision of an effective management structure and clerical support is essential for effective and efficient service delivery.

10

PROFESSIONAL
NETWORKS

*This chapter provides information on professional networks and national
and international organisations concerned with individuals with
communication disability and the professions who serve them.
Further information and contact addresses can be obtained from College.*

PROFESSIONAL NETWORKS

ADVISORY COMMITTEE OF THE THERAPEUTIC PROFESSIONS ALLIED TO MEDICINE (NORTHERN IRELAND)

The Advisory Committee of the Therapeutic Professions Allied to Medicine was appointed to advise the Department of Health and Social Services on the planning and provision of therapeutic paramedical services in Northern Ireland. This includes consideration of manpower policy, professional training needs and staffing. The remuneration and conditions of service of staff do not come within the remit of the Committee. The Committee is an advisory body to the Department and it has no executive functions.

Matters are referred to the Committee by the Department and the Committee also initiates matters to be brought under consideration. Some of the issues referred to the Committee may involve consultation with other bodies and the outcome may only emerge over a period of time.

Membership of the Committee is made up of two representatives of each discipline. The paramedical disciplines represented on the Committee are physiotherapy, occupational therapy, speech and language therapy, chiropody, orthoptics, nutrition and dietetics. Members are appointed after consultation with professional or other interested bodies. Members serve, however, in an individual capacity and not as representatives of the nominating bodies.

The Committee may appoint sub-committees and may appoint to each sub-committee persons who are not members of the Committee.

THE ASSOCIATION OF SPEECH AND LANGUAGE THERAPISTS IN INDEPENDENT PRACTICE (ASTIIP)

The Association of Speech and Language Therapists in Independent Practice (ASTIIP) is the officially recognised and affiliated body for speech and language therapists working in independent practice. Its role and function is:

■ to ensure provision of the highest possible standards of patient care, personal conduct and professionalism on the part of the therapists in independent practice. ASTIIP publishes detailed professional standards and guidelines for the independent practitioner in association with the College.;

■ to offer support for therapists in independent practice;

■ to provide an organised forum for advice (to other therapists and to the public) and the exchange of views and information of particular concern to private practice.

The constitution of ASTIIP reflects the philosophy and working practices of the College. This ensures that issues are dealt with under the umbrella of the profession's representative body. This, in turn, should lead to less fragmentation and more cohesion within the profession as a whole, and to mutually beneficial liaison between therapists employed by health services and those in

THE ASSOCIATION OF SPEECH AND LANGUAGE THERAPY MANAGERS

The Association of Speech and Language Therapy Managers (TASLTM) was founded in 1974 and is the national body representing the membership in England, Scotland, Wales and Northern Ireland.

The Association's role and function is:

- to act as an advisory body on national issues concerning the management of speech and language therapy services;

- to develop management skills and promote professional growth;

- to examine the role of speech and language therapy managers and formulate nationally acceptable guidelines;

- to promote and co-ordinate research projects relating to the management of speec and language therapy services;

- to collect and disseminate relevant information.

The membership of TASLTM is open to two categories of speech and language therapist: those responsible for the management of speech and language services in any health authority or trust in the United Kingdom or British forces posted overseas (BFPO); and those whose role is to advise purchasers or providers within a health authority, Board or trust in the United Kingdom or BFPO. There is also a facility for Associate Membership.

The Association has links with College, CREST (see below), the Department of Health and the Department for Education and has representation on various committees concerning management of speech and language therapy services.

COMMITTEE OF REPRESENTATIVES OF EDUCATION IN SPEECH AND LANGUAGE THERAPY (CREST)

CREST is the acronym of the Committee of Representatives of Education in Speech and Language Therapy. Membership consists of a senior speech and language therapist from each of the educational establishments which offer programmes leading to a qualification in speech and language therapy.

Although an independent group, CREST has links with the College Council and Academic Board through reciprocal observer status, and with TASLTM and the Department of Health, representatives of both being invited to participate in meetings.

The role of the Committee is to collate and share information, to address areas of common interest in the education of speech and language therapists and to discuss aspects of work practice which relate to this. The Committee has a long history, existing as the Principals' Panel and then as the Training Schools' Consultative Committee before assuming its current name.

Contact with the current chair of CREST can be made via the Academic Officer of the College.

COMMUNICATIONS FORUM

The Communications Forum is a national forum established in 1994 to bring together organisations concerned with speech and language impairments.

The Forum does not itself provide services, but will promote initiatives on behalf of the two and a half million people in the UK with communication impairments. Its membership comprises national professional and voluntary organisations whose main concern is communication disability. Associate members include national and local organisations which have communication as one of their concerns.

The Forum's aims include:

- putting communication concerns on the public agenda;
- co-operating to achieve positive developments in communications issues;
- promoting awareness; campaigning for equal access;
- informing purchasers and providers; networking with interested organisations;
- researching common concerns.

Contact with the Forum and further details of its member organisations can be made in writing to PO Box 854, 3 Dufferin Street, London EC1Y 8NB or through the Royal College of Speech and Language Therapists.

COMMUNICATION THERAPY INTERNATIONAL (CTI)

Communication Therapy International (CTI) is a United Kingdom-based non-profit making association whose members have an interest in services for people with communication disabilities in less developed countries. Membership is open to any professional working with individuals who have a communication disability.

The role and function of CTI is:

- to encourage, promote and support the development of appropriate services in less developed countries by sharing experience and knowledge and providing training for members planning to work in less developed countries.

- to raise awareness of relevant issues such as the global shortage of speech and language therapy services, the importance of providing services which can be sustained in the long-term by local personnel, the need for appropriate training and technology and the need to train other professionals and relatives in local settings.

CTI maintains links with other relevant organisations such as IALP, ASHA, VSO, and Action Health 2000.

INTERNATIONAL ASSOCIATION OF LOGOPEDICS AND PHONIATRICS (IALP)

The International Association of Logopedics and Phoniatrics is a non-governmental, non-political, world-wide organisation. It has two major fields, logopedics and phoniatrics and works for the benefit of those with speech and language, voice and hearing disabilities throughout the world.

The membership of the organisation is open to any individual with professional qualifications in the field of communication disorders and sciences. Affiliated members include national professional organisations of logopedics and phoniatrics, and multi-national, regional or local organisations who have parallel concerns.

The role and function of the organisation are:

- to promote development and standards of rehabilitative and preventive work, research and training in logopedics and phoniatrics in all countries and at all age levels;

- to distribute information on logopedics and phoniatrics in various countries;

- to organise periodic international congresses for the exchange of the most recent theoretical and practical knowledge in the field of logopedics, phoniatrics and communication pathology;

- to maintain and propagate an international journal dedicated to all questions of logopedic and phoniatrics;

- to establish contact with kindred scientific and therapeutic organisations and to assist in the establishment of such organisations in countries where there are none;

- to maintain international recognition for logopedics and phoniatrics as a special and separate science;

- to co-operate with UNESCO, UNICEF, WHO, ECOSOC, CIOMS and specifically to adopt their policies regarding the practice of non-discrimination with respect to race, nationality, origin, religion, handicapping conditions and sex.

NATIONAL ADVISORY COMMITTEES (SCOTLAND)

Six National Advisory Committees form part of the advisory function
of the Scottish Office Home and Health Department. Their membership reflects
the organisational structures of the professions they represent and,
as far as possible, is evenly distributed throughout Scotland.
These Committees are:

National Advisory Committee for Scientific Services
National Dental Advisory Committee
National Medical Advisory Committee
National Nursing, Midwifery and Health Visiting Advisory Committee
National Paramedical Advisory Committee
National Pharmaceutical Advisory Committee

The role of these Committees is to provide advice on the formulation of national policy and health care
provision in respect of the professions they represent. Separate machinery exists for discussion
of questions relating to remuneration and terms and conditions of service, and these are not therefore
included in the remit of the National Advisory Committees.

The Committee may be invited by the Department to act in a consultative capacity
to comment on work in which the Department or other bodies have been engaged.
It may also be invited to act in an advisory capacity to consider a particular issue and to give
its views. In addition, the Committee has a general remit to bring to the attention of the
Department matters of concern or interest to the relevant profession or service.

The membership of the National Paramedical Advisory Committee (NPAC) comprises 21 members,
two for each of the professions represented, and three members representing undergraduate
professional education. The professions represented on NPAC are chiropody, clinical psychology,
dietetics, occupational therapy, orthoptics, physiotherapy, diagnostic radiotherapy, therapeutic
radiography and speech and language therapy.

A representative of the NHS Management Executive attends meetings of NPAC as an observer.
Staff from the Health Policy and Public Health Directorate provide administrative support to the
Committee and its ad hoc working groups.

NPAC meets three times a year and produces a newsletter following each meeting.

SPEECH AND LANGUAGE THERAPISTS' EDUCATION PARTNERSHIP
(NORTHERN IRELAND)

The Speech and Language Therapists' Education Partnership (Northern Ireland) is a forum for collaboration among speech and language therapists in higher education and health and social services and education in Northern Ireland (NI).

The membership comprises speech and language therapists who are nominated representatives from TASLTM (NI), the University of Ulster, active or recent researchers, post-graduates and clinical supervisors of students.

The partnership's role and function is:

- to review, evaluate and act on policy affecting professional education of speech and language therapists in Northern Ireland;

- to formulate policies regarding professional education and to facilitate the implementation of such policies;

- to exchange information and address operational issues related to clinical education;

- to promote and support research within the profession in Northern Ireland.

It normally meets three times per year, although this may vary according to the amount of business or in response to particular initiatives.

SPEECH AND LANGUAGE THERAPY OFFICER AT THE DEPARTMENT OF HEALTH

The Speech and Language Therapy Officer at the Department of Health is a full-time civil service post, to which appointment is made by the Civil Service Appointments Board for a period of five years.

The post holder is required to provide advice for the Secretary of State, for Ministers and for officials at the Department of Health, on the effect of current policies on speech and language therapy services, and the formulation of future policies relating to those services.

The post holder is also required to act as a link between the Department of Health, other government departments, speech and language therapy professional organisations and the relevant voluntary bodies.

**STANDING LIAISON COMMITTEE OF SPEECH AND LANGUAGE THERAPISTS/
LOGOPEDISTS OF THE EUROPEAN UNION (CPLOL)**

The Standing Liaison Committee of Speech and Language Therapists/Logopedists of member countries of the European Union (EU) was established in Paris in 1988. Its membership is made up of representatives of the professional organisations from member countries of the European Union.

The aims and objectives of the Committee are:

- to represent the views of member professional organisations to the political, parliamentary and administrative authorities of the EU;

- to promote, within member countries of the EU: freedom of movement, co-ordination of conditions, harmonisation of education and exchange of information;

- to study regulations and decisions made by European authorities affecting speech and language therapy/logopedy, and to submit projects and proposals to these authorities;

- to promote meetings with EU liaison committees representing other professions which have common interests with speech and language therapists/logopedists.

- to provide assistance to member associations if the proposals made are of common interest.

British Dyslexia Association

The Royal National Institute for the Deaf

HEADWAY

NATIONAL
HEAD INJURIES
ASSOCIATION

CANCER LARYNGECTOMEE TRUST

'I CAN'

INVALID CHILDREN'S
AID NATIONWIDE

THE CHEST, HEART
AND STROKE ASSOCIATION

MNDA

WORKING FOR THE CONQUEST
OF MOTOR NEURONE DISEASE

THE ASSOCIATION FOR STAMMERERS

CLAPA

Cleft Lip and Palate Association

ACTION FOR
DYSPHASIC ADULTS

THE NATIONAL ASSOCIATION OF LARYNGECTOMEE CLUBS

THE INDEPENDENT PRACTITIONER

1   The College advocates that all therapists who practice independently are members of the Association of Therapists in Independent Practice (ASTIIP). Only fully registered members of the College are accepted as members of ASTIIP. Membership of ASTIIP represents a commitment to agreed standards of professional conduct for independent practice and to the standards of the College.

2   It is advisable that an independent practitioner should have at least two years post-qualification clinical experience before practising independently.

3   If a speech and language therapist has had a break from professional practice of over three years and wishes then to practise independently she/he should have attended an approved refresher course.

4   Practitioners should take steps to protect themselves from suspicion of unethical conduct by careful consideration of their activities. Therapists who have any current health service involvement with a particular client may not normally undertake private therapy with that client. Where necessary, therapists should seek advice from ASTIIP for clarification.

ETHICS OF PRIVATE PRACTICE

1   Practitioners should observe the courtesy of contacting all established private practitioners within an area when intending to establish a new private practice.

2   A therapist, on leaving a group practice, should not canvass clients who were referred to that practice to move with them.

PRACTICE MANAGEMENT

1   The practice should define its scope and objectives and make these clear in any literature describing the practice. It is the responsibility of practitioners to offer therapy only in areas where adequate clinical experience has been gained.

2   The practice should publish terms and conditions of therapy. This will ensure that clients are fully aware of the practitioner's expectations for fee settlement, and of what constitutes a therapy session in terms of duration and content. The terms and conditions should also specify whether or not reports are included in the initial consultation fee, and whether or not there are mileage charges for home visits etc. A scale of charges should be made available before the initial consultation.

3   After the initial assessment, clients should be given, where possible, an approximation of the amount of therapy (and therefore the cost) which may be necessary.

4 Practitioners should ensure that accurate accounts are kept and receipts given for all client and practice transactions, and that those records which are necessary for annual financial audit are in place.

5 The practice or practitioner should consider implementing a quality assurance programme. This provides a systematic way of evaluating the quality of the services provided and offers an opportunity to address identified weaknesses. Practices are advised to undertake regular internal audits which include examination of administrative and clinical procedures.

INTERFACE WITH MEDICAL PRACTITIONERS AND OTHER SPEECH & LANGUAGE THERAPISTS

1 Communication with the client's medical practitioner should be maintained at appropriate stages of the intervention. The therapist should send a communication stating that an initial consultation has taken place and outline the planned course of action arising from this. A note of discharge should follow when applicable.

2 Independent practitioners should advise the appropriate speech and language therapy service of the names of any clients being seen, although due consideration must be taken of individual circumstances. In certain instances, for example, where a client seeks a confidential second opinion, the practitioner should make discretionary decisions in order to act in their client's best interests. Serious and due consideration of the possibility of

test score invalidation and any deleterious effects of possible dual involvement should be borne in mind in such circumstances. In summary, recommended good practice is notification to health service departments. In discretionary circumstances the procedure may be circumvented. In these instances the therapist may consider requiring the client to sign an insertion to their records agreeing or requesting that the consultation remains confidential to the practice.

3 It is recommended good practice to advise enquirers of the availability of speech and language therapy within the health service to avoid situations where a member of the public may be unaware of the existence of statutory provision. Beyond this, independent practitioners should avoid involvement in discussions relating to levels and merits of local provision etc.

4 Where it is considered in the client's best interests to receive professional help from two practitioners, one must undertake the lead role in the co-ordination of case management. This responsibility should be delegated after discussion, and steps should be taken to clarify with the client the nature of the arrangement that has been reached.

5 Written permission to circulate reports to other professionals should be obtained from the client.

CLINICAL RECORD KEEPING

1 Clear, accurate and up-to-date records should be maintained. These should be made in a clear and logical form in legible writing using permanent ink. Any corrections should be initialled.

2 All written, audio and video records should be stored securely. All records should be retained for 10 years after the last entry. In addition to this, clients seen as children should have their records retained until their 25th birthday has occurred.

3 Computerised client records should be registered under the Data Protection Act (1984).

EMERGENCY PROCEDURES

Practitioners should consider the following:

1 whether working from home, undertaking domiciliary practice or working in specially designated premises, identification of the possible emergencies which may occur and the establishment of appropriate systems to deal with such emergencies as effectively as possible;

2 competence in cardiopulmonary resuscitation;

3 a procedure for the recording and reporting of accidents.

LEGAL AND BUSINESS PROTECTION:

Practitioners should consider:

1 familiarity with the Law of Negligence;

2 familiarity with the Law of Assaults;

3 familiarity with local planning regulations that affect their practice;

4 familiarity with Health & Safety legislation that affects their practice;

5 familiarity with employment legislation that effects their practice;

6 familiarity with the Children Act (1989), The Children Act, (Scotland) (1995), the Children Act (Northern Ireland) (1995) as applicable;

7 practitioners must carry appropriate and adequate current insurance cover during their working career and continue this for a period of years into their retirement to cover the lapse of this allowed in law for possible claims to be made against them;

8 practitioners must have adequate Public Liability Insurance;

9 practitioners must have adequate Professional Premises and Contents Insurance including insurance against fire and theft;

10 practitioners must have, if appropriate, Employers Liability Insurance;

11 practitioners should consider the necessity of Partnership Insurance, Personal Health and Accident Insurance and the necessity to organise adequate Pension Funding.

ADVERTISING AND MARKETING

1 Speech and language therapists should advertise and market their practices

according to the guidelines on advertising and marketing published by ASTIIP.

2 Paid-up members and paid-up members only of ASTIIP will be permitted to use the Corporate Logo of that organisation in ways permitted by the organisation.

CONTRACT SPEECH AND LANGUAGE THERAPY SERVICES

1 No therapist should canvass contract employment as an independent practitioner without having the minimum recommended clinical experience and any specialist experience appropriate to the post.

2 It is recommended that, as part of the negotiation process, therapists prepare and submit written proposals to the purchasing body detailing the services to be provided by the practice or individual therapist, the terms under which the services will be provided, and the ways in which quality of provision will be assured. Therapists should inform purchasers of their registration with the College and their membership of ASTIIP.

3 Practices offering contract services should only do so if they have the appropriate facilities to manage efficient invoicing and accounting practices. It is expected that ASTIIP members should offer basic standards of administration, including the use of stationery which clearly states the practice details, and the adherence to accepted practice in invoice presentation etc.

(ASTIIP members should seek advice from the ASTIIP Business Helpline if unsure.)

4 When finalising details, therapists should be careful to obtain explicit confirmation of their position as independent practitioners, particularly if employed in an environment alongside health service employees. Considerations may include whether or not the independent therapist is permitted to, or expected to, use their corporate identity on contract business, or whether all interface with clients and other professionals should be carried out under the name of the purchaser. The independent practitioner's position regarding departmental meetings, staff training etc. are further example of areas requiring clarification in advance of contract finalisation. ASTIIP members are expected to clarify this type of issue avoiding at all costs unforeseen compromise to their professionalism as contractors.

5 When negotiating fees, members should refer to current guidelines published by ASTIIP.

6 ASTIIP members are advised to keep time-management records of their attendances on contract business that should be submitted to corroborate invoices or for use as appropriate to the purchaser.

7 Requirements for statistical data collection will vary depending on the purchaser. Contractors should check these requirements thoroughly. In the absence of definite requirements ASTIIP members are expected to keep efficient records of client contacts whilst on contract business and to conform to ASTIIP standards in clinical record-keeping etc.

8 ASTIIP members are advised to make

explicit their wish to be involved with quality standard or monitoring programmes for independent practitioners. This may involve the practitioner requesting a liaison agreement with a senior health service therapist to discuss service and professional issues etc. ASTIIP strongly advises that members actively seek this type of monitoring to promote professionalism and co-operation between service providers. These recommendations should not interfere with the independent practitioner's right to operate within the parameters of their contract to provide independent services which may differ in style and organisation from that provided by health service counterparts.

ACCOMMODATION AND EQUIPMENT

Practitioners should pay due attention and regard to the following where relevant:

1   compliance with the Health & Safety Act and relevant local policies on Health & Safety;

2   local planning regulations;

3   use of equipment that is produced to nationally recognised safety standards and reflects up-to-date good practice.

12

HEALTH PROMOTION

HEALTH PROMOTION

INTRODUCTION

In 1974, the World Health Organisation took the lead in setting targets to achieve a clearly defined and quantifiable strategy for the promotion of health and the prevention of disease throughout its member states (WHO 1974).

Health Promotion is not a medical service. However, health professionals, particularly those in primary health care, have an important role in nurturing and enabling health promotion activities.

The United Kingdom Faculty of Community Medicine has defined the aims of any successful public health strategy to be:

1 EQUITY IN HEALTH so that everyone has the best possible opportunity to develop healthily and obtain required health care;

2 THE ADDITION OF YEARS TO LIFE for the prevention of premature death;

3 THE ADDITION OF HEALTH TO LIFE so that preventable disease and disability are minimised;

4 THE ADDITION OF LIFE TO YEARS so that the highest attainable level of health continues to be enjoyed by both elderly people and people disabled by chronic illness or permanent impairment.

These aims can be achieved through the implementation of two approaches to public health action:

- the 'Population-Based' approach, which focuses on measures to improve health throughout the entire community;

- the 'High Risk' approach, which concentrates on those who are at the highest risk of 'ill health'.

Until the mid-1980s, the emphasis in disease prevention/health promotion in the United Kingdom was primarily on the individualistic 'high risk' approach rather than the 'population-based' approach. The concept of health as the responsibility of the individual, rather than society or government, had been emphasised in the government's previous strategy documents, such as 'Prevention and Health, Everybody's Business' (DOH, 1976). In 1988, the White Paper 'Promoting Better Health' (DOH,1988) was published. It suggested that for many major public health problems, such as coronary heart disease, high blood pressure, cancer and alcohol-related disease, exclusive focus on a high risk approach was unlikely to reduce overall mortality and morbidity rates, and that the adoption of a combined population-based and individualistic approach was likely to achieve the greatest success.

In 1993, the Department of Health published 'The Health of the Nation' (DOH,1993). This document further emphasised the importance of disease prevention, promotion of health as well as prioritisation of resources. Its key objectives were to reduce the incidence of coronary heart disease, stroke, specific cancers, mental illness, HIV/Aids, and accidents in the young and old. A further target was to increase uptake of immunisation in the general population. Local services for those with physical disabilities and ethnic minority groups, together with palliative care for terminally ill people had to meet regional health authorities requirements.

Speech and language therapists may be involved in all these areas as part of their primary health care role. They have a corporate responsibility to provide information to clients, potential clients, their carers, and consumer representatives on issues relating to the promotion of health, particularly in the province of communication. Some communication disorders occur as a result of a preventable disease/disorder. Examples include: a voice problem, resulting from vocal nodules caused by vocal abuse; dysphasia in a stroke victim, where the stroke has resulted from diet-related hypertension; or aphonia as a result of a laryngectomy in a heavy smoker. Speech and language therapists therefore have a role in implementing the 'population-based' approach and the targeted 'high risk' approach.

CHILDREN'S SERVICES

Speech and language therapists have an important role to play in supporting other professionals in advising carers as to ways of developing play, symbolic understanding and communication skills in children. This may take the form of direct intervention, e.g. talks to ante-natal/post-natal groups or playgroups, or participating in the informal and formal training of other health care professionals, e.g. midwives and health visitors. For children with special needs, 'child health promotion' recognises that the early detection and treatment of potentially disabling conditions should be seen as a priority in child health services.

The role of speech and language therapists in developing feeding skills is acknowledged, especially for children with developmental problems resulting from prematurity, pre- or post-natal damage, or genetic conditions. Children with a progressive condition, such as muscular dystrophy should have access to therapy expertise in order to maximise function and prevent health complications. Speech and language therapy may offer support to planning groups designing playgroups, nurseries and classes for young children especially in areas of identified need. The speech and language therapist's role in child health promotion is crucial, particularly in the promotion of parenting skills which lead to the development of speech and language in early childhood (Hall, 1996).

ADULTHOOD AND OLD AGE

In adulthood and old age, disease and disability can cause a loss of functional capacity. The World Health Organisation suggests that key objectives in the care of the adults and the elderly should be:

■ to prevent unnecessary loss of functional capacity;

■ to maintain the quality of life in old age by preventing distressing symptoms;

■ to assist elderly people to live in their own homes and prevent unnecessary admissions to residential care.

■ to prevent the breakdown of informal networks of care, particularly families;

■ to prevent unnecessary decline in functional capacity and quality of life if admission to long-stay care is essential;

- to prevent iatrogenic (doctor-induced) diseases including the distress that can be caused by inappropriate interventions in old age.

The speech and language therapist has a role to play in both a preventative and reactive way enabling a number of these targets to be achieved. Whilst a therapist may not be able to eradicate 'stroke or Parkinson's Disease', participation in preventative activities may reduce disability and can have a major impact for an individual in relation to the targets outlined above.

The speech and language therapist's role may include encouraging early referral of those with problems and providing advice to those at risk, e.g. teachers, singers. It may involve education of clients and their carers through increasing awareness of environmental influences on communication, and promoting awareness of the importance of communication in building and maintaining relationships. The speech and language therapist may be involved in facilitating reading and writing skills, highlighting the effect of sensory deficits on communication, and encouraging appropriate support and management. There may also be a role in advising on statutory/legal requirements with appropriate information/advice.

The means of achieving these aims may include:

- involvement in training programmes;

- talks to carer/voluntary groups, e.g. Age Concern, Parkinson's Disease Society;

- distribution of appropriate literature;

- fostering awareness that communication is everyone's business;

- using multi-disciplinary notes;

- channelling information into the public domain via public campaigns such as Speak Week.

The speech and language therapist also has a role in improving awareness of swallowing difficulties amongst adult clients. This may involve setting up nurse/doctor screening systems to facilitate appropriate referral, encouraging referral of those at risk of aspiration, working with nurses and others to implement recommendations and facilitate good practice regarding positioning and feeding techniques. It may include establishing monitoring systems and discussing anxieties about swallowing/ choking with clients and carers.

The means of achieving these aims may include:

- training sessions;

- input to undergraduate/post-graduate medical and nurse training;

- giving specific advice to clients and carers.

In summary, the speech and language therapist has a role to play in 'promoting health' in the widest sense, through her/his participation in screening, public awareness campaigns and locally-based training and education events.

The College recognises this important dimension to the work of the speech and language therapist and supports the extension of this role into appropriate health promotion activities.

HEALTH PROMOTION AND PREVENTION IN RELATION TO SPEECH AND LANGUAGE DIFFICULTIES IN CHILDREN

Speech and language difficulties are probably the most common of all the difficulties experienced in the pre-school population (Drillien and Drummond, 1983). Many of these difficulties continue throughout the school years and frequently act as markers for a wide range of educational and behavioural difficulties. The identification and provision of services for such children at an early stage in their development is seen as a priority in view of the potentially negative implications for the child and the resource implications that these difficulties are likely to have.

The increased awareness of the long term implications of such difficulties has to be seen in the context of the role of prevention in Child Health Services. Prevention is conventionally divided into three levels, and the speech and language therapist has a contribution to make at each of these levels.

1 Primary Prevention

Primary prevention focuses on promoting good practice in all areas relating to the health and development of the young child. Examples include safety in the home, feeding, management of behavioural difficulties etc. Primary prevention is carried out by health visitors and GPs. This area used to be referred to as Health Education, but in recent years this has changed to Child Health Promotion. It has been suggested that Child Health Promotion should also replace the current , more restricted concept of Child Health Surveillance (Hall, 1996). The change

in terminology aims to reduce the somewhat paternalistic overtone associated with both health education and surveillance.

To date, speech and language therapists have had relatively little direct involvement in Primary Prevention work. However, they do have a role to play in increasing parent and professional awareness of communication patterns which promote language development. Speech and language therapists can achieve this through the use of relevant literature and training materials, as well as by providing input into ante-natal groups or providing in service training for nursery staff or health visitors. Speech and language therapists can also contribute to the Personal Child Health Record (PCHR) (formerly Parent Held Record), a recent innovation designed to empower parents in making choices about their child's early health and development.

2 Secondary Prevention

Secondary prevention focuses on identifying developmental, behavioural and health problems and making necessary referrals. Examples include delayed motor skills, low growth trajectory, behavioural difficulties, hearing and visual defects and developmental speech and language delay/disorder. Identification may take the form of specific screening procedures or judgements based on observation of the child. Secondary prevention is carried out by health visitors, medical officers and GPs.

Speech and language therapists often provide considerable input into the training of other professionals, in particular, what to look for and how and when to refer children for specialist help. In some settings, speech and language therapists are involved in developing specific screening measures. Whilst it is recognised that such measures may make a contribution to secondary prevention, it is not yet possible to advocate universal screening for speech and language difficulties. There is, however, a case for therapists to develop professional training packages which provide input into the identification process along with other professionals such as psychologists, paediatricians, health visitors, audiologists etc.

There is also a need for speech and language therapy departments to make explicit the channels of referral within their trusts and to audit the effects of such procedures.

3 Tertiary Prevention

Tertiary Prevention focuses on remediation of the impairment, disability or handicap of a condition. This may involve the amelioration of the central impairment or the prevention or reduction of associated difficulties. In some cases this may mean the removal of the symptoms altogether, but it is not necessary for the concept of a 'cure' to be implicit in the application of 'tertiary prevention'. Tertiary prevention is carried out by professionals with specialist knowledge and skills. Although this level of prevention has been the primary role of speech and language therapists to date, it is only one aspect of the service offered under the umbrella of Health Promotion.

Early Identification and the concept of evidence based health care

The relationship between identification and intervention poses a number of problems which affect the delivery of speech and language therapy services to children. The first problem relates to the understanding of the natural history of speech and language difficulties. It would be misleading to assume that all children with language scores falling below a given level have a potentially persistent difficulty, whilst those children who do not are probably free from such difficulties. Rather, it is necessary to calculate the risk of the child experiencing persistent difficulty against the potentially harmful effects of inappropriate intervention.

As the probability of the child experiencing persisting difficulties recedes, so the potential benefits of intervention decline. The implication of this argument is that children with less severe difficulties should receive a lower priority weighting in the identification process and resources should be targeted to children with more pervasive problems (Hall, 1996). To date, the evidence suggests that children in the pre-school age group with specific difficulties in single expressive modalities, notably phonology and vocabulary in the absence of other difficulties, should be considered lower priorities than those with difficulties across a range of modalities, particularly those involving receptive language and those with marked impairments in social skills. In essence, early identification should reflect current clinical practice based upon the best available evidence.

The second problem which has a direct influence on the early identification process is the need for evidence of the value of intervention. It is likely that commissioning authorities will be looking for such evidence before they allocate resources to early identification. There is now extensive evidence that specific intervention techniques and more general programmes of intervention, particularly those involving parents, can be shown to work (Enderby and Emerson, 1995, Law, forthcoming). However, there needs to be more research into the long term natural history of the developmental disorders. Speech and language therapists need to be actively involved in disseminating existing research evidence amongst purchasers, and undertaking systematic caseload analysis which will inform their practice and contribute to existing evidence of the value of intervention.

REFERENCES

Access to Health Records Act (1990). London; HMSO.

Advisory Committee on Dangerous Pathogens (ACDP) (1990) HIV: the Causative Agent of AIDS and Related Conditions.

AHCPR (1992) US Department of Health and Human Services. Agency for Health Service Policy and Research Publications. Rockville, M.D. AHCPR Publication 92/0038.

American Psychiatric Association (1994) *Diagnostic and Statistical Manual for Mental Disorders (DSM IV, R).* American Psychiatric Association; Washington, D.C.

American Speech Hearing Association (ASHA) (1981) Position Statement on Non Speech Communication. Rockville; ASHA.

Anderson, R. (1996) Clinical system security; interim guidelines. *BMJ*, 312, 109-111.

Bebbington, D. (1995) *Recruitment, Retention and Returners: a study of the career paths of people with a speech and language therapy qualification* London; RCSLT.

British Medical Association (1996) *Security in Clinical Information Systems.* London: BMA.

Bryan, K, Maxim, J, McIntosh, J, McClelland, A, Wirz, S, Edmondson, A, Snowling, M. (1991) The facts behind the figures: a reply to Enderby and Davies. *British Journal of Disorders of Communication* 26, 253-261.

Care Sector Consortium (1996) *National Occupational Standards for Care Level 3; Speech and Language Therapy Support* (distributed by the Local Government Management Board on behalf of the Care Sector Consortium).

Children Act (1989) London, HMSO.

Children Act (Scotland) (1995) London; HMSO.

Children and Young Persons Act (1969) London: HMSO.

Chronically Sick and Disabled Persons Act (1970). London; HMSO.

Crombie, I, Davies, H, Abraham, S, Florey, C duV. (1993) *The Audit Handbook London;* Wiley.

CSLT (1991) *Communicating Quality.* London; CSLT .

CSLT (1993) *Audit : A Manual for Speech and Language Therapists.* London; CSLT.

CSLT(1989) Position Paper on Aphasia.

CSLT (1989) Position Paper on Augmentative and Alternative Communication.

CSLT (1990) Position Paper on AIDS and HIV Infection.

CSLT (1990) Position Paper on Dysphagia.

CSLT(1990) Position Paper on Good Practice for Speech and Language Therapists Working with Clients from Linguistic Minorities.

CSLT (1992) Policy Review Forum: Dysphagia.

CSLT (1992) Schools and Speech and Language Therapy Working Together; Guidelines to Good Practice (Second Edition).

CSLT (1993) Technology, Alternative and Augmentative Communication File (TAAC).

CSLT (1993) Position Paper on Dementia.

Data Protection Act (1984) London; HMSO.

Davies, P, Enderby, P. (1991) A reply to Bryan et al's the facts behind the figures; a reply to Enderby and Davies. *British Journal of Disorders of Communication* 26, 262-267.

Department for Education (1978) *Report on the Education of Pupils with Learning Difficulties in Scottish Schools* London; HMSO.

DES Circular 1/83. Assessments and Statements of Special Educational Needs.

DES Circular 22/89. Assessments and Statements of Special Educational Needs; Procedures within the Education, Health and Social Services.

DHSS (1991) *Working Together Under the Children Act (1989); A Guide to Arrangements for Inter-Agency Co-operation for the Protection of Children from Abuse.* London; HMSO.

Disabled Persons (Services, Consultation and Representation) Act (1986). London; HMSO.

Department for Education and Science (1978) *Special Educational Needs (Warnock Report)* London; DES/HMSO.

Department for Education (1994) *Code of Practice on the Identification and Assessment of Special Educational Needs.* London; Department for Education.

DOH (1976) *Prevention of Health: Everybody's Business.* London: HMSO.

DOH (1988) *Promoting Better Health: The Government's Programme for Improving Primary Health Care.* London; HMSO.

DOH (1989) *Caring for People; the Next Decade and Beyond.* London; HMSO.

DOH (1989) *Working for Patients.* London; HMSO.

DOH (1990) *Guide to the Access to Health Records Act* London; HMSO.

DOH (1992) *The Health of the Nation.* London, HMSO, CM 1986.

DOH (1991) *The Patient's Charter* London; HMSO.

DOH (1991) *Research for Health.* London; HMSO.

DOH (1991) *Assessing the Effects of Health Technologies.* London; Department of Health.

DOH (1994) *Research and Development in Occupational Therapy, Physiotherapy and*

Speech and language Therapy: A Position Statement. London: Department of Health.

DOH (1995)*HIV and AIDS Health Promotion; an Evolving Strategy.* London; Department of Health.

DOH Circular HN (88) 26. Health Service Development; the Development of Services for People with Physical or Sensory Disabilities.

DOH Circular HC (89) 20. Health Service Management; Preservation, Retention and Destruction of Records.

DOH Circular (89) 29. Health Service Management Data Protection Act 1984; Modified Access to Personal Health Information.

DOH Circular EL (90) 161. Starting Specifications; A DHA Project Paper.

DOH Circular EL (91) 21. Professional Advice for Purchasers; a DHA Project Discussion Paper.

DOH Circular EL (93) 115. Improving clinical effectiveness.

DOH Circular EL (94) 74. Improving the effectiveness of the NHS.

DOH Circular HSG (95) 11. Ensuring the Effective Involvement of Professionals in Health Authority Work.

DOH Circular HSG (95) 19. GP Fundholding; a list of goods and services.

DOH Circular HSG (95) 65. GP Fundholding; a revised list of goods and services

DOH Circular HSG (95) 64. GP Fundholding; Inclusion of Community Specialist Nursing and Other Services in Standard and Community Fundholding from April 1996.

Drillien, C, Drummond, M. (1983) *Developmental Screening and the Child with Special Needs* London: Heinemann.

Education Act (1981) London, HMSO.

Education Act (1993) London; HMSO.

Education Act (Scotland) (1980) London; HMSO.

Enderby, P. (1992) An alphabet of Audit. *Therapy Weekly* 21, 151-165.

Enderby, P and Emerson, J (1995) *Does Speech and Language Therapy Work? A Review of the Literature.* London: Whurr Publishers.

Enderby, P, Davies, P. (1989) Communication disorders; planning a service to meet the needs. *British Journal of Disorders of Communication* 24, 301-332.

Enderby, P, Phillip, R. (1986) Speech and language handicap; towards knowing the size of the problem *British Journal of Disorders of Communication* 21, 151-166.

Farrer, A, Harvey, J, Morris, S. (1994) *Audit for the Therapy Professions.* London; Mercia Publications.

Gillham, B, Boyle, J, Smith, N, Cheyne, B. (1995) Language Screening at 18-36 months; the First Words and First Sentences Tests and the First Words Comprehension Cards. *Journal of Child Language Teaching and Therapy,* 11, (2) 193-208.

Gordon, M. (1993) Greater Glasgow Health Board Manpower Analysis. Glasgow; GGHB.

Hall, DMB. (1996) *Health for all Children; The Report of the Joint Working Party on Child Health Surveillance (Third Edition)* Oxford; OUP.

ICAC (1995) Communication Aids for Children ; a Briefing for Purchasers and Managers. (Available from AFASIC, 336, Brixton Road, London, SW9 7AA).

Law, J (forthcoming) Evaluating intervention for language impaired children; a review of the literature. European Journal of Disorders of Communication.

National Aids Manual (1995) *National Aids Manual*; Volumes 1,2,3.

National Health Service Regulations (1974) England & Wales: Statutory instrument no. 485 The National Health Service (Speech Therapists) Regulations 1974, as amended by no. 47 1985; Scotland: National Health Service (Speech Therapists) (Scotland) Regulations 1974 (3a) amended by no. 208 (S. 20) 1985.

National Health Service Act (1977) London; HMSO.

National Health Service and Community Care Act (1990) London; HMSO.

Normand, C. (1991) *Clinical Audit in Professions Allied to Medicine and Related Therapy Professions.* Report to the Department of Health on a Pilot Study.

Manpower Planning Advisory Group (MPAG) (1991) Speech Therapy; an Examination of Staffing Issues. A Report by SW Regional Health Authority. London; Department of Health

Mental Health Act (1983) London; HMSO.

Miller,C, Morrison,K, Pentland,B, Stansfield,J. (1995) Specialists and generalists. *CSLT Bulletin* 513, p 6-7.

Moving to Audit (1995) *Moving to Audit: An Education Package for Professions Allied to Medicine* University of Dundee Clinical Resource and Audit Group.

O'Brien, J, Tyne, A. (1981) *The Principle of Normalisation; a Foundation for Effective Services.* London: CMH.

Patients Charter (1989) London; HMSO.

Patients Charter in Scotland (1991) Edinburgh; The Scottish Office.

Public Health (Control of Disease) Act (1984) London; HMSO.

Office of Population, Census and Surveys, England and Wales (1984) *Population Trends,* 38,37.

Quirk, R. (1972) *Speech Therapy Services.* London; HMSO.

Roulstone, S. (1994) Expertise and speech and language therapy. Paper presented to

CSLT Policy Review Forum: Education for Practice; London.

RCSLT (1991) Registration Summary Papers.

RCSLT (1995) Guidelines on the Content of Post Qualification Education in Dysphagia.

RCSLT (1995a) Guidelines on the Accreditation of Courses Leading to a Qualification in Speech and Language Therapy.

RCSLT (1995b) Continuing Professional Development for Speech and Language Therapists - A Policy for the Future.

RCSLT, Professional Standards Board, (1996) The Role of the Mentor in Speech and Language Therapy . (S. Walker, 1996).

RCSLT, Professional Standards Board, (1996) Specialist and Generalists: Differentiation of Roles and Responsibilities by Function. (S Walker, 1996).

RCSLT, Professional Standards Board, (1996) Staffing Formula: A Working Paper. (S. Walker, 1996).

RCSLT (1996) Guidelines on Endoscopic Evaluation of the Nasal and Vocal Tract. (M. Lockhart, 1996).

RCSLT (1996) Guidelines on the Use of Hypnosis in Speech and Language Therapy.

Social Work Act (1976) London; HMSO.

Scottish Local Government Information Unit (1995) *The Children (Scotland) Act (1995)* - A Guide. (0141 226 4636).

Scottish Office (1993) *COSLA Speech and Language Therapy Provision for Young People under Twenty.* Edinburgh: Scottish Office.

Spencer,C. (1994) Working with volunteers. *CSLT Bulletin,* 504, p11.

Teasdale, G, Jennett, P. (1974) Assessment of coma and impaired consciousness; a practical scale. *Lancet,* 2, 81-84.

The Association of Speech Therapy Managers (1993) *Core curriculum for speech and language therapy assistants.* Ponteland: STASS Publications.

The Association of Speech ans Language Therapy Managers (1995) Notional Caseload Survey. TASLTM.

Welsh Language Act (1993) London; HMSO.

World Health Organisation (1974) *Health Education: a Programme Review.* Geneva: WHO.

World Health Organisation (1994) *International Classification of Diseases (10th Edition).* Geneva: WHO.

Wolfensberger, W. (1972) *The Principle of Normalisation in Human Services.* Toronto: National Institute on Mental Retardation.

Subject Index

© 1996

The Royal College of Speech and Language Therapists
7 Bath Place Rivington Street
London EC2A 3DR

First published 1991
Second edition 1996

British Library Cataloguing in Publication Data

ISBN 0 947589 04 X